Epistemological
Problems of Economics

The Institute for Humane Studies Series in Economic Theory

Distributed by New York University Press

Published by New York University Press

Epistemological Problems of Economics

by

LUDWIG VON MISES

TRANSLATED BY GEORGE REISMAN

NEW YORK UNIVERSITY PRESS

NEW YORK *AND* LONDON

Library of Congress Cataloging in Publication Data

Von Mises, Ludwig, 1881-1973.
  Epistemological problems of economics.

  Translation of Grundprobleme der Nationalökonomie.
  The "Institute for Humane Studies Series in Economic Theory.
  Includes bibliographical references and index.
  1. Economics.   2. Economics—Methodology.
I. Title.
HB71.V6313   1981   330.1   80-24604
ISBN 0-8147-8757-6
ISBN 0-8147-8758-4 (pbk.)

HB
71
V6313
1981

10 9 8 7 6 5 4 3 2
PRINTED IN THE UNITED STATES OF AMERICA

Foreword

In 1960, in the preface to the first English-language edition of this volume of essays, Mises wrote, "They represent . . . the necessary preliminary study for the thorough scrutiny of the problems involved such as I tried to provide in my book *Human Action, a Treatise of Economics*" (p. VII).

This brief indication of the position these essays occupy in the evolution of Mises' thought is certainly helpful. It is easy to see, for instance, that the first essay "The Task and Scope of the Science of Human Action"—which had not been published before 1933, the date of the German edition of the volume—is in fact an extensive sketch of the main ideas of the methodological Part One of *Human Action*.

Most of the other essays originally appeared in German journals devoted to the social sciences in the late 1920s. In them, the critical purport is evident. In a number of forays directed against rival methodological positions, Mises attempts to safeguard his own edifice, as yet under construction. As he put it in 1960:

> In order to examine the legitimacy of all these objections, it seemed to me imperative not only to demonstrate positively the logical character of the propositions of economics and sociology, but also to evaluate critically the teachings of a few representatives of historicism, empiricism, and irrationalism. This, of necessity, determined the outward form of my work. It is divided into a number of independent essays which, with the exception of the first and most comprehensive, were published previously. From the outset, however, they were conceived and planned as parts of a whole. [p. xvi]

Almost half a century has passed since these essays saw the light of day. To appreciate them, we have to recall not only the circumstances of the time in which they were written, but also Mises' own position and temperament as a man of ideas.

The essays were written in the last years of the Weimar Republic and were addressed to a German academic audience in which

v

support for, and understanding of, the market economy, never very strong in these circles, had almost vanished. It was not a good time for subtlety. Nor could we expect the nuances of enlightened thought to find ready understanding. We have all the more reason to admire the high level on which Mises conducts his argument, his endeavour to demonstrate that problems of epistemology underlie disputes on the mundane matters of economic policy.

When Mises wrote these essays, he was of course already well known (to his German readers) as a monetary theorist; and in the early 1920s, he had established his reputation as a foremost critic of socialism in all its forms. In these essays, however, he is staking a new claim to be listened to—namely as a methodologist.

For most Austrian and German economists of the 1920s the *Methodenstreit* was a quarrel of the past, a most unhappy affair best forgotten. How could sensible people doubt that theory and history were both equally legitimate forms of the pursuit of knowledge? Since both protagonists in the dispute, Menger and Schmoller, appeared to accept this, it was hard to see what the violent quarrel was about.

Mises took an altogether different view. For him, the *Methodenstreit* was by no means over. In his view, what was at stake was not theory as such, viz., empirical generalizations; but the particular kind of theory Menger had defended, based on necessary, not on contingent knowledge. Menger had seen the task of economics as establishing what he called "exact laws," laws which require no experience to confirm or disconfirm them. He admitted of course the existence of empirical generalizations, but took little interest in them. His was an Aristotelian position. Our knowledge of essences permits us to arrive at "exact laws" by means of deduction. He regarded the law of value as an instance of such a law. In respect of their search for such laws, he saw no difference between natural and social sciences.

But about the turn of the century, a change in the philosophy of science associated with the names of Mach and Poincaré took place, which stressed the provisional and hypothetical nature of all scientific knowledge and the consequent need for empirical confirmation of all theories.

Mises regarded himself as Menger's true heir, certainly in the

field of methodology. Owing to the change in the climate of
opinion mentioned, Menger's position in this field had, by the
1920s, become difficult to defend. But Mises did not flinch from
his task. He distinguished between our abstract knowledge of
action and our knowledge of concrete situations in which action
has to be taken. He admits that "if we pursue definite plans, only
experience can teach us how we must act vis-à-vis the external
world in concrete situations" (p. 13). He continues,

> However, what we know about our action under given
> conditions is derived not from experience, but from reason.
> What we know about the fundamental categories of action—
> action, economizing, preferring, the relationship of means
> and ends, and everything else that together with these, con-
> stitutes the system of human action—is not derived from
> experience. We conceive all this from within, just as we
> conceive logical and mathematical truths, a priori, without
> referring to any experience. Nor could experience ever lead
> anyone to the knowledge of these things if he did not com-
> prehend them from within himself. [pp. 13-14]

Thus to swim against the tide took courage, a quality Mises
never lacked. It also meant that in his endeavor he had many
enemies and few friends, even in his own Vienna. For his was a
challenge to positivists and empiricists of almost every school,
not merely to the somewhat attentuated remnants of what by 1930
was left of the German Historical School. We have to remember
that at precisely this time Vienna had become the headquarters of
logical positivism, of the Vienna Circle of Carnap and Schlick.
With this in mind, it is possible to feel that his critical ardour was
somewhat unevenly distributed among his enemies, far too much
of it devoted to the German historians and too little to logical
positivism—not to mention the rising school of existentialism.

What, then, did he accomplish in these essays? In the first of
them he accomplished two things. First, he detached subjective
value theory from its older dependence on a theory of wants. For
Menger, wants were almost physiological facts, hence we were
able to distinguish between "real" and "imaginary" ones. Mises
established human preferences as the ultimate springs of action
and showed that they find a place within the framework of a logic

of means and ends which must form the basis of any theory of
action that is to satisfy the demands of our reason. We freely
choose our ends within the constraints nature imposes upon us. It
is the universal scarcity of means that limits the range of our
action.

Second, Mises opened the way for others to make use of the
logic of means and ends as the basis of economic science. The first
step on this way was successfully taken by Lord Robbins in 1932
with his famous definition of the subject matter of economics in
terms of ends and means. That definition soon won almost universal acclaim. What Professor Hayek in "Economics and Knowledge" (1937) described as "The Pure Logic of Choice" is of course
identical with the Misesian notion. Unfortunately, in the decade
of the 1940s, it fell into oblivion. What is today known as neo-
classical economics rests on a theory of choice in which ends are
not freely chosen by economic agents, but "given" to them in the
form of indifference curves: a badly misnamed theory of choice
forced into the Procrustean bed of determinism.

The second essay, "Sociology and History," stirred up a good
deal of interest when it was first published in 1929. There, Mises
makes an attempt to come to terms with the work of Max Weber. It
was an ambitious undertaking, and Mises faced a formidable task.
It would be impossible for us to describe all the nuances of this
encounter in these few pages. The reader must bear in mind that,
when Mises first published the essay, nine years after Weber's
death, the literature on Weber was scanty even in German. So
Mises had little guidance.

In one sense, the two thinkers were allies in the endeavour to set
up a science of action, a generalizing discipline concerned with
matters of culture. In this sense, they are both "sociologists," even
though Mises later came to prefer the term "praxeology," he tells
us. Both were philosophically Neo-Kantians, though of different
brands. Both agreed that economics has to be regarded as part of
the wider discipline concerned with human action.

But they were at odds in the way they conceived of the new
science. Mises, following Menger, drew a sharp distinction
between Theory and History and attributed great importance to
it. To Weber on the other hand, as to the whole German Historical

School, this difference was entirely a matter of degree, and not of kind. Mises recognizes and deplores that for Weber

> the difference between sociology and history is considered as only one of degree. In both, the object of cognition is identical. Both make use of the same logical method of forming concepts. They are different merely in the extent of their proximity to reality, their fullness of content and the purity of their ideal-typical constructions. Thus Max Weber has implicitly answered the question that had once constituted the substance of the Methodenstreit entirely in the sense of those who denied the logical legitimacy of a theoretical science of social phenomena. According to him, social science is logically conceivable only as a special, qualified kind of historical investigation. [p. 77]

In his critique of Weber's methodology, Mises makes two important points. First, he criticises Weber's distinction between "purposive-rational" (zweckrational) and "value-rational" (wertrational) action.

> This leads us to an examination of the types of behavior that Weber contrasts with rational (zweckrational) behavior. To begin with, it is quite clear that what Weber calls "valuational" (wertrational) behavior cannot be fundamentally distinguished from "rational" behavior. The results that rational conduct aims at are also values and as such they are beyond rationality.... What Weber calls "valuational" conduct differs from rational conduct only in that it regards a definite mode of behavior also as a value and accordingly arranges it in the rank order of values. [p. 83]

That seems a rather conclusive argument.

Second, Mises is highly critical of the Ideal Type, Weber's fundamental concept to be employed in social studies. Here, he was not alone. A fierce controversy developed on the meaning and merits of this elusive notion, a controversy in the course of which some of Weber's admirers turned into his most severe critics. In the end everybody seemed to agree that the Ideal Type is much too wide a concept to be useful and that it would have to be narrowed down, but it appeared impossible to reach agreement on the direction in which this should be done.

In *The Legacy of Max Weber* (Berkeley, California: Glendessary Press, 1971), I have suggested that we make The Plan, and not the Ideal Type, the starting point and fundamental concept of a theory of social action. As means and ends, the two notions to which Mises assigned the character of fundamental concepts of the theory of action, are combined and given concrete shape in plans, it would seem that in this way Mises' objection may be met. (See *ibid*, pp. 26-34.)

The last essay, "Inconvertible Capital," was originally Mises' contribution to a *festschrift* for the Dutch economist C.M. Verrijn Stuart.

There, in dealing with "the influence of the past on production" and "the malinvestment of capital," Mises indicated some problems to which Austrian capital theory later devoted attention. His argument has important implications.

The capital stock at any point of time never is what it would be had the present been correctly foreseen at those moments in the past when the relevant investment decisions were made, when the present was still the future. Hence, the capital stock never has its "equilibrium composition," and the general equilibrium model cannot be applied to problems concerning capital.

In the essay, Mises does not actually point out this implication, though Professor Hayek in chapter II of his *Pure Theory of Capital* (1941) did. As often happens to pioneers of thought, Mises did not at once grasp all the implications of the facts the general importance of which he had discovered.

For most of his life Mises, as we saw, had to swim against the tide. Undaunted, he may well have derived some satisfaction from his lonely struggle. With the rather grotesque exception of the market socialists, who on occasion did pay him their regards, the academic world ignored him. His few friends admired his courage and tenacity, even though in their hearts they may often have wished there were fewer occasions to display these qualities.

Of late, however, the high tide of logical positivism appears to be receding, even in the Anglo–Saxon world. In certain circles, we notice, it has even become fashionable to say that different disciplines may have to use different languages. Perhaps it is not too much to hope that in the climate of opinion now taking shape various nuances of enlightened discourse, hitherto neglected, will find a readier understanding and that the "language" of means and ends will come to be recognised as a legitimate medium in which to express human thought about action.

Johannesburg
March/April 1978   Ludwig M. Lachmann

Preface to the English-Language Edition

The popular epistemological doctrines of our age do not admit that a fundamental difference prevails between the realm of events that the natural sciences investigate and the domain of human action that is the subject matter of economics and history. People nurture some confused ideas about a "unified science" that would have to study the behavior of human beings according to the methods Newtonian physics resorts to in the study of mass and motion. On the basis of this allegedly "positive" approach to the problems of mankind, they plan to develop "social engineering," a new technique that would enable the "economic tsar" of the planned society of the future to deal with living men in the way technology enables the engineer to deal with inanimate materials.

These doctrines misrepresent entirely every aspect of the sciences of human action.

As far as man can see, there prevails a regularity in the succession and concatenation of natural phenomena. Experience, especially that of experiments performed in the laboratory, makes it possible for man to discern some of the "laws" of this regularity in many fields even with approximate quantitative accuracy. These experimentally established facts are the material that the natural sciences employ in building their theories. A theory is rejected if it contradicts the facts of experience. The natural sciences do not know anything about design and final causes.

Human action invariably aims at the attainment of ends chosen. Acting man is intent upon diverting the course of affairs by purposeful conduct from the lines it would take if he were not to interfere. He wants to substitute a state of affairs that suits him better for one that suits him less. He chooses ends and means. These choices are directed by ideas.

The objects of the natural sciences react to stimuli according to

xiii

regular patterns. No such regularity, as far as man can see, determines the reaction of man to various stimuli. Ideas are frequently, but not always, the reaction of an individual to a stimulation provided by his natural environment. But even such reactions are not uniform. Different individuals, and the same individual at various periods of his life, react to the same stimulus in a different way.

As there is no discernible regularity in the emergence and concatenation of ideas and judgments of value, and therefore also not in the succession and concatenation of human acts, the role that experience plays in the study of human action is radically different from that which it plays in the natural sciences. Experience of human action is history. Historical experience does not provide facts that could render in the construction of a theoretical science services that could be compared to those which laboratory experiments and observation render to physics. Historical events are always the joint effect of the cooperation of various factors and chains of causation. In matters of human action no experiments can be performed. History needs to be interpreted by theoretical insight gained previously from other sources.

This is valid also for the field of economic action. The specific experience with which economics and economic statistics are concerned always refers to the past. It is history, and as such does not provide knowledge about a regularity that will manifest itself also in the future. What acting man wants to know is theory, that is, cognition of the regularity in the necessary succession and concatenation of what is commonly called economic events. He wants to know the "laws" of economics in order to choose means that are fit to attain the ends sought.

Such a science of human action cannot be elaborated either by recourse to the methods praised—but never practically resorted to—by the doctrines of logical positivism, historicism, institutionalism, Marxism and Fabianism or by economic history, econometrics and statistics. All that these methods of procedure can establish is history, that is, the description of complex phenomena that happened at a definite place on our globe at a definite date as the consequence of the combined operation of a multitude of factors. From such cognition it is impossible to derive knowledge that could tell us something about the effects to be expected in the future from the application of definite measures and policies, e.g., inflation, price ceilings, or tariffs. But it is precisely this that people want to learn from the study of economics.

It is the aim of the essays collected in this volume to explode the errors implied in the negativistic doctrines rejecting economic theory and thereby to clear the way for the systematic analysis of the phenomena of human action and especially also of those commonly called economic. They represent, as it were, the necessary preliminary study for the thorough scrutiny of the problems involved such as I tried to provide in my book, *Human Action, a Treatise of Economics.**

*   *   *

Some of the authors whose statements I analyzed and criticized in these essays are little known to the American public. But the ideas which they developed and which I tried to refute are not different from the doctrines that were taught by many other authors, either American or foreign, whose books were written in English or are available in English-language translations and are amply read in this country. Such is, for instance, the case with the doctrines of the late professor of the University of Berlin, Alfred Vierkandt. In order to pass over in silence the fact that men, guided by ideas and resorting to judgments of value, choose between different ends and between different means for the attainment of the ends chosen, Vierkandt tried to reduce the actions and achievements of men to the operation of instincts. What man brings about is, he assumed, the product of an instinct with which he has been endowed for this special purpose. Now this opinion does not differ essentially from that of Frederick Engels as especially expressed in his most popular book, the *Anti-Dühring*,† nor from that of William McDougall and his numerous American followers.

In examining the tenets of Mr. Gunnar Myrdal I referred to the German-language edition of his book, *Das Politische Element in der Nationalökonomischen Doktrinbildung*, published in 1932.

---

* Yale University Press, 1949.

† See my book *Theory and History* (Yale University Press, 1957), pages 194 f.

Twenty-one years later this German-language edition served as the basis for the English translation by Mr. Paul Streeten.*

In his "Preface to the English Edition" Mr. Myrdal declares that this edition is "apart from a few cuts and minor editorial re-arrangements" an "unrevised translation of the original version." He does not mention that my criticism of his analysis of the ends that wage-earners want to attain by unionism induced him to change essentially the wording of the passage concerned. In perusing my criticism, the reader is asked to remember that it refers to the literally quoted passage from pages 299 f. of the German edition and not to the purged text on page 200 of the English edition.

A further observation concerning the terminology used is needed. When, in 1929, I first published the second essay of this collection, I still believed that it was unnecessary to introduce a new term to signify the general theoretical science of human action as distinguished from the historical studies dealing with human action performed in the past. I thought that it would be possible to employ for this purpose the term *sociology,* which in the opinion of some authors was designed to signify such a general theoretical science. Only later did I realize that this was not expedient and adopted the term *praxeology.*

*   *   *

Mr. George Reisman translated from the text published in 1933 under the title *Grundprobleme der Nationalökonomie* and the subtitle *Untersuchungen über Verfahren, Aufgaben und Inhalt der Wirtschafts- und Gesellschaftslehre.* The translation was prepared for publication by Mr. Arthur Goddard. The translator and the editor carried on their work independently. I myself did not supply any suggestions concerning the translation nor any deviations from the original German text.

It remains for me to extend my heartiest thanks both to Mr. Reisman and to Mr. Goddard. I am especially grateful to the directors and staff members of the foundation that is publishing this series of studies.

LUDWIG VON MISES

* *The Political Element in the Development of Economic Theory* (Routledge & Kegan Paul Ltd., London, 1953).

Preface to the German Edition

Misunderstandings about the nature and significance of economics are not due exclusively to antipathies arising from political bias against the results of inquiry and the conclusions to be necessarily drawn from them. Epistemology, which for a long time was concerned solely with mathematics and physics, and only later began to turn its attention to biology and history as well, is presented with apparently insuperable difficulties by the logical and methodological singularity of economic theory. These difficulties stem for the most part from an astonishing unfamiliarity with the fundamental elements of economics itself. When a thinker of Bergson's caliber, whose encyclopedic mastery of modern science is virtually unparalleled, expresses views that show he is a stranger to a basic concept of economics,[1] one can well imagine what the present situation is with regard to the dissemination of knowledge of that science.

Under the influence of Mill's empiricism and psychologism, logic was not prepared for the treatment of the problems that economics presents to it. Moreover, every attempt at a satisfactory solution was frustrated by the inadequacy of the objective theory of value then prevailing in economics. Nevertheless, it is precisely to this epoch that we owe the most valuable contributions to the elucidation of the problems of the scientific theory of economics. For the successful treatment of these questions, Senior, John Stuart Mill, and Cairnes satisfied in the highest degree the most important prerequisite: they themselves were economists. From their discussions, which are set in the framework of the psychologistic logic prevailing at that time, emerged ideas that required only fecundation by a more perfect theory of the laws of thought to lead to entirely different results.

The inadequacy of empiricist logic hampered the endeavors of Carl Menger still more seriously than those of the English thinkers. His brilliant *Untersuchungen über die Methode der Sozialwissenschaften* is even less satisfactory today than, for example,

Cairnes' book on methodology. This is perhaps due to the fact that Menger wanted to proceed more radically and that, working some decades later, he was in a position to see difficulties that his predecessors had passed over.

Elucidation of the fundamental logical problems of economics did not make the progress that might have been expected from these splendid beginnings. The writings of the adherents of the Historical and the *Kathedersozialist* Schools in Germany and England and of the American Institutionalists confused, rather than advanced, our knowledge of these matters.[2]

It is to the investigations of Windelband, Rickert, and Max Weber that we owe the clarification of the logical problems of the historical sciences. To be sure, the very possibility of a universally valid science of human action escaped these thinkers. Living and working in the age of the Historical School, they failed to see that sociology and economics can be and, indeed, are universally valid sciences of human action. But this shortcoming on their part does not vitiate what they accomplished for the logic of the historical sciences. They were impelled to consider these problems by the positivist demand that the traditional historical disciplines—the moral sciences—be repudiated as unscientific and replaced by a science of historical laws. They not only demonstrated the absurdity of this view, but they brought into relief the distinctive logical character of the historical sciences in connection with the doctrine of "understanding," to the development of which theologians, philologists, and historians had contributed.

No notice was taken—perhaps deliberately—of the fact that the theory of Windelband and Rickert also involves an implicit repudiation of all endeavors to produce an "historical theory" for the political sciences. In their eyes the historical sciences and the nomothetic sciences are logically distinct. A "universal economics," that is, an empirical theory of economic history that could be derived, as Schmoller thought, from historical data, must appear just as absurd, in their view, as the effort to establish laws of historical development, such as Kurt Breysig, for example, attempted to discover.

In Max Weber's view also, economics and sociology completely merge into history. Like the latter, they are moral or cultural sciences and make use of the same logical method. Their most important conceptual tool is the ideal type, which possesses the same logical structure in history and in what Max Weber regarded as economics and sociology. But bestowing on ideal types names like "economic style," "economic system," or "economic stage" in no way changes their logical status. They still remain the conceptual instrument of historical, and not of theoretical, investigation. The delineation of the characteristic features of a historical period and the understanding of its significance, which ideal types make possible, are indisputably tasks of the historical sciences. The very expression "economic style" is an imitation of the jargon and conceptual apparatus of art history. Thus far, however, no one has thought of calling art history a theoretical science because it classifies the historical data with which it deals into types or "styles" of art.

Moreover, these distinctions among art styles are based on a systematic classification of works of art undertaken in accordance with the methods of the natural sciences. The method that leads to the differentiation of art styles is not the specific understanding of the moral sciences, but the systematic division of objects of art into classes. Understanding makes reference only to the results of this work of systematizing and schematizing. In the distinctions among economic styles these conditions are lacking. The result of economic activity is always want-satisfaction, which can be judged only subjectively. An economic style does not make its appearance in the form of artifacts that could be classified in the same way as works of art. Economic styles cannot be distinguished, for example, according to the characteristics of the goods produced in the various periods of economic history, as the Gothic style and the Renaissance style are differentiated according to the characteristics of their architecture. Attempts to differentiate economic styles according to economic attitude, economic spirit, and the like, do violence to the facts. They are based not on objectively distinguishable, and therefore rationally incontrovertible, characteristics, but on understanding, which is inseparable from subjective judgment of qualities.

Furthermore, everyone would find it completely absurd if an art historian were to presume to derive laws of style for the art of the present and the future from the relationships discovered among the styles of the past. Yet this is precisely what the adherents of the Historical School presume to do with the economic laws that they purport to discover from the study of history. Even if one were to grant that it is possible to empirically derive laws of economic action applicable within temporal, national, or otherwise delimited historical periods, from the data of economic history, it would still be impermissible to call these laws economics and to treat them as such. No matter how much views about the character and content of economics may differ, there is one point about which unanimity prevails: economics is a theory capable of making assertions about future economic action, about the economic conditions of tomorrow and the day after tomorrow. The concept of theory, in contradistinction to the concept of history, is, and always and universally has been, understood as involving a regularity valid for the future as well as the past.

If the adherents of the Historical School were, in accordance with the logic and epistemology of their program, to confine themselves to speaking only of the economic conditions of the past, and if they were to decline to consider any questions touching on the economic conditions of the future, they could at least spare themselves the reproach of inconsistency. However, they maintain that what they write about and deal with is economics. Moreover, they engage in discussions of economic policy from the standpoint of scientific theory, as if their science, as they themselves conceive it, were in a position to make predictions about the economic conditions of the future.

We are not concerned here with the problems dealt with in the debate over the permissibility of value judgments in science. What is at issue is rather the question whether an adherent of the Historical School has not debarred himself from participating in the discussion of purely scientific problems, apart from all questions concerning the desirability of the ultimate ends being aimed at: whether, for example, he may make predictions about the future effects of a proposed change in currency legislation. Art historians speak of the art and the styles of the past. If they were to undertake to speak of the paintings of the future, no painter would pay any attention to what they said. Yet the economists of the Historical School talk more about the future than about the past. (As far as the historian is concerned, there are fundamentally only the past and the future. The present is but a fleeting instant between the two.) They speak of the effects of free trade and protection and of the consequences of the formation of cartels. They tell us that we must expect a planned economy, autarky, and the like. Has an art historian ever presumed to tell us what art styles the future holds in store for us?

The consistent adherent of the Historical School would have to confine himself to saying: There are, to be sure, a small number of generalizations that apply to all economic conditions.[3] But they are so few and insignificant that it is not worth while to dwell on them. The only worthy objects of consideration are the characteristics of changing economic styles that can be ascertained from economic history, and the historical theories relevant to these styles. Science is able to make statements about such matters. But it should be silent about economic conditions in general, and therefore about the economic conditions of tomorrow. For there cannot be an "historical theory" of future economic conditions.

If one classifies economics as one of the moral sciences that make use of the method of historical "understanding," then one must also adopt the procedure of these sciences. One may, accordingly, write a history of the German economy, or of all economies thus far, in the same way as one writes a history of German literature or of world literature; but one may certainly not write a "universal economics." Yet even this would be possible, from the point of view of the Historical School, if one were to contrast "universal economics," understood as universal economic history, to an alleged "special economics" that would deal with individual branches of production. However, the standpoint of the Historical School does not permit economics to be differentiated from economic history.

The purpose of this book is to establish the logical legitimacy of the science that has for its object the universally valid laws of human action, i.e., laws that claim validity without respect to the place, time, race, nationality, or class of the actor. The aim of these investigations is not to draw up the program of a new science, but to show what the science with which we are already acquainted has in view. The area of thought encompassed here is one to which Windelband, Rickert, and Max Weber were strangers. However, if they had been familiar with it, they would certainly not have disputed its logical legitimacy. What is denied is the possibility of deriving *a posteriori* from historical experience empirical laws of history in general, or of economic history in particular, or "laws" of "economic action" within a definite historical period.

Consequently, it would be completely amiss to want to read into the results of these investigations a condemnation of theories which assign to the moral or cultural sciences that make use of the historical method the cognition of the historical, the unique, the nonrepeatable, the individual, and the irrational, and which consider historical understanding as the distinctive method of these sciences and the construction of ideal types as their most important conceptual instrument. The method employed by the moral and cultural sciences is not in question here. On the contrary, my criticism is leveled only against the impermissible confusion of methods and the conceptual vagueness involved in the assumption—which abandons the insights that we owe to the inquiries of Windelband, Rickert, and Max Weber—that it is possible to derive "theoretical" knowledge from historical experience. What is under attack here is the doctrine that would have us believe, on the one hand, that historical data can be approached without any theory of action, and, on the other hand, that an empirical theory of action can be derived by induction from the data of history.

Every type of descriptive economics and economic statistics falls under the heading of historical research. They too apprise us only of the past, albeit the most recent past. From the point of view of empirical science, the present immediately becomes past. The cognitive value of such inquiries does not consist in the possibility of deriving from them teachings that could be formulated as theoretical propositions. Whoever fails to realize this is unable to grasp the meaning and logical character of historical research.

One would also completely misunderstand the intention of the following investigations if one were to regard them as an intrusion into the alleged conflict between history and empirical science, on the one hand, and pure and abstract theory, on the other. All theory is necessarily pure and abstract. Both theory and history are equally legitimate, and both are equally indispensable. The logical contrast between them is in no sense an opposition. The goal of my analysis is, rather, to distinguish aprioristic theory from history and empirical science and to demonstrate the absurdity of the endeavors of the Historical and the Institutionalist Schools to reconcile the logically incompatible. Such endeavors are inconsistent with the aims of historical research precisely because they seek to draw from the past practical applications for the present and the future, even if only to the extent of denying that the propositions of the universally valid theory are applicable to the present and the future.

The virtue of historical inquiry does not lie in the derivation of laws. Its cognitive value is not to be sought in the possibility of its providing direct practical applications for our action. It deals only with the past; it can never turn toward the future. History makes one wise, but not competent to solve concrete problems. The psuedo-historical discipline that today calls itself sociology is essentially an interpretation of historical events and a proclamation of allegedly inevitable future developments in the sense of the absurd Marxian metaphysics of progress. This metaphysics seeks to secure itself against the strictures of scientific sociology on the one hand and of historical investigation on the other by its pretension to view things "sociologically," and not economically, historically, or in some other way that would be exposed to "nonsociological" criticism. The proponents of the pseudo-historical discipline that calls itself "the economic aspects of the sciences of the state" and the adherents of the Institutionalist School protect themselves from the economists' critique of their interventionist program by citing the relativity of all the economic knowledge that they purport to have acquired through the presuppositionless treatment of economic history. Both seek to substitute the irrational for logic and discursive reasoning.

In order to examine the legitimacy of all these objections, it seemed to me imperative not only to demonstrate positively the logical character of the propositions of economics and sociology, but also to evaluate critically the teachings of a few representatives of historicism, empiricism, and irrationalism. This, of necessity, determined the outward form of my work. It is divided into a number of independent essays which, with the exception of the first and most comprehensive, were published previously.[4] From the outset, however, they were conceived and planned as parts of a whole, and they have been given further unity by means of various revisions, especially in the case of the second investigation. Furthermore, I considered it essential to reformulate, in this context, several basic ideas of economic theory in order to free them of the inconsistencies and confusions that had generally attached to them in previous presentations. I thought it pertinent also to expose the psychological factors that nourish the opposition to the acceptance of economic theory. And finally, I was convinced of the necessity of showing, by way of example, what relation does subsist between historical and economic conditions and what problems would certainly have to be taken into consideration by a school that sought, in turning to history, not a pretext for rejecting theoretical results that are unacceptable to it for political reasons, but a means of furthering knowledge. A certain amount of repetition has been inevitable in my treatment of these topics, since the arguments against the possibility of a universally valid economic theory, although stated in various forms, are, in the last analysis, all rooted in the same errors.

In principle the universal validity of the propositions of economics is no longer disputed even by the adherents of the Historical School. They have had to abandon this maxim of historicism. They confine themselves to restricting to a very narrow range the phenomena that such propositions could explain. And they consider these propositions so self-evident and commonplace that they regard it as unnecessary for any science to deal with them. On the other hand, this school maintains—and in this lies its empiricism—that economic laws applicable to particular historical periods can be derived from the data of economic history. Yet whatever the proponents of historicism exhibit in the way of such laws proves, on closer examination, to be the characterization of particular periods of history and their economic usages and to require, therefore, the specific understanding of the past. Thus far they have not succeeded in establishing a single thesis that would have the same logical status as the propositions of the universally valid theory. According to the Historical School, the laws of the universally valid theory are applicable only to the capitalism of the liberal era. Nevertheless, these laws enable us to grasp conceptually, under a single principle, the process by which the value of money changed in ancient Athens and in the "early capitalism" of the sixteenth century. A proposition essentially different from the laws of the universally valid theory that would also enable us to do this has yet to be adduced.

Accordingly, one is at a loss to understand why the adherents of the Historical School carefully avoid coming to grips directly with the teachings of the universally valid theory, why they persistently decline to undertake any general treatment of it,[5] and why they still stubbornly cling to such inappropriate designations as economics and economic theory for their historical arguments. The explanation can be found only when it is observed that political, and not scientific, considerations are decisive here: one combats economics because one knows no other way to protect an untenable political program against unfavorable criticism that employs the findings of science. The Historical School in Europe and the Institutionalist School in America are the harbingers of the ruinous economic policy that has brought the world to its present condition and will undoubtedly destroy modern culture if it continues to prevail.

These political considerations are not treated in this book, which concerns itself with the problems in their fundamental significance, quite apart from all politics. Perhaps, however, in an age that turns its back upon everything that does not, at first glance, appear to be immediately useful, it is not out of place to point out that abstract problems of logic and methodology have a close bearing on the life of every individual and on the fate of our entire culture. And it may be no less important to call attention to the fact that no problem of economics or sociology, even if it appears quite simple to superficial consideration, can be fully mastered without reverting to the logical foundations of the science of human action.

Ludwig von Mises
Vienna, January, 1933

NOTES

1. Bergson on exchange: *et l'on ne peut le pratiquer sans s'être demandé si les deux objects échangés sont bien de même valeur, c'est-à-dire échangeables contre un même troisieme.* (Bergson, *Les deux sources de la morale et de la religion* (Paris, 1932), p. 68.

2. Not until this book was already at the printer's did the volume devoted to Werner Sombart, presented in honor of his seventieth birthday by *Schmollers Jarbuch* (56th Yearbook, Volume 6) come into my hands. The first part is devoted to the treatment of the problem of "Theory and History." In discussing questions of logic and methodology, the articles in this volume make use of the traditional arguments of historicism and empiricism and pass over in silence the arguments against the view of the Historical School. This is true also of the most important contribution, that of Spiethoff ("Die Allgemeine Volkswirtschaftslehre als geschichtliche Theorie"), which is a brilliant presentation of the methodology of the school. Like the other contributors, Spiethoff comes to grips only with the ideas of the adherents of the Historical School; he does not even seem to be acquainted with Robbin's important work. Spiethoff says: "The theory of the capitalist market economy starts from the idea that individuals are guided by selfish motives. We know that charity is practiced as well, and that still other motives are operative, but we regard this as so insignificant in the aggregate as to be unessential . . ." (p. 900). This shows that Spiethoff's conception of the theory is far indeed from what modern subjectivist economics teaches. He still views the *status controversiae* as it presented itself in the eighties and nineties of the last century. He fails to see that from the point of view of economics, what is significant is not the economy, but the economic action of men. The universally valid aprioristic theory is not, as he thinks, an "unreal construction," though it is certainly a conceptual construction. There can be no theory other than an aprioristic and universally valid theory (i.e., a theory claiming validity independent of place, time, nationality, race, and the like), because human reasoning is unable to derive theoretical propositions from historical experience. All this escapes him entirely. In the investigations of this book the views of Spiethoff and the Historical School are critically examined in detail and rejected.

3. Consistent historicism, however, would not even have to grant this much.

4. I am indebted to the publishing house of Duncker and Humblot for permission to print the essays published in the 183rd volume of the publications of the Verein für Sozialpolitik.

5. The fact that Sombart calls Gossen "the brilliant idiot" can hardly be regarded as a sufficient critique. Cf. Sombart, *Die drei Nationalokonömien* (Munich, 1930), p. 4.

Contents

1

The Task and Scope
of the Science of
Human Action

I. *The Nature and Development of the Social Sciences*

1. ORIGIN IN THE HISTORICAL AND NORMATIVE SCIENCES

It is in accounts of history that we find the earliest beginnings of knowledge in the sciences of human action. An epistemology that is today rejected required of the historian that he approach his subject matter without theory and simply depict the past as it was. He has to describe and portray past reality, and, it was said, he will best succeed in doing this if he views events and the sources of information about them with the least possible amount of prejudice and presupposition.

Not until very late was it realized that the historian cannot duplicate or reproduce the past; on the contrary, he interprets and recasts it, and this requires that he make use of some ideas that he must have already had before setting about his work.[1] Even if, in the course of his work, the treatment of his material leads him to new ideas, concepts are always logically prior to the understanding of the individual, the unique, and the non-repeatable. It is impossible to speak of war and peace unless one has a definite conception of war and peace before one turns to the historical sources. Nor can one speak of causes and effects in the individual case unless one possesses a theory that treats certain connections between cause and effect as having a universal range

1

of applicability. The reason why we accept the sentence, "The king defeated the rebels and therefore remained in power," but are not satisfied with the logically contradictory sentence, "The king defeated the rebels and therefore fell from power," is that the first conforms to our theories about the results of military victory, while the latter contradicts them.

The study of history always presupposes a measure of universally valid knowledge. This knowledge, which constitutes the conceptual tool of the historian, may sometimes seem platitudinous to one who considers it only superficially. But closer examination will more often reveal that it is the necessary consequence of a system of thought that embraces all human action and all social phenomena. For example, in using an expression such as "land hunger," "lack of land," or the like, one makes implicit reference to a theory that, if consistently thought through to its conclusion, leads to the law of diminishing returns, or in more general terms, the law of returns. For if this law did not hold, the farmer who wanted to obtain a greater net yield would not require more land; by means of an increased expenditure of labor and capital goods he would be able to obtain from even the smallest piece of tillage the same result he wanted to achieve by increasing the amount of acreage at his disposal. The size of the area available for cultivation would then be a matter of indifference to him.

However, it is not only in history and in the other sciences that make use of the conceptual tools of historical investigation that we find universally valid statements about human action. Such knowledge also constitutes the foundation of the normative sciences—ethics, the philosophy of law, and systematic jurisprudence. The primary task of political philosophy, the philosophy of law, and political science is the attainment of universally valid knowledge of social phenomena. If they have failed in this endeavor, the reason is to be sought not only in the fact that they often strayed from their goal and aimed at others, and—like the philosophy of history—instead of seeking the universally valid in the vicissitudes of particular events, began to search for the objective meaning of things. The determining factor in their failure was that from the very outset they made use of a scientifically unfruitful method: they began not with the individual and his action, but with attempts to view the totality. What they wanted to discover was not the regularity prevailing in the action of men, but the whole course of mankind's progression from its origin to the end of all things.

Psychology, in turning to the individual, found the right starting point. However, its path necessarily leads in another direction than that of the science of human action. The subject matter of the latter is action and what follows from action, whereas the subject matter of psychology is the psychic events that result in action. Economics begins at the point at which psychology leaves off.

2. ECONOMICS

The scattered and fragmentary insights of the historical and normative sciences themselves achieved scientific status only with the development of economics in the eighteenth century. When men realized that the phenomena of the market conform to laws, they began to develop catallactics and the theory of exchange, which constitutes the heart of economics. After the theory of the division of labor was elaborated, Ricardo's law of association enabled men to grasp its nature and significance, and thereby the nature and significance of the formation of society.

The development of economics and rationalistic sociology from Cantillon and Hume to Bentham and Ricardo did more to transform human thinking than any other scientific theory before or since. Up to that time it had been believed that no bounds other than those drawn by the laws of nature circumscribed the path of acting man. It was not known that there is still something more that sets a limit to political power beyond which it cannot go. Now it was learned that in the social realm too there is something operative which power and force are unable to alter and to which they must adjust themselves if they hope to achieve success, in precisely the same way as they must take into account the laws of nature.

This realization had enormous significance for men's action. It led to the program and policies of liberalism and thus unleashed human powers that, under capitalism, have transformed the world. Yet it was precisely the practical significance of the theories of the new science that was responsible for its undoing. Whoever wished to combat liberal economic policy was compelled to challenge the character of economics as a science. Enemies arose against it for political reasons.

The historian must never forget that the most momentous occurrence in the history of the last hundred years, the attack launched against the universally valid science of human action and its hitherto best developed branch, economics, was motivated from the very beginning not by scientific ideas, but by political considerations. However, the science of human action itself is not concerned with these political backgrounds, but with the arguments with which it has been confronted. For it has also been confronted with arguments and attacked by objective reasoning. Its nature remained problematical as long as no one succeeded in achieving clarity about the question what this science really is and what character its propositions have.

3. THE PROGRAM OF SOCIOLOGY AND THE QUEST FOR HISTORICAL LAWS

Concurrently with the achievements that stemmed from the foundation of the science of human action came grandiloquent programmatic declarations that demanded a science of social phenomena. The discoveries made by Hume, Smith, Ricardo, Bentham, and many others may be regarded as constituting the historical beginning and foundation of a truly scientific knowledge of society. The term "sociology," however, was coined by August Comte, who, for the rest, in no way contributed to social science. A great number of authors with him and after him called for a science of society, most of them without appreciating what had already been done toward founding it and without being able to specify how one would go about achieving it. Many lost themselves in empty trivialities, the most frightful example of which may be considered the attempt to conceive of society as a biological organism. Others concocted an ostensible science to justify their political schemes. Still others, for example Comte himself, added new constructions to the philosophy of history and called the result sociology.

These prophets of a new epoch, who professed to have developed for the first time a science of the social realm, not only failed in this domain, which they had declared to be the proper field of their activity, but unhesitatingly set out to destroy history and all the sciences that make use of the historical method. Prepossessed by the idea that Newtonian mechanics constitutes the model for all the genuine sciences, they demanded of history that it at last begin to raise itself to the status of an exact science through the construction of "historical laws."

Windelband, Rickert, and their school opposed these demands and brought into clear relief the special and peculiar characteristics of historical investigation. Nevertheless, their arguments are weakened by their failure to conceive of the possibility of universally valid knowledge in the sphere of human action. In their view the domain of social science comprises only history and the historical method.[2] They regarded the findings of economics and historical investigation in the same light as the Historical School. Thus, they remained bound to historicism. Moreover, they did not see that an intellectual outlook corresponding to the empiricism that they had attacked in the field of the sciences of human action often went hand in hand with historicism.

4. THE STANDPOINT OF HISTORICISM

In the view of historicism the field of the science of human action is constituted only by history and the historical method. Historicism maintains that it is a waste of effort to search after universally valid regularities that would be independent of time, place, race, nationality, and culture. All that sociology and economics can tell us is the experience of a historical event, which can be invalidated by new experience. What was yesterday can be otherwise tomorrow. All scientific knowledge in the social realm is derived from experience; it is a generalization drawn from past experience that can always be upset by some later experience. Therefore, the only appropriate method of the social sciences is the specific understanding of the historically unique. There is no knowledge whose validity extends beyond a definite historical epoch or at most beyond several historical epochs.

It is impossible to think this view through consistently to its conclusion. If one attempts to do so, one must sooner or later reach a point at which one is forced to admit that there is something in our knowledge that comes before experience, something whose validity is independent of time and place. Even Sombart, who is today the most outspoken representative of the view that economics must make use of the method of understanding, is compelled to acknowledge that also in the "field of culture, and in particular of human society, there is such a thing as logically necessary relationships." He believes that "they constitute what we call the mind's conformity to law; and we call these principles, deduced a priori, laws." [3] Thus, unintentionally and unawares, Sombart has admitted all that is required to prove the necessity of a universally valid science of human action fundamentally different from the historical sciences of human action. If there are such principles and laws at all, then there must also be a science of them; and this science must be logically prior to every other treatment of these problems. It will not do simply to accept these principles as they are conceived in daily life. It is absurd to want to forbid science to enter a field and to demand tolerance for received misconceptions and unclear, contradictory ideas. Nor is Sombart able to offer anything more than a few sarcastic remarks in support of his disapproval of any attempt to treat economics as a universally valid theory. He thinks it is "occasionally very amusing to observe how an empty trifle lying concealed behind a great show of words makes its appearance in all its pitiful meagreness and almost arouses our scorn." [4] This is, of course, a quite inadequate attempt to defend the procedure adopted by Sombart and other supporters of historicism. If, as Sombart expressly admits, there are "fundamental economic concepts . . . that are universally valid for all economic action," [5] then science may not be prevented from concerning itself with them.

Sombart admits still more. He states explicitly that "all theory is 'pure,' that is, independent of time and space." [6] Thus he takes issue with Knies, who opposed the "absolutism of theory," i.e., its "pretension to set forth propositions in the scientific treatment of political economy that are unconditional and equally valid for all times, countries, and nationalities." [7]

Perhaps it will be objected that it is belaboring the obvious to insist that economics provides us with universally valid knowledge. Unfortunately, such a reproach would have no justification; in the eyes of many people it is not obvious. Whoever has undertaken to present the teachings of historicism in a coherent form has generally been unable to avoid revealing, at some point in the process, the impossibility of systematically developing the doctrine. However, the importance of historicism does not lie in the entirely abortive attempts that have been made to treat it as a coherent theory. Historicism by its very nature is not a system, but the rejection and denial in principle of the possibility of constructing a system. It exists and operates not within the structure of a complete system of thought, but in critical *aperçus*, in the propaganda of economic and socio-political programs, and between the lines of historical, descriptive, and statistical studies. The politics and the science of the last decades have been completely dominated by the views of historicism and empiricism. When it is recalled that an author who, during his lifetime, stood in the highest regard in the German-speaking countries as a theorist of "the economic aspects of political science," explained the necessity to economize as a specific feature of production in a money economy,[8] one will certainly appreciate the need of emphasizing the untenability of historicism before embarking upon the task of setting forth the logical character of the science of human action.

5. THE STANDPOINT OF EMPIRICISM

It is indisputable that there is and must be an aprioristic theory of human action. And it is equally indisputable that human action can be the subject matter of historical investigation. The protest of the consistent representatives of historicism, who do not want to admit the possibility of a theory that would be independent of time and place, need disturb us no more than the contention of naturalism, which wants to challenge the scientific character of history so long as it has not reached the point where it can establish historical laws.

Naturalism presupposes that empirical laws could be derived a posteriori from the study of historical data. Sometimes it is assumed that these laws are valid without respect to time or place, sometimes that they have validity only for certain periods, countries, races, or nationalities.[9] The overwhelming majority of historians reject both varieties of this doctrine. Indeed, it is generally rejected even by those who are in accord with historicism and who do not want to admit that, without the aid of the aprioristic theory of human action, the historian would be completely at a loss to deal with his material and would be unable to solve any of his problems. Such historians generally maintain that they are able to carry on their work completely free of theory.

We need not enter here into the investigation of whether historicism must lead necessarily to the one or to the other of these two views. Whoever is of the opinion that the doctrine of historicism cannot be consistently thought through to its conclusion will consider it futile to undertake such an investigation. The only point worth noting is that a sharp opposition exists between the view of the adherents of the Historical School and that of the majority of historians. Whereas the former believe that they can discover empirical laws from the data of history and want to call the compilation of such laws sociology and economics, most historians would not be willing to agree that this can be done.

The thesis of those who affirm the possibility of deriving empirical laws from historical data we shall call empiricism. Historicism and empiricism are, consequently, not the same thing. As a rule, though certainly not always, if they take any position on the problem at all, historians profess their adherence to historicism. With few exceptions (Buckle, for example) they are opponents of empiricism. The adherents of the Historical and the Institutionalist Schools take the point of view of historicism, although they find it impossible to maintain this doctrine in its purity as soon as they attempt to state it in a logically and epistemologically coherent manner; they are almost always in accord with empiricism. Thus, a sharp contrast of view generally exists between the historians and the economists and sociologists of the Historical School.

The question with which we are now concerned is no longer whether a prevailing regularity can be discovered in human action, but whether the observation of facts without any reference to a system of aprioristic knowledge of human action can be considered a method capable of leading us to the cognition of such a regularity. Can economic history furnish "building stones" for an economic theory, as Schmoller maintains? [10] Can the "findings of economic history's specialized description become elements of theory and lead to universal truths"? In this connection we shall not take up the question of the possibility of universal "historical laws" (which would therefore not be economic laws) that has often been exhaustively discussed.[11] We shall limit ourselves to examining whether, by means of the observation of facts, that is, by an a posteriori method, we could arrive at statements of the kind sought for by the system of economic theory.

The method used by the natural sciences for the discovery of the laws of phenomena begins with observation. However, the decisive step is taken only with the construction of an hypothesis: a proposition does not simply emerge from observation and experience, for these always present us only with complex phenomena in which various factors appear so closely connected that we are unable to determine what role should be attributed to each. The hypothesis is already an intellectual elaboration of experience, above all in its claim to universal validity, which is its decisive characteristic. The experience that has led to the construction of the proposition is always limited to the past; it is always an experience of a phenomenon that occurred in a particular place and at a particular time. However, the universal validity claimed for the proposition also implies applicability to all other past and future occurrences. It is based on an imperfect induction. (No universal theorems emerge from perfect induction, but only descriptions of an event that occurred in the past.)

Hypotheses must be continually verified anew by experience.

In an experiment they can generally be subjected to a particular method of examination. Various hypotheses are linked together into a system, and everything is deduced that must logically follow from them. Then experiments are performed again and again to verify the hypotheses in question. One tests whether new experience conforms to the expectations required by the hypotheses. Two assumptions are necessary for these methods of verification: the possibility of controlling the conditions of the experiment, and the existence of experimentally discoverable constant relations whose magnitudes admit of numerical determination. If we wish to call a proposition of empirical science true (with whatever degree of certainty or probability an empirically derived proposition can have) when a change of the relevant conditions in all observed cases leads to the results we have been led to expect, then we may say that we possess the means of testing the truth of such propositions.

With regard to historical experience, however, we find ourselves in an entirely different situation. Here we lack the possibility not only of performing a controlled experiment in order to observe the individual determinants of a change, but also of discovering numerical constants. We can observe and experience historical change only as the result of the combined action of a countless number of individual causes that we are unable to distinguish according to their magnitudes. We never find fixed relationships that are open to numerical calculation. The long cherished assumption that a proportional relationship, which could be expressed in an equation, exists between prices and the quantity of money has proved fallacious; and as a result the doctrine that knowledge of human action can be formulated in quantitative terms has lost its only support.

Whoever wants to derive laws of human action from experience would have to be able to show how given situations influence action quantitatively and qualitatively. It is psychology that generally has sought to provide such a demonstration, and for that reason all those who assign this task to sociology and economics are prone to recommend to them the psychological method. What is more, by the psychological method they understand not what was called psychological—in a rather inappropriate and even misleading sense—in the method of the Austrian School, but rather the procedures and discoveries of scientific psychology itself.

However, psychology has failed in this sphere. With the use of its methods it can, of course, observe unconscious reactions to stimuli in the manner of the biological sciences. Beyond this it can accomplish nothing that could lead to the discovery of empirical laws. It can determine how definite men have behaved in definite situations in the past, and it infers from its findings that conduct will be similar in the future if similar men are placed in a similar situation. It can tell us how English school boys behaved in the last decades when confronted with a definite situation, for example, when they encountered a crippled beggar. Such information tells us very little about the conduct of English school children in the coming decades or about the conduct of French or German school children. Psychology can establish nothing more than the occurrence of an historical incident: the cases observed have shown such and such; but the conclusions drawn from the observed cases, which refer to English school children of a definite period, are not logically justified when applied to other cases of the same historical and ethnological character that have not been observed.

All that observation teaches us is that the same situation has a different effect on different men. The attempt to arrange men in classes whose members all react in the same way has not been successful because even the same men react differently at different times, and there is no means of ascribing unequivocally definite modes of reaction to different ages or other objectively distinguishable periods or conditions of life. Consequently, there is no hope of achieving knowledge of a regularity in the phenomena by this method. This is what one has in mind when one speaks of free will, of the irrationality of what is human, spiritual, or historical, of individuality in history, and of the impossibility of rationally comprehending life in its fullness and diversity. One expresses the same idea in pointing out that it is not possible for us to grasp how the action of the external world influences our minds, our will, and, consequently, our action. It follows from this that psychology, in so far as it deals with such things, is history or, in the terminology of current German philosophy, a moral science.

Whoever declares that the method of historical understanding used by the moral sciences is appropriate also for economics should be aware of the fact that this method can never lead to the discovery of empirical laws. Understanding is precisely the method that the historical sciences (in the broadest sense of the term) employ in dealing with the unique, the non-repeatable, that is, in treating what is simply historical. Understanding is the mental grasp of something that we are unable to bring under rules and explain through them.[12] This is true not only of the field traditionally designated as that of universal history, but also of all special fields, above all that of economic history. The position taken by the empiricist school of German economics in the struggle against economic theory is untenable also from the standpoint of the logic of the historical sciences as developed by Dilthey, Windelband, Rickert, and Max Weber.

In the empirical sciences the controlled experiment is indispensable for the a posteriori derivation of propositions whenever experience presents only complex phenomena in which the effect is produced by several interlinked causes. In historical experience we can observe only complex phenomena, and an experiment is inapplicable to such a situation. Sometimes it is said that a mental experiment (*Gedankenexperiment*) could take its place. However, a mental experiment, logically considered, has an entirely different meaning from a real experiment. It involves thinking through the implications of a proposition in the light of its compatibility with other propositions that we accept as true. If these other propositions are not derived from experience, then the mental experiment makes no reference to experience.

6. THE LOGICAL CHARACTER OF THE UNIVERSALLY VALID SCIENCE OF HUMAN ACTION

The science of human action that strives for universally valid knowledge is the theoretical system whose hitherto best elaborated branch is economics. In all of its branches this science is a priori, not empirical. Like logic and mathematics, it is not derived from experience; it is prior to experience. It is, as it were, the logic of action and deed.[13]

Human thought serves human life and action. It is not absolute thought, but the forethought directed toward projected acts and the afterthought that reflects upon acts done. Hence, in the last analysis, logic and the universally valid science of human action are one and the same. If we separate them, so as to contrast logic and practice, we must show at what point their paths diverge and where the special province of the science of action is to be found.

One of the tasks with which thought must cope in order to fulfill its function is that of comprehending the conditions under which human action takes place. To treat these in their concrete detail is the work of the natural sciences and, in a certain sense, also of history and the other historical sciences. Our science, on the other hand, disregarding the accidental, considers only the essential. Its goal is the comprehension of the universal, and its procedure is formal and axiomatic. It views action and the conditions under which action takes place not in their concrete form, as we encounter them in everyday life, nor in their actual setting, as we view them in each of the sciences of nature and of history, but as formal constructions that enable us to grasp the patterns of human action in their purity.

Only experience makes it possible for us to know the particular conditions of action in their concrete form. Only experience can teach us that there are lions and microbes and that their existence can present definite problems to acting man; and it would be absurd, without experience, to indulge in speculations about the existence or nonexistence of some legendary beast. The existence of the external world is given through experience; and if we pursue definite plans, only experience can teach us how we must act vis-a-vis the external world in concrete situations.

However, what we know about our action under given conditions is derived not from experience, but from reason. What we know about the fundamental categories of action—action, economizing, preferring, the relationship of means and ends, and everything else that, together with these, constitutes the system of human action—is not derived from experience. We conceive all this from within, just as we conceive logical and mathematical truths, a priori, without reference to any experience. Nor could experience ever lead anyone to the knowledge of these things if he did not comprehend them from within himself.

As an a priori category the principle of action is on a par with the principle of causality. It is present in all knowledge of any conduct that goes beyond an unconscious reaction. "In the beginning was the deed." In our view the concept of man is, above all else, also the concept of the being who acts. Our consciousness is that of an ego which is capable of acting and does act. The fact that our deeds are intentional makes them actions. Our thinking about men and their conduct, and our conduct toward men and toward our surroundings in general, presuppose the category of action.

Nevertheless, we are quite incapable of thinking of this fundamental category and the system deduced from it without also thinking, at the same time, of the universal prerequisites of human action. For example, we are unable to grasp the concept of economic action and of economy without implying in our thought the concept of economic quantity relations and the concept of an economic good. Only experience can teach us whether or not these concepts are applicable to anything in the conditions under which our life must actually be lived. Only experience tells us that not all things in the external world are free goods. However, it is not experience, but reason, which is prior to experience, that tells us what is a free and what is an economic good.

Consequently, it would be possible to construct, by the use of the axiomatic method, a universal praxeology so general that its system would embrace not only all the patterns of action in the world that we actually encounter, but also patterns of action in worlds whose conditions are purely imaginary and do not correspond to any experience. A theory of money would still be meaningful even if throughout history there had never been any indirect exchange. That such a theory would have no practical importance in a world that did not use money would in no way detract from the truth of its statements. Because we study science for the sake of real life—and, it should be remembered, the desire for pure knowledge for its own sake is also a part of life—and not as a form of mental gymnastics, we generally do not mind forgoing the gratification that could be offered by a perfect, comprehensive system of the axioms of human action, a system so universal that it would comprise all thinkable categories of the conditions of action. Instead, we are satisfied with the less universal system that refers to the conditions given in the world of experience.

Nevertheless, this reference to experience in no way changes the aprioristic character of our knowledge. In this connection, experience is of absolutely no concern to our thinking. All that we owe to experience is the demarcation of those problems that we consider with interest from problems that we wish to leave aside because they are uninteresting from the point of view of our desire for knowledge. Hence, experience by no means always refers to the existence or nonexistence of the conditions of action, but often only to the presence of an interest in the treatment of a problem. In experience there is no socialist community; nevertheless, the investigation of the economy of such a community is a problem that in our age arouses the greatest of interest.

A theory of action could conceivably be constructed on the assumption that men lacked the possibility of understanding one another by means of symbols, or on the assumption that men— immortal and eternally young—were indifferent in every respect to the passage of time and therefore did not consider it in their action. The axioms of the theory could conceivably be framed in such universal terms as to embrace these and all other possibilities; and it would be conceivable to draw up a formal praxeological system patterned after the science of logic or the science built upon the axioms of, for example, Hilbertian geometry.[14] We forgo these possibilities because conditions that do not correspond to those we encounter in our action interest us only in so far as thinking through their implications in imaginary constructions enables us to further our knowledge of action under given conditions.

The method actually employed by economists in the treatment of their problems can be seen with particular clarity in the case of the problem of imputation. Conceivably it would be possible to formulate the theory of the appraisement and pricing of the factors of production (goods of higher order, producers' goods) in the broadest generality so that, for one thing, we would work only with an unqualified concept, viz., means of production. We could then elaborate the theory in such a way that the three factors of production that are enumerated in the customary presentation would appear as special cases. But we proceed differently. We do not bother to furnish a universal imputation theory of the means of production as such, but proceed immediately to the treatment of the three categories of means of production: land, labor, and capital. This practice is altogether warranted by the object of our investigation, of which we must never lose sight.

However, the renunciation of axiomatic universality and precision also conceals many dangers, and it has not always been possible to avoid them. It is not only the Marxist theory of classes[15] that has failed to grasp the categorial character of each of these specific groups of factors of production. To be sure, it was noted that the peculiarity of land as a factor of production lies in the difference in the usefulness of individual pieces of land from the point of view of the goals of action; the theory of ground rent never lost sight of the fact that land is appraised differently according to its quality and location. However, the theory of wages did overlook the fact that labor too is of different quality and intensity and that on the market there is never a supply of or a demand for "labor" as such, but only a supply of and a demand for labor of a definite kind. Even after this fact was recognized, an attempt was made to evade its consequences by assuming that what forms the bulk of the supply and is chiefly in demand is unskilled labor and that it is permissible to ignore, as quantitatively negligible, skilled, "higher" labor. The theory of wages would have been spared many errors had it been kept in mind what function the special treatment of labor in the theory of distribution is called upon to fulfill and at what point it becomes necessary to speak no longer simply of labor, but of labor of a definite quality that is offered or sought at a given time in a given place. It was still more difficult for the theory of capital to free itself of the idea of abstract capital, where the categorial difference between land, labor, and capital is no longer in question, but where the appraisement of definite capital goods, supplied or demanded in a definite place at a definite time, is to be considered. Likewise in the theory of distribution and in the theory of imputation, it was not easy to shake off the influence of the universalist view.[16]

Our science deals with the forms and patterns of action under the various categories of its conditions. In pointing this out we are not drafting a plan for a future science. We do not maintain that the science of human action should be made aprioristic, but that it is so already. We do not want to discover a new method, but only to characterize correctly the method that is actually used. The theorems of economics are derived not from the observation of facts, but through deduction from the fundamental category of action, which has been expressed sometimes as the economic principle (i.e., the necessity to economize), sometimes as the value principle or as the cost principle. They are of aprioristic derivation and therefore lay claim to the apodictic certainty that belongs to basic principles so derived.

7. SOCIOLOGY AND ECONOMICS: SOME COMMENTS ON THE HISTORY OF ECONOMIC THOUGHT

It is in sociology and above all in economics that we encounter the universally valid science of human action. Whatever has hitherto been accomplished in this science is to be considered either sociology or economics in the traditional sense. Names are conventional designations that in no way can directly—that is, without reference to an existing terminology—express the essence of what is designated, as a still widespread view demands. Consequently, there is no point in examining the appropriateness of the terms "economics" (theory of the economy) and "sociology" (theory of society) as names for the universally valid science of human action. Inherited from the past, they have accompanied the science on its way to the development of a completely comprehensive theoretical system. That is why these terms, in accordance with the way in which words are coined, refer to the historical starting point of the investigation and not to the logical foundation of the developed theory or to the central idea of the theory itself. Unfortunately, this fact has not always been appreciated, and repeated attempts have been made to define and comprehend the scope and task of the science on the basis of nomenclature. In the spirit of a crude form of conceptual realism, society was designated as the subject matter assigned to sociology, and the economy, or the economic aspect of culture, as the theme of economics. And then no pains were spared in the attempt to ascertain what, after all, society and the economy really are.

If today we may take the view that the subject of our science is human action, without fear of thereby arousing more hostility than that which every scientific theory encounters, it is because of the work of several generations of scholars. The investigations of such completely different thinkers as Cairnes, Bagehot, Menger, Max Weber, and Robbins show that they are all guided by this idea. In view of the history of science it is understandable that the claim of economics to be aprioristic and not empirical may still give rise to opposition because the existing literature has only slightly prepared the way for it. The two hundred years in which the development of our science has taken place have not been favorable to the acknowledgment of a new field of aprioristic knowledge. The successes achieved by the use of the empirical methods of the natural sciences and by the careful investigation of sources on the part of the historical sciences have attracted so much attention that no notice was taken of the advances that the aprioristic sciences were making at the same time, although without them the progress made by empiricism would not have been possible. An age that wanted to deny the aprioristic character even of logic was certainly not prepared for the recognition of the aprioristic character of praxeology.

A glance at the theories of Senior, John Stuart Mill, Cairnes, and Wieser will show that, in spite of different terminologies and divergent views of the logical character of economics and of its place among the sciences, the conception of it as an aprioristic discipline was not, in fact, very far from the position taken not only by the economists who adhered to the views of the classical school, but also by the authors of the subjective theory of value. However, in this connection, one should be careful not to draw too sweeping conclusions from their statements, in view of the profound changes that have taken place since then in the conception of the fundamental logical and methodological questions and, correspondingly, also in the terminology of the literature devoted to their treatment.

According to Senior, there is no doubt that the science of economics "depends more on reasoning than observation." [17] Concerning the method of the economist he states: "His premises consist of a few general propositions, the result of observation, or consciousness, and scarcely requiring proof, or even formal statement, which almost every man, as soon as he hears them, admits, as familiar to his thoughts, or at least as included in his previous knowledge." [18] Here both the observation of the external world and self-consciousness are mentioned as the sources of our knowledge. However, it is said that these propositions, which originate from within, either are immediately evident or follow necessarily from immediately evident propositions. Consequently, they are of aprioristic derivation and are not dependent upon experience, unless one wishes to call aprioristic cognition inner experience.

John Stuart Mill recognizes only empirical science and rejects in principle "a supposed mode of philosophizing, which does not profess to be founded upon experience at all." He distinguishes two methods of scientific thought: the method a posteriori, "which requires, as the basis of its conclusions, not experience merely, but specific experience," and the method a priori, by which he understands "reasoning from an assumed hypothesis." In addition, he says of the latter method that it is "not a practice confined to mathematics, but is of the essence of all science which admits of general reasoning at all." Political economy is to be characterized "as essentially an abstract science, and its method as the method a priori." [19]

It would lead us far from our subject to point out and examine what separates us today from Mill's conception of the a priori and of economics. In his view, even axioms are "but a class, the most universal class, of inductions from experience"; indeed, logic and mathematics are empirical sciences.[20] Just as geometry "presupposes an arbitrary definition of a line: that which has length, but not breadth," so "does political economy presuppose an

arbitrary definition of man, as a being who invariably does that
by which he may obtain the greatest amount of necessaries, con-
veniences and luxuries, with the smallest quantity of labor and
physical self-denial with which they can be obtained in the existing state of knowledge." [21] Here the only important thing for us
to note is that Mill places logic, mathematics, and the "moral
sciences" in the category of disciplines for which the appropriate
method is the "method a priori." For the "moral sciences" this
is "the only method," since the impossibility of performing experiments precludes the "method a posteriori." [22]

Even the contrast that Cairnes drew between the inductive and
the deductive methods does not correspond to the distinction that
we make between empiricism and apriorism. His terminology was
that of the philosophy of his age, which was completely under
the influence of empiricism and psychologism. When Cairnes proceeds to answer the question whether economics is to be studied
according to the deductive method or—as is generally assumed—
according to the inductive method, and concludes by ascribing
principal importance to the former, he employs a terminology
that is so far removed from that of modern logic and epistemology
that it would require intensive analysis to translate the meaning
of his words into language familiar to the contemporary reader.
But his actual reasoning, even though formulated in different
terms, is closer to our own conception than would appear at first
sight. Cairnes points out that the position of the natural scientist
and that of the economist in relation to the subject matter of
their investigations are entirely different. There is no other
method available to the natural scientist than that of inductive—
we would say: empirical—investigation, for "mankind have no
direct knowledge of ultimate physical principles." [23] It is otherwise
in the case of the economist. "The economist starts with a knowledge of ultimate causes." [24] We have at our disposal "direct knowledge . . . of causes in our consciousness of what passes in our
own minds, and in the information which our senses convey, or
at least are capable of conveying, to us of external facts." [25] Thus,
the economist is "at the outset of his researches . . . already in

possession of those ultimate principles governing the phenomena which form the subject of his study." [26]

Even more obviously than Cairnes, Wieser tends toward the view that economics is an aprioristic science. He failed to reach this conclusion only because the prevailing epistemological theories barred the way.[27] The function of economic theory, according to Wieser, consists in "scientifically explicating and developing the content of common economic experience." The consciousness of every economically active human being, he continues, provides him with

a fund of experiences that are the common possession of all who practice economy. These are experiences that every theorist already finds within himself without first having to resort to special scientific procedures. They are experiences concerning facts of the external world, as for instance, the existence of goods and their orders; experiences concerning facts of an internal character, such as the existence of human needs, and concerning the consequences of this fact; and experiences concerning the origin and course of economic action on the part of most men.

The scope of economic theory extends

exactly as far as common experience. The task of the theorist always ends where common experience ends and where science must collect its observations by historical or statistical investigation or by whatever other means may be deemed reliable.[28]

It is clear that what Wieser calls "common experience," in contradistinction to the other kind, is not the experience with which the empirical sciences are concerned. The method of economics, which Wieser himself calls the psychological method, but which at the same time he also sharply distinguishes from psychology, consists, he says, in "looking outward from within the consciousness," while the natural scientist (and therefore empirical science) observes the facts "only from without." Wieser sees the cardinal error of Schumpeter precisely in his belief that the method of the natural sciences is suitable also for economic theory. Economics, Wieser maintains, finds "that certain acts are performed in the consciousness with the feeling of necessity." Why, then, "should it first go to the trouble of deriving a law from a long chain of induction when everyone clearly hears the voice of the law within himself?" [29]

What Wieser calls "common experience" is to be sharply distinguished from experience acquired "through observations collected in the manner of historical or statistical studies." Clearly, this is not experience in the sense of the empirical sciences, but the very opposite: it is that which logically precedes experience and is, indeed, a condition and presupposition of every experience. When Wieser seeks to mark off economic theory from the historical, descriptive, and statistical treatment of economic problems, he enters upon a path that must lead, if one follows it consistently, to the recognition of the aprioristic character of economic theory. Of course, it should occasion no surprise that Wieser himself did not draw this conclusion. He was unable to rid himself of the influence of Mill's psychologistic epistemology, which ascribed an empirical character even to the laws of thought.[30]

NOTES

1. Cf. Rickert, *Kulturwissenschaft und Naturwissenschaft* (3rd ed.; Tübingen, 1915), pp. 28 ff.
2. Cf. below p. 74.
3. Sombart, *Die drei Nationalökonomien* (Munich and Leipzig, 1930), p. 253.
4. *Ibid.*
5. Sombart, *op. cit.,* p. 247.
6. Sombart, *op. cit.,* p. 298.
7. Knies, *Die politische Ökonomie vom geschichtlichen Standpunkte* (Braunschweig, 1883), p. 24.
8. Cf. Lexis, *Allgemeine Volkswirtschaftslehre* (3rd ed.; Berlin and Leipzig, 1926), p. 14.
9. For a critique of this second point of view, cf. below pp. 25 ff. and pp. 119 ff.
10. Schmoller, "Volkswirtschaft, Volkswirtschaftslehre und Methode," *Handwörterbuch der Staatswissenschaften* (3rd ed.), VIII, 464.
11. Concerning historical laws, cf. below pp. 108 ff.
12. Cf. below pp. 130 ff.
13. Several great economists were at the same time great logicians: Hume, Whately, John Stuart Mill, and Stanley Jevons.
14. Cf. Slutsky, "Ein Beitrag zur formal-praxeologischen Grundlegung der Ökonomik," *Annales de la classe des sciences sociales-économiques* (Kiev: Académie Oukraïenne des Sciences, 1926), Vol. IV.

15. On this point cf. my *Socialism,* trans. by J. Kahane (new ed.; New Haven, 1951), pp. 331 f.
16. On the universalist view cf. below pp. 153 f. For a special application of the reasoning outlined in the text to the theory of capital, cf. below pp. 217 ff.
17. Senior, *Political Economy* (6th ed.; London, 1872), p. 5.
18. *Ibid.,* p. 3.
19. John Stuart Mill, *Essays on Some Unsettled Questions of Political Economy* (3rd ed.; London, 1877), p. 143.
20. John Stuart Mill, *System of Logic Ratiocinative and Inductive* (8th ed.; London, 1872), I, 290 ff.
21. John Stuart Mill, *op. cit.,* p. 144.
22. John Stuart Mill, *op. cit.,* pp. 146 ff.
23. Cairnes, *The Character and Logical Method of Political Economy* (3rd ed.; London, 1888), p. 83.
24. *Ibid.,* p. 87.
25. *Ibid.,* p. 88.
26. *Ibid.,* pp. 89 ff.
27. Menger's pioneering investigations are still further weakened by their dependence on Mill's empiricism and psychologism. In this connection I wish to emphasize that I employ terms like "empiricism," "historicism," etc. without any connotation of a value judgment. Cf. Husserl, *Logische Untersuchungen* (3rd ed.; Halle, 1922), I, 52, footnote.
28. Wieser, "Theorie der gesellschaftlichen Wirtschaft," *Grundriss der Sozialökonomik* (Tübingen, 1914), p. 133.
29. Wieser, "Das Wesen und der Hauptinhalt der theoretischen Nationalökonomie," *Gesammelte Abhandlungen,* edited by Hayek (Tübingen, 1929), p. 17.
30. Among the most recent works devoted to the logic and methodology of the science of human action are those of Engliš: *Grundlagen des wirtschaftlichen Denkens,* trans. by Saudek (Brünn, 1925); *Begrundung der Teleologie als Form des empirischen Erkennens* (Brünn, 1930); and *Teleologische Theorie der Staatswirtschaft* (Brünn, 1933). The opposition between causality and teleology, which is the chief concern of Engliš, is not within the scope of the problems dealt with here.

II. *The Scope and Meaning of the System of A Priori Theorems*

1. THE BASIC CONCEPT OF ACTION AND ITS CATEGORIAL CONDITIONS

The starting point of our reasoning is not behavior, but action, or, as it is redundantly designated, rational action. Human action is conscious behavior on the part of a human being. Conceptually it can be sharply and clearly distinguished from unconscious activity, even though in some cases it is perhaps not easy to determine whether given behavior is to be assigned to one or the other category.

As thinking and acting men, we grasp the concept of action. In grasping this concept we simultaneously grasp the closely correlated concepts of value, wealth, exchange, price, and cost. They are all necessarily implied in the concept of action, and together with them the concepts of valuing, scale of value and importance, scarcity and abundance, advantage and disadvantage, success, profit, and loss. The logical unfolding of all these concepts and categories in systematic derivation from the fundamental category of action and the demonstration of the necessary relations among them constitutes the first task of our science. The part that deals with the elementary theory of value and price serves as the starting point in its exposition. There can be no doubt whatever concerning the aprioristic character of these disciplines.

The most general prerequisite of action is a state of dissatisfaction, on the one hand, and, on the other, the possibility of removing or alleviating it by taking action. (Perfect satisfaction and its concomitant, the absence of any stimulus to change and action, belong properly to the concept of a perfect being. This, however, is beyond the power of the human mind to conceive. A perfect being would not act.) Only this most general condition is necessarily implied in the concept of action. The other categorial conditions of action are independent of the basic concept; they are not necessary prerequisites of concrete action. Whether or not they are present in a particular case can be shown by experience only. But where they are present, the action necessarily falls under definite laws that flow from the categorial determinacy of these further conditions.

It is an empirical fact that man grows old and dies and that therefore he cannot be indifferent to the passage of time. That this has been man's experience thus far without exception, that we do not have the slightest evidence to the contrary, and that scarcely any other experience points more obviously to its foundation in a law of nature—all this in no way changes its empirical character. The fact that the passage of time is one of the conditions under which action takes place is established empirically and not a priori. We can without contradiction conceive of action on the part of immortal beings who would never age. But in so far as we take into consideration the action of men who are not indifferent to the passage of time and who therefore economize time because it is important to them whether they attain a desired end sooner or later, we must attribute to their action everything that necessarily follows from the categorial nature of time. The empirical character of our knowledge that the passage of time is a condition of any given action in no way affects the aprioristic character of the conclusions that necessarily follow from the introduction of the category of time. Whatever follows necessarily from empirical knwledge—e.g., the propositions of the agio theory of interest—lies outside the scope of empiricism.

Whether the exchange of economic goods (in the broadest sense, which also includes services) occurs directly, as in barter, or indirectly, through a medium of exchange, can be established only empirically. However, where and in so far as media of exchange are employed, all the propositions that are essentially valid with regard to indirect exchange must hold true. Everything asserted by the quantity theory of money, the theory of the relation between the quantity of money and interest, the theory of fiduciary media, and the circulation-credit theory of the business cycle, then becomes inseparably connected with action. All these theorems would still be meaningful even if there had never been any indirect exchange; only their practical significance for our action and for the science that explains it would then have to be appraised differently. However, the heuristic importance of experience for the analysis of action is not to be disregarded. Perhaps if there had never been indirect exchange, we would not have been able to conceive of it as a possible form of action and to study it in all its ramifications. But this in no way alters the aprioristic character of our science.

These considerations enable us to assess critically the thesis that all or most of the doctrines of economics hold only for a limited period of history and that, consequently, theorems whose validity is thus limited historically or geographically should replace, or at least supplement, those of the universally valid theory. All the propositions established by the universally valid theory hold to the extent that the conditions that they presuppose and precisely delimit are given. Where these conditions are present, the propositions hold without exception. This means that these propositions concern action as such; that is, that they presuppose only the existence of a state of dissatisfaction, on the one hand, and the recognized possibility, on the other, of relieving this dissatisfaction by conscious behavior, and that, therefore, the elementary laws of value are valid without exception for all human action. When an isolated person acts, his action occurs in accordance with the laws of value. Where, in addition, goods of higher order are introduced into action, all the laws of the theory of imputation are valid. Where indirect exchange takes place, all the laws of monetary theory are valid. Where fiduciary media are created, all the laws of the theory of fiduciary media (the theory of credit) are valid. There would be no point in expressing this fact by saying that the doctrines of the theory of money are true only in those periods of history in which indirect exchange takes place.

However, the case is entirely different with the thesis of those who would subordinate theory to history. What they maintain is that propositions derived from the universally valid theory are not applicable to historical periods in which the conditions presupposed by the theory are present. They assert, for example, that the laws of price determination of one epoch are different from those of another. They declare that the propositions of the theory of prices, as developed by subjective economics, are true only in a free economy, but that they no longer have any validity in the age of the hampered market, cartels, and government intervention.

In fact, the theory of prices expounds the principles governing the formation of monopoly prices as well as of competitive prices. It demonstrates that every price must be either a monopoly price or a competitive price and that there can be no third kind of price. In so far as prices on the hampered market are monopoly prices they are determined in accordance with the laws of monopoly price. Limited and hampered competition that does not lead to the formation of monopoly prices presents no special problem for the theory. The formation of competitive prices is fundamentally independent of the extent of competition. Whether the competition in a given case is greater or smaller is a datum that the theory does not have to take into account since it deals with categorial, and not concrete, conditions. The extent of the competition in a particular case influences the height of the price, but not the manner in which the price is determined.

The Historical School has not succeeded in providing any proof of its assertion that the laws derived from the universally valid theory do not hold for all human action independently of place, time, race, or nationality. In order to prove this it would have had to show that the logical structure of human thinking and the categorial nature of human action change in the course of history and are different for particular peoples, races, classes, etc. This it could never demonstrate; indeed, philosophy has established the very opposite as the truth.[1]

Nor were the adherents of the Historical School ever able to point to any instance of a proposition for which the claim could be made that observation had established it as an economic law with merely temporal, local, national, or similarly limited validity. They were unable to discover such a proposition either a priori or a posteriori. If thinking and action were really conditioned by place, time, race, nationality, climate, class, etc., then it would be impossible for a German of the twentieth century to understand anything of the logic and action of a Greek of the age of Pericles. We have already shown why the a posteriori discovery of empirical laws of action is not possible.[2] All that the "historical theory" could present was history—very poor history, to be sure, but, considered from a logical point of view, history nevertheless, and in no sense a theory.

2. A PRIORI THEORY AND EMPIRICAL CONFIRMATION

New experience can force us to discard or modify inferences we have drawn from previous experience. But no kind of experience can ever force us to discard or modify a priori theorems. They are not derived from experience; they are logically prior to it and cannot be either proved by corroborative experience or disproved by experience to the contrary. We can comprehend action only by means of a priori theorems. Nothing is more clearly an inversion of the truth than the thesis of empiricism that theoretical propositions are arrived at through induction on the basis of a presuppositionless observation of "facts." It is only with the aid of a theory that we can determine what the facts are. Even a complete stranger to scientific thinking, who naively believes in being nothing if not "practical," has a definite theoretical conception of what he is doing. Without a "theory" he could not speak about his action at all, he could not think about it, he could not even act. Scientific reasoning is distinguished from the daily thinking of everyone only in seeking to go further and in not stopping until it reaches a point beyond which it cannot go. Scientific theories are different from those of the average man only in that they attempt to build on a foundation that further reasoning cannot shake. Whereas in everyday living one is usually content to accept uncritically ideas that have been handed down, to carry a burden of prejudices and misunderstandings of all kinds, and to allow fallacies and errors to pass as true in cases where it is not easy to avoid them; scientific theories aim at unity and compactness, clarity, precision, apodictic evidence, and freedom from contradiction.

Theories about action are implicit in the very words we use in acting, and still more in those we use in speaking about action. The frequently lamented semantic ambiguities[3] that plague our efforts to achieve precision in science have their roots precisely in the fact that the terms employed are themselves the outcome of definite theories held in common-sense thinking. The supporters of historicism were able to believe that facts can be understood without any theory only because they failed to recognize that a theory is already contained in the very linguistic terms involved in every act of thought. To apply language, with its words and concepts, to anything is at the same time to approach it with a theory. Even the empiricist, who allegedly works without presuppositions, makes use of theoretical tools. They are distinguished from those produced by a scientific theory only in being less perfect and therefore also less useful.

Consequently, a proposition of an aprioristic theory can never be refuted by experience. Human action always confronts experience as a complex phenomenon that first must be analyzed and interpreted by a theory before it can even be set in the context of an hypothesis that could be proved or disproved; hence the vexatious impasse created when supporters of conflicting doctrines point to the same historical data as evidence of their correctness. The statement that statistics can prove anything is a popular recognition of this truth. No political or economic program, no matter how absurd, can, in the eyes of its supporters, be contradicted by experience. Whoever is convinced a priori of the correctness of his doctrine can always point out that some condition essential for success according to his theory has not been met. Each of the German political parties seeks in the experience of the second Reich confirmation of the soundness of its program. Supporters and opponents of socialism draw opposite conclusions from the experience of Russian bolshevism. Disagreements concerning the probative power of concrete historical experience can be resolved only by reverting to the doctrines of the universally valid theory, which are independent of all experience. Every theoretical argument that is supposedly drawn from history necessarily becomes a logical argument about pure theory apart from all history. When arguments based on principle concern questions of action, one should always be ready to admit that nothing can "be found more dangerous and more unworthy of a philosopher than the vulgar pretension to appeal to an experience to the contrary," [4] and not, like Kant and the socialists of all schools who follow him, only when such an appeal shows socialism in an unfavorable light.

Precisely because the phenomena of historical experience are complex, the inadequacies of an erroneous theory are less effectively revealed when experience contradicts it than when it is assessed in the light of the correct theory. The iron law of wages was not rejected because experience contradicted it, but because its fundamental absurdities were exposed. The conflict between its most clearly controvertible thesis—that wages tend toward the minimum needed for subsistence—and the facts of experience should have been easily recognized. Yet it is even today just as firmly entrenched in lay discussion and public opinion as in the

Marxian theory of surplus value, which, incidentally, professes to reject the iron law of wages. No past experience prevented Knapp from presenting his state theory of money,* and no later experience has forced his supporters to give up the theory.

The obstinacy of such unwillingness to learn from experience should stand as a warning to science. If a contradiction appears between a theory and experience, we always have to assume that a condition presupposed by the theory was not present, or else that there is some error in our observation. Since the essential prerequisite of action—dissatisfaction and the possibility of removing it partly or entirely—is always present, only the second possibility —an error in observation—remains open. However, in science one cannot be too cautious. If the facts do not confirm the theory, the cause perhaps may lie in the imperfection of the theory. The disagreement between the theory and the facts of experience consequently forces us to think through the problems of the theory again. But so long as a re-examination of the theory uncovers no errors in our thinking, we are not entitled to doubt its truth.

On the other hand, a theory that does not appear to be contradicted by experience is by no means to be regarded as conclusively established. The great logician of empiricism, John Stuart Mill, was unable to find any contradiction whatever between the objective theory of value and the facts of experience. Otherwise he would certainly not have made the statement, precisely on the eve of a radical change in the theory of value and price, that as far as the laws of value were concerned, there remained nothing more to be explained either in the present or in the future; the theory was quite perfect.[5] An error of this kind on the part of such a man must ever stand as a warning to all theorists.

3. THEORY AND THE FACTS OF EXPERIENCE

The science of action deals only with those problems whose solution directly or indirectly affects practical interests. It does not concern itself, for reasons already explained,[6] with the complete devlopment of a comprehensive system embracing all the

* Cf. the English translation of his book with this title by H. M. Lucas and J. Bonar (London, 1924).

conceivable categories of action in their broadest generality. The peculiar advantage of this procedure is that, by giving preference to the problems encountered under the actual conditions in which action takes place, our science is obliged to direct its attention to the facts of experience. It is thereby prevented from forgetting that one of its tasks consists in the determination of the boundary between the conditions of action accessible to and requiring categorial comprehension, on the one hand, and the concrete data of the individual case, on the other. The theory must constantly concern itself with the actual facts of the individual and non-repeatable case because only this offers it the possibility of showing where (conceptually, though perhaps not spatially, temporally, or in some other respect that would be perceptible to the senses) the realm of theoretical comprehension ends and that of historical understanding begins. When the science that aims at universally valid knowledge has so perfected its methods as to reach the furthest limit to which the theory can be pursued—that is, the point at which no condition of action open to categorial comprehension remains outside its range if experience has demonstrated the advisability of its inclusion—that science will still be obliged to treat also a part of the problems of descriptive, statistical, and historical research. Otherwise it could in no way succeed in recognizing and marking off its own domain. This task of demarcation is proper to it, and not to the empirical, descriptive sciences, because it is logically prior to them.

To be sure, even this procedure conceals many dangers. Sometimes one neglects to distinguish the universally valid from the historical; the methods are confounded, and then unsatisfactory results are obtained. Thus Böhm-Bawerk's ingenious exposition of the theory of interest, for example, suffered especially from an insufficient separation between the two modes of procedure.

4. THE DISTINCTION BETWEEN MEANS AND ENDS: THE "IRRATIONAL"

Most of the objections raised against the science of action stem from a misconception of the distinction between means and ends. In the strict sense, the end is always the removal of a dissatisfaction. However, we can doubtless also designate as an end the attainment of that condition of the external world which brings about our state of satisfaction either directly or indirectly, or which enables us to perform, without further difficulties, the act through which satisfaction is to be obtained. If the removal of the feeling of hunger is the end sought, the procuring of food and its preparation for eating can also be considered as ends; if one seeks the removal of the feeling of cold as an end, the heating of one's quarters can just as well be called an end. If additional measures are needed for the removal of dissatisfaction, then the attainment of any particular step along the way toward the desired final condition is also designated as an end. In this sense the acquisition of money in the market economy and, proximately, the division of labor are designated as ends of action; in this sense too the attainment of all things that indirectly promote the end of want-satisfaction appear as proximate or intermediate ends.

In the course of attaining the primary end, secondary ends are attained. A man walks from A to B. He would choose the shortest route if other, secondary ends did not demand satisfaction. He makes a detour if he can walk in the shade a little longer; if he can include in his walk another place, C, which he wants to look for; if, by doing so, he can avoid dangers that may be lying in wait for him on the shortest route; or if he just happens to like the longer route. If he decides on a detour, we must infer that at the moment of decision the attainment of such secondary ends was of greater importance in his judgment than the saving of distance. Consequently, for him the "detour" was no detour at all, since his walk brought him greater satisfaction or—at least from the point of view that he took of his situation at the moment of decision—was expected to bring greater satisfaction than the attainment of his destination by the shorter route. Only one who does not have these secondary ends in mind can call the longer way a detour. As far as our stroller was concerned, it was the correct route, that is, the route that promised the greatest satisfaction.[7]

Since satisfaction and dissatisfaction depend only on the subjective view of the individual, there is no room for argument on this question in a science that does not presume to establish a scale of values or to make judgments of value. Its conception of an end, in the strict sense, is more deductive than empirical: ends are determined by the wishes and the desires of the individual. Whenever reference is made to the greater or lesser appropriateness of means, this can only be from the point of view of the acting individual.

We must next deal with the objection of those who never weary of asserting that man does not act rationally at all. It has never been disputed that man does not always act correctly from the objective point of view; that is, that either from ignorance of causal relations or because of an erroneous judgment of the given situation, in order to realize his ends he acts differently from the way in which he would act if he had correct information. In 1833 the method of healing wounds was different from that used in 1933, and in 2033 still another way will presumably be thought suitable. Statesmen, field marshals, and stock-market speculators act differently at present from the way in which they would act if they knew exactly all the data needed for an accurate judgment of conditions. Only a perfect being, whose omniscience and omnipresence would enable him to survey all the data and every causal relationship, could know how each erring human being would have to act at every moment if he wanted to possess the divine attribute of omniscience. If we were to attempt to distinguish rational action from irrational action, we should not only be setting ourselves up as a judge over the scales of value of our fellow men, but we should also be declaring our own knowledge to be the only correct, objective standard of knowledge. We should be arrogating to ourselves the position that only an all-knowing being has the power to occupy.

The assertion that there is irrational action is always rooted in an evaluation of a scale of values different from our own. Whoever says that irrationality plays a role in human action is merely saying that his fellow men behave in a way that he does not consider correct. If we do not wish to pass judgment on the ends and the scales of value of other people and to claim omniscience for ourselves, the statement, "He acts irrationally," is meaningless, because it is not compatible with the concept of action. The "seeking to attain an end" and the "striving after a goal" cannot be eliminated from the concept of action. Whatever does not strive after goals or seek the attainment of ends reacts with absolute passivity to an external stimulus and is without a will of its own, like an automaton or a stone. To be sure, man too is as far outside the effective range of his action as a reed in the wind. But in so far as he is able to do anything, he always acts: even negligence and passivity are action if another course of conduct could have been chosen. And the conduct that is determined by the unconscious, in the Freudian sense, or by the subconscious, is also action in so far as conscious behavior could prevent it but neglects to do so. Even in the unconscious and apparently senseless behavior of the neurotic and the psychopath there is meaning, i.e., there is striving after ends and goals.[8]

Everything that we say about action is independent of the motives that cause it and of the goals toward which it strives in the individual case. It makes no difference whether action springs from altruistic or from egoistic motives, from a noble or from a base disposition; whether it is directed toward the attainment of materialistic or idealistic ends; whether it arises from exhaustive and painstaking deliberation or follows fleeting impulses and passions. The laws of catallactics that economics expounds are valid for every exchange regardless of whether those involved in it have acted wisely or unwisely or whether they were actuated by economic or noneconomic motives.[9] The causes of action and the goals toward which it strives are data for the theory of action: upon their concrete configuration depends the course of action taken in the individual case, but the nature of action as such is not thereby affected.

These considerations have an evident bearing on the widespread tendency of the present age to appeal to the irrational. The concepts rational and irrational are not applicable to ends at all. Whoever wishes to pass judgment on ends may praise or condemn them as good or evil, fine or vulgar, etc. When the expressions "rational" and "irrational" are applied to the means employed for the attainment of an end, such a usage has significance only from the standpoint of a definite technology. However, the use of means other than those prescribed as "rational" by this technology can be accounted for in only two possible ways: either the "rational" means were not known to the actor, or he did not employ them because he wished to attain still other ends—perhaps very foolish ones from the point of view of the observer. In neither of these two cases is one justified in speaking of "irrational" action.

Action is, by definition, always rational. One is unwarranted in calling goals of action irrational simply because they are not worth striving for from the point of view of one's own valuations. Such a mode of expressions leads to gross misunderstandings. Instead of saying that irrationality plays a role in action, one should accustom oneself to saying merely: There are people who aim at different ends from those that I aim at, and people who employ different means from those I would employ in their situation.

NOTES

1. See below pp. 102 f. for a further discussion of this point.
2. *Supra,* pp. 9 ff.
3. Cf. Wieser, *Über den Ursprung und die Hauptgesetze des wirtschaftlichen Wertes* (Wien, 1884), pp. 1 ff.
4. Kant, *Critique of Pure Reason,* "Transcendental Doctrine of Elements," Part II, Second Division, Book I, Section I.
5. J. S. Mill, *Principles of Political Economy* (London, 1867), III, 265.
6. *Supra,* pp. 14 ff.
7. Cf. Robbins, *An Essay on the Nature and Significance of Economic Science* (London, 1932), p. 23.
8. Cf. Freud, *Lectures on the Introduction to Psychoanalysis,* 17th lecture.
9. Cf. Wicksteed, *The Common Sense of Political Economy,* ed. by Robbins (London, 1933), I, 28.

III. *Science and Value*

1. THE MEANING OF NEUTRALITY WITH REGARD
   TO VALUE JUDGMENTS

The fact that the science of economics had its origin in economic policy explains why most economists use expressions in the presentation of the theory that involve judgments and standards of value accepted by all mankind, or certainly by almost all men.

If, for example, one is discussing the effects of tariffs, one usually employs, or at least one used to employ, terms that call a situation in which a given amount of capital and labor was able to produce a definite quantity of material economic goods "better" than a situation in which the same amount could produce only a smaller quantity.

The use of such expressions can hardly be said to imperil seriously the scientific character of the investigation, which precludes all standards and judgments of value. Whoever is of the opinion that economic policy ought to be differently oriented, i.e., in such a way that men become not richer in material goods, but poorer, can learn from the doctrine of free trade all that he needs to know in order to enter upon the path that leads to the goal he aspires to reach. If he himself were to undertake to develop the theory, he would, provided his reasoning were correct, arrive at the same results as other theorists, except that in his presentation he would use different expressions in a few incidental remarks and digressions that are unimportant from the point of view of what is essential in the theory. The objectivity of bacteriology as a branch of biology is not in the least vitiated by the fact that the researchers in this field regard their task as a struggle against the viruses responsible for conditions harmful to the human organism. Their theories are completely objective even though their presentation may be interlaced with terms like "harmful" and "useful," "favorable," and "unfavorable," and the like, implying judgments of value. They neither raise nor answer questions concerning the value of life and health; and their findings are independent of the individual researchers' valuation of these endowments. Whether one wishes to destroy rather than preserve human life, or whether, like the doctor, one seeks to cure and not to kill, he will, in either case, be able to draw from the results of their research all that he needs to know to accomplish his purpose.

One can be of the opinion that the "unfavorable" effects of tariffs, as set forth by the theory of free trade, are more than counterbalanced by other effects that warrant paying the price of the former. In that case one has the task, if one wishes to be scientific, of first of all pointing out and demonstrating these other effects as exactly and as clearly as possible. It then becomes the concern of politics to make the decision. In this connection it is by no means undesirable for the economist to take part in the discussion of policy. No one is better qualified to explain the matter at issue clearly and completely to those who have to make the decision. Of course, in doing so the economist is always under the obligation to make clear where the scientific explanation of causal relationships ends and where a clash of values requires to be resolved.

What is impermissible, however, is the obliteration of the boundary between scientific explanation and political value judgment. Although themselves guilty of this very failing, there are those who continually reproach economics for its alleged political bias because in writings on this subject one often employs terms that do not call into question generally accepted standards of value. Precisely these critics know only too well that they would be unable to attain their political goals if they were to admit that their proposals do not prove acceptable when gauged by such standards. The protectionists are well aware of the fact that they would have no hope of achieving their objectives if those called upon to decide the issue were to realize that protectionism lowers the productivity of labor as regards material goods. Because they know this, and because they want to set up protective tariffs notwithstanding, they go to great lengths to try to prove that protective tariffs are to be regarded as advantageous even "from the economic point of view." And because they fail lamentably in these endeavors, they charge economics with political bias.

2. SCIENCE AND TECHNOLOGY: ECONOMICS AND LIBERALISM

Whether science seeks knowledge for its own sake or in order thereby to obtain information for the sake of action, or whether it aims at both ends at the same time, it is in any case permissible to make practical use of the results of scientific investigation. Man thinks not only for the sake of thinking, but also in order to act. There would be no need to repeat these truisms were it not for the fact that antiliberal, partisan propaganda in the guise of science day after day vehemently seeks to deny them.

The fact that economics, as a science, is neutral with regard to judgments of value and that it can express neither approval nor disapproval does not prevent us from trying to learn from economics how we must arrange our action in order to achieve the ends at which we aim. The ends can be diverse. Caligula, who wished that the whole Roman people had but one head so that he might decapitate them at a single stroke, had different ends in mind from those of other mortals. However, such exceptional cases are rare; and their tendency to be self-destructive (Caligula, indeed, would hardly have long survived the fulfilment of his wish) makes an exhaustive concern with their ideals unnecessary. No matter how much their wishes, desires, and valuations may differ in details, men aim, for biological reasons, at the same basic ends. Regardless of world view, religion, nationality, race, class, position, education, personal abilities, age, health, or sex, they aspire above all to be able to pass their lives under the most favorable physiological conditions possible. They want to eat and drink; they seek clothing, shelter, and various other things in addition. Moreover, they are of the opinion that more food, clothing, and the like, is better than less.

Every individual desires life, health, and well-being for himself and for his friends and close relations. At the same time, the life, health, and well-being of others may be indifferent to him. Filled with the atavistic instincts of a beast of prey, he may even believe that others stand in his way, that they are depriving him of foraging grounds, and that the satisfaction of his wants must involve the killing and robbing of his fellow men. But the technology based on the cognitions of the science of human action shows him that this is not so. Work performed under the division of labor is more productive than the isolated labor of the individual. Even when superior men combine with those less favored in every respect and inferior to them in capacity for work and intellectual and physical abilities, both sides gain, as is demonstrated by Ricardo's law of association (usually called the law of comparative costs). Consequently, every individual is better able to attain his ends by the social cooperation of labor than by isolated work.

Social cooperation, however, can be based only on the foundation of private ownership of the means of production. Socialism —the public ownership of the means of production—would make impossible any economic calculation and is therefore impracticable. The absurdity of syndicalism is undisputed. As for interventionist encroachments, they prove—when judged from the point of view of those who advocate them—senseless and contrary to purpose, because they not only do not bring about the results desired by their supporters, but involve consequences that they themselves must deprecate.

Therefore, when one reaches the conclusion, strictly by adherence to the canons of scientific procedure, that private ownership of the means of production is the only practicable form of social organization, this is neither an apology for capitalism nor an improper attempt to lend the authority of science to the support of liberalism. To the man who adopts the scientific method in reflecting upon the problems of human action, liberalism must appear as the only policy that can lead to lasting well-being for himself, his friends, and his loved ones, and, indeed, for all others as well. Only one who does not want to achieve such ends as life, health, and prosperity for himself, his friends, and those he loves, only one who prefers sickness, misery, and suffering may reject the reasoning of liberalism on the ground that it is not neutral with regard to value judgments.

The defenders of the prevailing etatist and interventionist system completely misunderstand this. They think that the acceptance of liberalism, on the assumptions mentioned, presupposes a definite world view.[1] Liberalism has nothing to do with world views, metaphysics, or value judgments.

We can imagine beings similar to men who would want to extinguish their humanity and, by putting an end to all thought and action, to attain to the unthinking, passive, vegetative existence of plants. It is doubtful whether there are or have ever been such men. Even St. Aegidius, the most radical advocate of asceticism, was not altogether consistent in his zeal for austerity when he recommended the birds and the fish as a model for man. To be entirely consistent, together with the Sermon on the

Mount, he would have had to extol the lilies of the field as the embodiments of the ideal of complete abandonment of all concern for the improvement of one's lot.

We have nothing to say to men of this kind, consistent ascetics who by their self-denying passivity give themselves up to death, just as they would have nothing to say to us. If one wishes to call their doctrine a world view, then one must not forget to add that it is not a human world view, since it must lead to the extinction of mankind. Our science sees men only as acting men, not as plants having the appearance of men. Acting man aims at ends, i.e., he wants to overcome dissatisfaction as far as possible. Our science shows that aiming at ends is necessary to existence and that human ends, whatever they may be, are better attained by the social cooperation of the division of labor than in isolation. (It is worthy of note that no historical experience has been found in conflict with this proposition.) Once one has appreciated this fact, one realizes that no standard of value of any kind is contained in the system of economic or sociological theory or in the teachings of liberalism, which constitute the practical application of this theory to action in society. All objections to the effect that economics, sociology, and liberalism are predicated on a definite world view prove untenable once it is recognized that the science of action is concerned only with acting men and that it can say nothing about plant-like beings living with no thought of tomorrow, whom we can scarely consider as human.

3. THE UNIVERSALIST CRITIQUE OF METHODOLOGICAL INDIVIDUALISM

The reproach of individualism is commonly levelled against economics on the basis of an alleged irreconcilable conflict between the interests of society and those of the individual. Classical and subjectivist economics, it is said, give an undue priority to the interests of the individual over those of society and generally contend, in conscious denial of the facts, that a harmony of interests prevails between them. It would be the task of genuine science to show that the whole is superior to the parts and that the individual has to subordinate himself to, and conduct himself for, the benefit of society and to sacrifice his selfish private interests to the common good.

In the eyes of those who hold this point of view society must appear as a means designed by Providence to attain ends that are hidden from us. The individual must bow to the will of Providence and must sacrifice his own interests so that its will may be done. His greatest duty is obedience. He must subordinate himself to the leaders and live just as they command.

But who, one must ask, is to be the leader? For many want to lead, and, of course, in different directions and toward different goals. The collectivists, who never cease to pour scorn and derision on the liberal theory of the harmony of interests, pass over in silence the fact that there are various forms of collectivism and that their interests are in irreconcilable conflict. They laud the Middle Ages and its culture of community and solidarity, and with romantic sentimentality they wax ecstatic over the communal associations "in which the individual was included, and in which he was kept warm and protected like fruit in its rind." [2] But they forget that papacy and empire, for example, opposed each other for hundreds of years and that every individual could find himself at any time in the position of having to choose between them. Were the inhabitants of Milan also "kept warm and protected like fruit in its rind" when they had to hand over their city to Frederick Barbarossa? Are there not various factions fighting today on German soil with bitter anger, each of which claims to represent the only true collectivism? And do not the Marxian socialists, the national socialists, the church, and many other parties approach every individual with the demand: Join us, for you belong in our ranks, and fight to the death the "false" forms of collectivism? A collectivist social philosophy that did not designate a definite form of collectivism as true and either treat all others as subordinate to it or condemn them as false would be meaningless and vain. It must always tell the individual: Here you have an unquestionably given goal, because an inner voice has revealed it to me; to it you must sacrifice everything else, yourself above all. Fight to victory or death under the banner of this ideal, and concern yourself with nothing else.

Collectivism, in fact, can be stated in no other way than as partisan dogma in which the commitment to a definite ideal and the condemnation of all others are equally necessary. Loyola did not preach just any faith, but that of the Church of Rome. Lagarde did not advocate nationalism, but what he regarded as German nationalism. Church, nation, state *in abstracto* are concepts of nominalistic science. The collectivists idolize only the one true church, only the "great" nation—the "chosen" people who have been entrusted by Providence with a special mission—only the true state; everything else they condemn.

For that reason all collectivist doctrines are harbingers of irreconcilable hatred and war to the death.

The theory of the division of labor—the starting point of sociology—demonstrates that there is no irreconcilable conflict, as collectivist metaphysics maintains, between the interests of society and those of the individual. In isolation the individual cannot attain his ends, whatever they may be, or at least not to the same extent as by social cooperation. The sacrifices he makes for the maintenance of social cooperation are therefore only temporary: renunciation of a momentary benefit for the sake of an advantage that endures throughout the continued existence and evolution of the division of labor. Society comes into being and develops not by virtue of a moral law imposed on mankind by mysterious powers bent on forcing the individual, against his interests, into subordination to the social whole, but through the action of individuals cooperating in the attainment of ends that they severally aim at, in order to take advantage of the higher productivity brought about by the division of labor. The sum and substance of the "individualistic" and "atomistic" theory of society is that every individual benefits from the existence of society and that no one would be better off as a freebooting individual in an imaginary state of isolation, searching for food on his own and engaging in the war of all against all, than as a member of society, though a thousand times more constrained and circumscribed.

The collectivists contend that "individualism" sees in society only the sum total of individuals, whereas society is really something specific.[3] However, science is not at all concerned with determining what society is, but with the effect of labor performed under conditions of social cooperation. And its first statement is that the productivity of social cooperation surpasses in every respect the sum total of the production of isolated individuals.

For the purposes of science we must start from the action of the individual because this is the only thing of which we can have direct cognition. The idea of a society that could operate or manifest itself apart from the action of individuals is absurd. Everything social must in some way be recognizable in the action of the individual. What would the mystical totality of the universalists be if it were not alive in every individual? Every form of society is operative in the actions of individuals aiming at definite ends. What would a German national character be that did not find expression in the Germanism of individuals? What would a church be that did not express the faith of individuals? That one is a member of a market society, a party comrade, a citizen, or a member of any other association must be shown through his action.

Spann, the most prominent present-day champion of universalism, strongly emphasizes that universalist sociology deals with spiritual facts that cannot be drawn from experience because they "possess, by virtue of their a priori character, a pre-empirical, supra-empirical existence." [4]

In the first place, this is not accurately expressed. Only the laws of human action can be derived a priori; but it is experience alone that can establish whether or not the categorial prerequisites of action are also present in the concrete case. (Here we may pass over the fact that every experience presupposes something given a priori.) One can infer from the a priori theory of action that the division of labor is not practicable without some way by which men can communicate with one another. But only experience can show whether the division of labor and language exist in fact. And experience alone can tell us that different linguistic systems are to be found in the world and that from this fact particular consequences must follow—consequences which, a priori, are at best recognized as possible, but certainly not as having been established as existing. It cannot be deduced a priori that between the totality constituted by humanity or the totality constituted by a world state, on the one hand, and the individual, on the other, stand the totalities constituted by people, race, state, and linguistic community; this can be ascertained only through experience.

However, what Spann has in mind when he declares the a priori method to be the only one appropriate for sociology as he conceives it is not at all a priori reasoning, but intuitive insight into a whole. Again and again science is reproached for its inability to grasp the whole of life, becoming, and being. In its hands the living whole becomes a dead patchwork; the brilliance and color of creation pale, and the infinite variety and beauty of the universe wither into a rational pattern. A new science must arise which would teach us to grasp the whole in its entirety. Only knowledge of this kind deserves the name of true science. Everything else is merely rational explanation and as such is untrue because it is unable to approach the splendor of creation.

4. THE EXPERIENCE OF A WHOLE AND SCIENTIFIC COGNITION

Science, which is dependent both on discursive reasoning and on experience, does not present us with a unified picture of the world. It reduces phenomena to a number of concepts and propositions that we must accept as ultimate, without being able to establish a connection between them. It proves incapable of closing the gap that exists between the system of the sciences of human thought and action and the system of the sciences of physical nature. It does not know how to find a bridge between sentience and motion or between consciousness and matter. What life and death are eludes its grasp.

But what reason and the experience of the natural sciences have denied us is given to us by personal experience, though in a different manner from that of science. We are unable to fathom life through reason, nor can we experience it through science. Reason and science deal only with isolated fragments detached from the living whole and thereby killed. They never refer to life as it is lived and never to life as a whole. But we experience life in living, and in living our life we live life as such: we experience the unity and indissoluble congenerousness of all life. We are unable to grasp the whole by reasoning, but we can experience it in living.

This personal experience of wholeness, unity, and infinity is the loftiest peak of human existence. It is the awakening to a higher humanity. It alone transforms everyday living into true living. It is not vouchsafed to us daily or at all places. The occasions on which we are brought closer to the world spirit must await a propitious hour. Such moments occur only seldom, but they are a thousandfold rewarding, and reflection upon them illumines the passing days, weeks, months, and years.

What we experience in these moments of exaltation fills our deepest and most personal thoughts and feelings. They are so private and personal that we are unable to communicate them to anyone else. They are so deep within us that they cannot make a clear impression on our own consciousness. Whoever in the presence of his beloved or in the contemplation of an aspect of nature or in the stirring of his own strength has experienced the power of the infinite finds it impossible to tell either himself or others what it is that moves him and how it moves him. The whole remains ineffable because reason and language are unable to enter here.

Art is nothing more than a faltering and inadequate attempt to express what has been thus experienced and to give some form to its content. The work of art captures not the experience, but only what its creator has been able to express of the experience. Missing are the content, the color, and the vitality of the experience, which come entirely from within. Of course, the work of art can kindle a new personal experience if one allows oneself to be affected by it. However, the experience that the work of art evokes is not adequate to what its creator wanted to express. The artist gives the work tone, melody, color, words, and form, but not personal experience. Yet we derive more from it than the mere sensation of tone, melody, color, words, and form: we experience it. And this personal experience is another and a new experience of a different kind. The same is true of all forms of mysticism and metaphysics. We grasp the words, but we ourselves must add the meaning, the personal experience. For our means of expression and of thought do not touch life in its fullness and wholeness. As the ancient Brahmin sages said, it is that "which words and thoughts seek without finding." [5]

That is why there can be no progress or evolution in metaphysics, mysticism, and art. The accuracy with which a work renders the likeness of the external world can be enhanced, but not what is essential, not what is artistic in it. The most primitive work of art also can express the strongest experience, and it speaks to us, if only we let it, and leads us into depths that science can never make accessible.

Again and again those who want to obliterate the boundary between scientific knowledge and mystical intuition in personal experience reproach science for stopping at the surface of things and not penetrating into the depths. One has to recognize that science is not metaphysics, and certainly not mysticism; it can never bring us the illumination and the satisfaction experienced by one enraptured in ecstasy. Science is sobriety and clarity of conception, not intoxicated vision.

It is true, as Bergson has seen with unsurpassed clarity, that between reality and the knowledge that science can convey to us there is an unbridgeable gulf.[6] Science cannot grasp life directly. What it captures in its system of concepts is always of a different character from the living whole.[7] One may therefore, if one wishes, even call it dead, because what is not life is death. But if one thinks that one has thereby pronounced an unfavorable judgment on science, one is mistaken. One can call science dead, but one cannot say that it is not useful. It is indispensable in a double sense: first, as the sole means that can lead us to whatever measure of knowledge we can attain at all; and then, as the only foundation for an action that brings us closer to the ends at which we aim. Whether we see the greatest value in wisdom or in action, in neither case may we scorn science. It alone shows us the way both to knowledge and to action. Without it our existence would be only vegetative.

5. THE ERRORS OF THE UNIVERSALIST DOCTRINE

Thus every argument of the universalist critique directed against the methodological individualism of sociology, and of economics in particular, proves unwarranted. Science cannot proceed otherwise than discursively. Its starting points must have as much certainty as human knowledge is capable of, and it must go on from there, making logical deductions step by step. It can begin as an aprioristic science with propositions necessary to thought that find their support and warrant in apodictic evidence; or as an empirical science it can start with experience. But never can it take as its starting point the vision of a whole.

One would misunderstand the nature and function of cartography if one were to demand that maps show mountains and forests in all their beauty and grandeur. The most exquisite description of the loveliness of the countryside could not in the least compensate us for the map. It would not be able to show us the path that leads to the goals we want to reach. It is not for botany to discuss the beauty and the charm of flowers; it may not take its starting point from forests and meadows, but from the individual plants, and it studies plants from the standpoint of vegetable physiology and plant biology by basing its knowledge on that of the cell.

When universalism opposes the thesis that "natural laws of mechanistic causality" underlie social phenomena, we can agree in so far as there is a fundamental difference between the observation of nature and the comprehension of meaning that is characteristic of the sciences of human action. The view of behaviorism is just as untenable as the epistemological position taken by Schumpeter in his first book.[8] All mechanistic analogies are misleading.

However, we can no more do without the category of causality in our scientific thinking than in everyday thinking; it is the only category that cannot be thought away.[9] Indeed, a mode of reasoning that did not involve reference to causality could not arrive at the concepts of God and the whole. That science means, above all, conceptual thinking will not, of course, be disputed. But thinking must always be causal and rational.

Human reasoning does not have the power to exhaust completely the content of the universe. In the sciences of human action it goes as far as conceptual thinking can go. Beyond this point nothing more can be done than to determine what the irrational facts are by means of the specific understanding of the moral sciences.

The error of universalism, as well as of other doctrines that attempt to deal with the methodological and logical uncertainties of the moral sciences, consists in the failure to see that understanding—i.e., insight into form and quality—is not the sole or the preeminent method of the moral sciences, but on the contrary, that it must be logically and temporally preceded by conception, i.e., the intellectual comprehension of meaning.

6. "OBJECTIVE" MEANING

The metaphysical systems of the philosophy of history presume to be able to detect behind the appearance of things their "true" and "real" essence, which is hidden to the profane eye. They imagine themselves capable of discovering the final purpose of all mundane activity. They want to grasp the "objective meaning" of events, which, they maintain, is different from their subjective meaning, i.e., the meaning intended by the actor himself. In this respect all systems of religion and all philosophies of history proceed according to the same principles. Notwithstanding the bitterness with which they fight one another, Marxian socialism, German national socialism, and the non-German movements related to it, which have taken a variety of forms, are all in agreement on logical method; and it is worth noting that they can all be traced back to the same metaphysical foundation, namely, the Hegelian dialectic.

The science of human action knows of no way that could lead reasoning men to knowledge of the hidden plans of God or Nature. It is unable to give any answer to the question of the "meaning of the whole" that could be logically established in the manner in which the findings of scientific thought must be in order to be acknowledged at least as provisional truths. It deliberately abstains from intruding into the depths of metaphysics.[10] It suffers lightly the reproach of its opponents that it stops at the "surface" of things.

It is not to be denied that the loftiest theme that human thought can set for itself is reflection on ultimate questions. Whether such reflection can accomplish anything is doubtful. Many of the most eminent minds of the past were of the opinion that thought and cognition overstep their domain of effectiveness when they apply themselves to such tasks. In any case, it is certain that differences of a fundamental nature exist between metaphysical speculations and scientific investigation—differences that may not be ignored without peril. It is the function of science to think out to their ultimate conclusions the a priori prerequisites of knowledge in their purity, to develop thereby a comprehensive theoretical system, and, with the aid of the results so obtained, to extract from the data of experience all that they can teach.

On the other hand, it is no part of the task of science to examine ultimate questions or to prescribe values and determine their order of rank. Nevertheless, one may call the fulfillment of these tasks higher, nobler, and more important than that of the simpler task of science, which is to develop a theoretical system of cause-and-effect relationships enabling us to arrange our action in such a way that we can attain the goals we aim at. One may hold poets, prophets, or promulgators of new values in higher esteem than scientists. But in no case is one free to confound these two fundamentally different functions. For example, one may not attempt, in compliance with Novalis' invitation, to "poetize" the science of finance.[11]

Metaphysics and science perform different functions. They cannot, therefore, adopt the same procedures, nor are they alike in their goals. They can work side by side without enmity because they need not dispute each other's domain as long as they do not misconstrue their own character. A conflict arises only when one or the other attempts to overstep the boundary between them. Positivism thought that, in place of uncertain speculations and poetry masquerading as philosophy, it would be able, through the application of the methods of science to the problems dealt with by metaphysics, to adopt a procedure guaranteeing the certainty of scientific demonstration to the treatment of the ultimate objects of knowledge. What it failed to see was that from the moment it undertook to treat of metaphysical problems, it itself also necessarily engaged in metaphysics. Precisely because it did not see this, its own metaphysics, notwithstanding its professions of scorn for everything metaphysical, was naive in the extreme.

On the other hand, securely established conclusions of scientific thought are again and again attacked on metaphysical grounds. Now, of course, nothing that is scientifically established can be brought against the assumption that things could present themselves to a mind other than human differently from the way in which we see and experience them, so that the science of this other mind would possess a different content from ours. Our own thinking is utterly powerless to discover anything whatever about what such a superhuman or divine being would think. But within the cosmos in which our action is effective and in which our thinking paves the way for action, the findings of our scientific reasoning are so securely established as to render meaningless the statement that, in a broader setting or in a deeper sense, they would have to lose their validity and yield to some other cognition.

Since we must concern ourselves here not with empirical science, but with the apriorism of the science of human action, we need not consider the encroachments of metaphysics upon the domain of the former. It is obvious that the attempts to use metaphysical arguments to refute what follows from a priori ratiocination are tantamount to replacing discursive reasoning by the arbitrariness of intuitive flights of fancy. No metaphysics is in any way able to undermine the concept of action. Consequently, metaphysics can detract nothing from whatever is necessarily deduced from that concept. When we seek to comprehend categorially the prerequisites of human action, one may criticize and correct our procedure, if it goes wrong, by resort to scientific reasoning. However, whatever firmly withstands the logical scrutiny of our reason can in no way be refuted by the assertions of metaphysics. It is no more permissible to deny recognition to any of the propositions of economics—for example, the theory of value and of price formation—by referring to the fact that one has a different "world view" or that one's "interests" give one a different—e.g., the "proletarian"—standpoint than it would be to use the statements of metaphysics to argue down the binomial theorem. No vision of totality, no universalism, and no "sociologism" can allow us to "understand" things differently from the way in which they must present themselves to our sober reasoning. If I am unable to show through arithmetical reasoning that arithmetic is contradictory in saying three times three equals nine, I am not warranted in asserting that in a "higher" or "deeper" sense another answer has to be true.

The conclusions that must be drawn from the findings of economics do not meet the approval of those whose immediate, momentary interests make it appear desirable that other teachings be recognized as correct. Inasmuch as they are at a loss to discover any error in the logical structure of economics, they call upon supramundane powers for help.

NOTES

1. E.g., Vleugel's "Probleme der Wertlehre," *Archiv für Sozialwissenschaft und Sozialpolitik,* LXVIII, 227 f. Liberalism has no thought of denying the existence of servilism and its world view. All that liberalism endeavors to demonstrate is that the realization of the goals of servilism would necessarily bring about consequences of whose inevitability its advocates are in ignorance and which, even in their own eyes, must appear as too high a price to have to pay for the attainment of their ideal.
2. Sombart, *Der proletarische Sozializmus* (10th ed.; Jena, 1924), I, 31.
3. Spann, article "Soziologie," *Handwörterbuch der Staatswissenschaften* (4th edition), VII, 655.
4. *Ibid.*
5. Cf. Deussen, *Vedânta, Platon und Kant* (Vienna, 1917), p. 67.
6. Cf. Bergson, *L'évolution créatrice* (7th ed.; Paris, 1911), pp. 1 ff.
7. This has never been denied, not even by the empiricism of the natural sciences. Erasmus Darwin wrote: "Following life, in creatures we dissect,/ We lose it, in the moment we detect." Quoted by J. S. Mill in his *System der deductiven und inductiven Logik,* trans. by von Gomperz (Leipzig, 1872), II, p. 163.
8. *Wesen und Hauptinhalt der theoretischen Nationalökonomie* (Leipzig, 1908).

9. Cf. Schopenhauer, *Die Welt as Wille und Vorstellung* (Collected Works, edited by Frauenstädt, 2nd ed.; Leipzig, 1916), II, 531.
10. Sulzbach, *Die Grundlagen der politischen Parteibildung* (Tübingen, 1921), pp. v f.
11. Quoted by Freyer in *Die Bewertung der Wirtschaft im philosophischen Denken des 19. Jahrhunderts* (Leipzig, 1921), p. 48.

IV. *Utilitarianism and Rationalism and the Theory of Action*

1. VIERKANDT'S INSTINCT SOCIOLOGY

None of the objections that have been raised for thousands of years against hedonism and utilitarianism has the least bearing upon the theory of action. When the correlative concepts of pleasure and pain, or utility and disutility, are grasped in their formal sense and are deprived of all material content, all the objections that have been repeated *ad nauseam* for ages have the ground cut from under them. It requires a considerable unfamiliarity with the present state of the argument to raise once again the old charges against "immoral" hedonism and "vulgar" utilitarianism.

Today it is customary, when one finds oneself compelled to acknowledge the logical impossibility of any other view, to say that the formal conception of pleasure and utility is devoid of all cognitive value. In grasping these ideas in their purity, the concept of action, it is said, becomes so empty that nothing more can be done with it. To answer this criticism one need only point to all that economic theory has been able to deduce from the allegedly empty concept of action.

If one attempts to engage in the scientific investigation of what, in our view, constitutes the subject matter of the science of human action without resort to the proscribed principle of hedonism, one falls unawares into empiricism, which cannot succeed in connecting into a system the multiplicity of facts it encounters or in using them for the explanation of the phenomena that are to be comprehended. An example may make this clear.

In his endeavor to construct a theory of society, Vierkandt

knows no other means than to ascribe to men a series of "social propensities." In this regard he follows the procedure of a great number of investigators. He understands by the social propensities of man

> such innate instincts (e.g., the instinct to be of help) and other innate characteristics and modes of behavior (e.g., understanding and susceptibility to influence) as presuppose for their manifestation the presence of other men, or, more precisely, the condition of society.

In addition, there are still other propensities such as also or only "manifest themselves in relation to other entities." [1] And here Vierkandt goes on to enumerate and describe a series of instincts, propensities, and impulses.

Such an enumeration can never, of course, be complete. The distinction between one instinct and another must necessarily be arbitrary. To be quite consistent one would have to link a corresponding instinct with every goal that has ever been aimed at anywhere and at any time. If, for example, one assumes the existence of an instinct for food, from which one distinguishes the instinct for means of enjoyment, there is no reason why one should not go further and speak also of an instinct for meat or, even more specifically, of an instinct for beef or, still more specifically, of an instinct for beefsteak. What one has in view in speaking simply of the instinct for food is a summary statement in terms of the end aimed at by the actions of men directed toward the provision of different foods. If one represents, in summary form, actions directed toward the consumption of carbohydrates, fats, and proteins as the result of the instinct for food, one can, in the same way and with the same justification, also look upon actions directed toward providing food, shelter, and clothing, as well as a great many other actions, as the result of the instinct for self-preservation. How far one goes in this process of generalization is entirely a matter of arbitrary choice, unless one makes a radical change in one's whole mode of reasoning and passes to the level of broadest generality, i.e., to the formal concept of the end devoid of all material content. Because

Vierkandt rejects utilitarianism and hedonism and therefore does not take this decisive step, he comes to a stop at an arbitrary division of the various human wants.

The innate social propensities appear, Vierkandt goes on to explain, "frequently in pairs of opposites." Thus, pitted against the "instinct of self-esteem" is "its opposite, the instinct of obedience"; against the "instinct to be of help," the "fighting instinct"; against the "sociable instinct," an "instinct of avoidance"; against the "communicative instinct," an "instinct of secretiveness and concealment." [2] Since nothing can be said about the strength with which these opposed instincts make themselves felt, one cannot understand how the rise of social cooperation is to be explained on the basis of them. Even if we pass over the impermissible hypostasis involved in the statement that the "social propensities" lead to the development of social cooperation, we still lack any adequate explanation for the fact that the social instincts are victorious over the antisocial instincts. Why is it that the fighting instinct, the instinct of self-esteem, and the instinct of avoidance do not frustrate the formation of social bonds?

The "instinct of self-esteem," Vierkandt maintains, cannot manifest itself "without the instinct of subordination being active at the same time." Here, he continues, one has to deal with the "characteristic coalescence of opposed instincts; in this regard the total picture is, of course, modified by the instinct of domination." [3] Assuming an "instinct of subordination," one is forced, if one does not choose to be completely blind to reality, to assume an opposite instinct: Vierkandt calls it the instinct of self-esteem. (Wiese objected with good reason that Vierkandt, when he recognizes an instinct of subordination, would have to "allow no less for an instinct of rebellion, which is, of course, very important in history and in the life of the individual." [4]) Yet Vierkandt is unable to produce any other proof that the instinct of subordination is victorious over the instinct of self-esteem than the fact that in his presentation he labels the former the stronger and better instinct. "Subordination," he asserts, "is a condition which is healthy, normal, and conducive to happiness; a condition in which the situation demands the replacement of self-esteem by the opposite attitude." [5] It is, after all, noteworthy that Vierkandt, the opponent of eudemonism, attributes to subordination effects conducive to happiness. Here Feuerbach's observation becomes pertinent: "Every instinct is an instinct for happiness." [6]

The self-esteem that Vierkandt has in mind is, however, of a peculiar kind. It is, as it were, a by-product of subordination. "Everywhere, acceding to the will of the superior means at the same time that one elevates oneself to his level: subordination means simultaneously an inner sharing of the greatness of the superior." He cites as an example "the relationship of the servant to his master under patriarchal conditions." [7] In another place Vierkandt again speaks of the "servant who shows off the castle of his master with enhanced self-esteem" because he feels "inwardly at one with his lord, his family, and their splendor." [8]

The self-esteem that Vierkandt has in view reveals itself, therefore, as nothing more than the pride of a flunky. Then, of course, there is no wonder that it does not stand in the way of the instinct of subordination. This subordination is tantamount to "unconditional obedience." The subordinate makes himself "blindly dependent within." He

submits completely to his superior's judgment, especially his value judgments: he receives his worth from his superior in that he regulates his conduct according to his superior's standards and by so doing satisfies his self-esteem. The subordinate is, as it were, absorbed by the superior: he loses his personality, but finds in community with the superior a new one again, which he experiences as his own personality ennobled.[9]

Vierkandt is able to point with particular satisfaction to the fact that all these instincts are to be found in animals.

In the dog the truly human inner devotion to its master shows itself in an elementary, but very powerful, form, e.g., enlivenment in the master's presence and the polarization brought about by him in general.

Vierkandt considers as very noteworthy

also the satisfaction of self-esteem shown by a dog and probably by other animals too when they succeed in the performance of a task for which they have been trained, because of the connection of this instinct with the instinct of subordination in the human being.[10]

Thus, as Vierkandt sees it, human society is, so to speak, already foreshadowed in the relationship of the master to the dog he trains. The relationship of leader and led corresponds to the relationship of master and dog: it is healthy and normal, and it is conducive to the happiness of both, the master as well as the dog.

One cannot argue this point further with Vierkandt because, in his view, the ultimate source of cognition is

phenomenological insight, i.e., what we directly experience personally in ourselves and can convey to our consciousness with apodictic evidence.[11]

Therefore, we do not doubt that he really has inwardly experienced all this. Indeed, we shall go still further and not deny his qualification to speak from direct personal experience and insight about the "truly human inner devotion of the dog to his master." But what if someone were to affirm that he had personally experienced and intuited something different? Suppose one chose to call "healthy, normal, and conducive to happiness" not the self-esteem of lackeys and dogs, but that of men? What if one chose to seek the basis of "inner communion" not in the "desire for subordination," like Vierkandt,[12] but in the desire for joint action?

Vierkandt rejects the individualist theory of action because he wants to champion a political program that appears senseless when viewed from the standpoint of scientific economics and sociology. He is unable to support his rejection of the latter except by repeatedly referring to the rationalist, individualist, and atomistic character of everything that does not meet with his approval.[13] Rationalism, individualism, and atomism are today condemned by *all* ruling parties for easily recognizable reasons; and so this mode of argumentation suffices for the sphere in which the official doctrine is accepted. In place of the sciences he attacks without having understood their teachings, Vierkandt provides an arbitrary enumeration and description of innate primary instincts and impulses that he alleges to have experienced and intuited just so and not otherwise, in order to found a political program on a basis that suits his purposes. Here we can disregard all this. What is noteworthy for us is that he who wants to avoid the path taken by the universally valid science of human action can explain the social cooperation of men in no other way than by reference to the working of inborn propensities that lead to association; that is, if he does not prefer to represent it still more simply as a work of God or Nature.

If anyone believes that he can explain every human want, or every class of human wants constructed by him, by correlating with it a particular impulse, instinct, propensity, or feeling, then he is certainly not to be forbidden to do so. Not only do we not deny that men desire, want, and aim at different things, but we start precisely from this fact in our reflections. When science speaks of pleasure, happiness, utility, or wants, these signify nothing but what is desired, wished for and aimed at, what men regard as ends and goals, what they lack, and what, if procured, satisfies them. These terms make no reference whatever to the concrete content of what is desired: the science is formal and neutral with regard to values. The one declaration of the science of "happiness" is that it is purely subjective. In this declaration there is, therefore, room for all conceivable desires and wants. Consequently, no statement about the quality of the ends aimed at by men can in any way affect or undermine the correctness of our theory.

The point at which the science of action begins its work is the mutual incompatibility of individual desires and the impossibility of perfect satisfaction. Since it is not granted to man to satisfy all his desires completely, inasmuch as he can attain one end only by forgoing another, he must differentiate among instincts: he must decide in favor of one thing and against something else; he must choose and value, prefer and set aside—in short, act. Even for one who calls the happiness of subordination desirable, a moment can come in which he has to choose between devotion to the leader and the satisfaction of another instinct, e.g., the instinct for food; as when a republican party at the head of the government threatens monarchist officials with dismissal. Everyone again and again finds himself confronted with a situation in which his conduct—whether it consist in an overt deed, an act of omission, or acquiescence—helps to determine whether or not his goals are attained.

However, a doctrine that rejects rationalism, individualism, and eudaemonism can say nothing about human action. It stops at the enumeration and description of a number of instincts. To be sure, it tells us that men love and hate, that they are garrulous and taciturn, that they are cruel and compassionate, that they are sociable and that they shun society. But it can say nothing about the fact that they act, work, labor, and toil to achieve goals. For one can speak of action only if one starts from the individual, if one takes rationality into consideration, and if one recognizes that the goal of action is the removal of dissatisfaction. If one wants to explain society without reference to the actions of men, the only expedient that remains is to view it as the outcome of mysteriously operating forces. Society is then the result of the instinct of association; it is "inner communion"; it is basic and intrinsic; it is not of this world.

2. MYRDAL'S THEORY OF ATTITUDES

Still another example may help to show how vain are all objections raised against the atomism, individualism, utilitarianism, and rationalism of the science of action. No less clearly than in the case just discussed, it will be seen here too that attempts to explain human action in terms of such psychological factors as the striving for power are incapable of refuting the conclusions that economics reaches by cogent logical reasoning. Under the guise of nonpartisan criticism of all the social sciences hitherto developed, an effort is made to justify interventionism, a policy whose inexpedience and futility (as seen from the standpoint of the goals that its advocates hope to attain by it) has been demonstrated by economics.

Myrdal thinks one understands

the pathos of the labor movement poorly if one believes that it fights chiefly for higher real wages. Viewed from the standpoint of social psychology, something else is involved here . . . The demands for higher wages, shorter working time, etc. are, of course, important in and of themselves, but viewed more deeply, they are only an expression of far more general strivings for power and demands for justice on the part of a social class which simply feels oppressed. Even if there were no hope of forcing through higher wages, the battle would go on. Even if the workers had reason to believe that a decline in productivity and wages would result, they would never-theless demand more power and codetermination in the conduct of business. In the last analysis, more is at stake for them than money; their joy of labor is involved, their self-esteem, or, if one will, their worth as men. Perhaps no great strike can be explained merely as a strike for higher wages.[14]

With this argument Myrdal, of course, believes he has deprived of its importance—from the point of view of the workers' judg-ment of the goals of trade unionism—the irrefutable proof pro-vided by economics that trade-union policy can never permanently raise wages for all workers. For whoever knows how to examine the matter "more deeply" or from the standpoint of "social psychology" will realize, he thinks, that in the eyes of the workers organized in unions, what is at issue is by no means the height of wages or a question of money; on the contrary, quite different things are at stake, such as their "joy of labor," their "self-esteem," and their "worth as men."

If this were really so, it would be impossible to understand why union leaders and the socialists of the chair who give them support place so much emphasis on again and again upholding in their public declarations the contention, pronounced untenable by economics, that wages can be raised permanently for all workers by trade unionism; and why they so ardently endeavor to pro-scribe and silence all who are of a different opinion. The reason for this behavior on the part of union leaders and their literary allies is that the unionized workers expect an increase in their real income. No worker would join a union if he were unable to hope for a wage increase from it, but, on the contrary, would have to reckon with a loss of wages. Even the prospect of being compensated through joy of labor, self-esteem, human worth, and the like could not make him a friend of the unions. Union leaders know quite well that the expectation of an increase in income is the one and only factor that has brought the unions into existence and still holds them together.

However, even if Myrdal were right in saying that the unions really do not fight chiefly for higher wages, but rather for other things, the statements of economics on the question of the influence that the combination of workers into trade unions has on the height of wages would remain unaffected. Economics is neither for nor against unions. It seeks only to show how the specific policy of trade unions affects the labor market.

Myrdal's position is not improved by his avoidance of plain and open speaking. In explaining that the demand for higher wages is "of course, important in and of itself," he no doubt thinks he has sufficiently protected himself against all criticism. We encounter here the vicious practice on the part of the socialists of the chair of concealing an inadequacy of logic by means of an imprecise and inexact mode of expression. Inasmuch as, in the further course of his argument, Myrdal goes so far as to assert that workers would adhere to trade unions even if they were to discover that this involved a sacrifice of wages, he holds the view that the wage increase—which, in his opinion and in that of all socialists of the chair and union leaders, union policy makes inevitable—is valued by the workers only as an agreeable, but secondary, success of measures directed at the attainment of other goals. However, such a statement makes no contribution whatever toward advancing the discussion of the question whether the employment of union tactics can result in a general and permanent wage increase, which is the only aspect of the matter that has any importance for economic theory and—as all unbiased critics will, of course, admit—in actual practice as well.

Myrdal is familiar with neither the history nor the present state of economics and is therefore fighting against windmills. According to him, economics maintains that only "economic interests" guide human action. By "economic interests" Myrdal understands "the desire for higher income and lower prices."

This, he contends, is an error: "Regrettably—or perhaps fortunately—the motives of human action are not exhausted with the mere recording of economic interests." [15]

The economists of an earlier age took the view that there is a definable province of the "economic" and that it is the function of economics to investigate this province. Modern economists adhered to this view for some time, although the line of demarcation between "economic" and "noneconomic" ends must have appeared still less clearly visible in the light of their subjectivism than in that of the objectivism of the classical economists. Even today this view has not yet been given up by everyone. But more and more the realization is spreading that neither the motivations nor the ends of action can be differentiated as economic and noneconomic. What is economic is only the conduct of acting men. Economic action consists in the endeavor to remedy the state of dissatisfaction or, expressed differently, to satisfy wants as far as the scarcity of means allows.

It cannot be maintained that either of these two views saw in the pursuit of economic interests (in the sense in which Myrdal employs this term) the only motive of human action. The older view distinguished between economic and noneconomic goals. According to the modern view, all action is economic. Modern economics makes no distinction among ends because it considers them all equally legitimate, even those that the older view and the popular mode of expression (adopted also by Myrdal) regard as noneconomic. Modern economists do not want valuations to be smuggled into their science. For example, they do not want efforts to obtain "ideal" goods to be considered different in any way from the striving for "material" goods. The fact that frequently a financial gain is eschewed or expenditures are made in order to attain political or other ends, which are usually called noneconomic, is not only not denied, but emphasized.

Myrdal works with a concept of "interest" that he equates with that of "economic interest" and thus with "the desire for higher income and lower prices." The conduct of men, he maintains, is not determined by interests alone, but by "attitudes." The term "attitude" is to be understood as "the emotional disposition of an individual to respond in certain ways toward actual or potential situations." There are "happily," he adds, "enough men with attitudes which do not at all coincide with their interests." [16] It certainly does not require a book of over three hundred pages to point this out. No one has denied, least of all economists, that there are men who aim at other things besides "higher incomes and lower prices." Böhm-Bawerk, for instance, explicitly stated that he used the word "well-being" in the broadest sense, in which it does "not embrace merely the self-centered interests of a subject, but everything that appears to him worthy of pursuit." [17] All the arguments advanced by Myrdal against the utilitarianism of economics collapse completely, because he has not understood the fundamental ideas of the modern doctrines he undertakes to criticize.

3. THE CRITIQUE OF RATIONALISM BY ETHNOLOGY AND PREHISTORY

Attempts to undermine the "rationalistic" starting point of economic theory by drawing on the research findings of ethnology and the history of primitive peoples also miss the mark.

Eduard Hahn traces the origin of the plow and plow farming back to ancient myths. Tillage with the plow, he tells us, was originally a ceremony in which the plow represented the phallus of the ox who drew it impregnating mother earth. The wagon, according to him, was not originally an "economic" means of conveyance. On the contrary, it was a sacred implement whose purpose was "to repeat on earth the wanderings of the rulers of fate in heaven." Only later did "the wagon sink to a commonplace implement of farming." [18]

By means of these discoveries, which, to be sure, are by no means uncontested, Hahn thinks he has cut the ground from under the utilitarian position and furnished complete proof of the correctness of his political program, which demands the "reestablishment of an active social aristocracy." [19] "Modern ethnology," Hahn believes,

finds itself . . . again and again and again in the strongest opposition to the current view, which, in the most regrettable contradiction of the facts of the real world, is bent on setting out pure utility as the only operative mainspring of all the economic activity of men, and, indeed, of all historical events in general. Gradually, however, it will have to be recognized that the ideal aspect certainly deserves very great consideration; that it is not true for all ages and peoples, as it is said to be for us, the children of the second half of the nineteenth century, that the result of every activity—whether it is a matter of a sack of potatoes or the greatest discovery in philosophy or physics—can be expressed in marks and pfennigs, or, for that matter, in dollars and cents.[20]

The peoples whose culture Hahn has studied had different ideas of the relationship between cause and effect from those of the men of the nineteenth century. Whereas today we are guided in our conduct by ideas derived from modern chemistry, biology, and physiology, they had notions that we are now accustomed to call beliefs in magic and myths. They were, says Hahn, imbued with the idea that

the life of the vegetable or the animal kingdom could be influenced by efficacious rites.[21]

The oldest agricultural botany, he further maintains, also certainly stemmed from the idea that

before one could demand something of the land, something would have to be done to further the growth of the vegetable kingdom; one had to have first contributed something to it.[22]

Thus, Hahn himself admits that the primitive husbandmen practiced their rites because of their supposed utility and their anticipated results. Their customs and magical rites were, according to Hahn's own presentation, actions consciously aiming at ends. When we call their technology "magic" and ours "scientific," all we are saying is that the fundamental orientation of men's conduct is the same in both cases and that the difference is determined by the disparity in their concrete ideas concerning the relationship between cause and effect. These mythological views saw a causal relationship between, for example, the nudity of the plowman and a rich harvest, and between many other customs that are offensive to us today and the fertility of the soil;[23] and rites were performed in accordance with these ideas in order to ensure the success of agricultural labor. But surely no one can find any support in all this for the statement that men of primitive times differed from us in that the mainspring of their actions was not utility, but idealism. Obviously the result of economic activity could not be computed in marks and pfennigs in an age that was not yet familiar with the use of money. But what the men of primitive times strove for, what they valued alone, and what they sought to attain precisely by means of their rites, religious acts, exorcisms, prayers, and orgies was the satisfaction of the "common" exigencies of life: the need for food, clothing, shelter, health, and safety. For the other things we value today they would have had no understanding—not even for "the greatest discovery in philosophy or physics."

The progress of civilization, Frobenius thinks, derives not from "need" and "uneasiness," but from "ideals." Among other things the history of cultivation with the hoe proves this.

The first step was apparently a gathering of grain that grew wild. Out of thankfulness, and in order to propitiate mother earth, who was wounded by the grain harvest, the custom arose, as an ideal, of again restoring grain to her, the fruits of which flowed back not so much to the profane life, but as holy testimony of sacrifice. Not until a later age did cultivation with the hoe assume a more and more profane and rational character . . . Only when provident causality let ideals atrophy, when sober facts came to dominate the spirit, did the practical, expedient utilization of the "discovery" of cultivation with the hoe appear as profane farming.[24]

It may well be true that cultivation with the hoe and the plow arose as ritual acts out of a technology of magic and mythology and that later, after the inefficacy of the rites was realized, these methods of tillage were retained because their suitability came to be recognized as a result of the knowledge of agricultural botany that had been acquired in the meantime. This discovery may be welcomed as a very interesting contribution to the history of technology and the application of technological knowledge. Yet for the purposes of the subject under discussion it tells us nothing beyond the fact that the technological notions of primitive ages were different from ours. It would be impermissible to infer from this that the action of men of distant times and lands was categorially different from the action of modern men. Berthold Schwarz intended to make gold, and in attempting to do so is said to have discovered the preparation for gunpowder. Columbus set sail to seek a sea route to the Indies and discovered America. Can one therefore maintain that these two men acted in ways fundamentally different from the way we act today? It has never been denied that human action does not always attain the ends it has set for itself and occasionally has results that would have appeared worth aiming at if they had been known earlier.

When the husbandmen of remote antiquity sought to increase the produce of their land by means of symbolic rites, their action was based on the prevailing "technological" notions of their time. When today we proceed differently, our action conforms to the technological notions prevailing at the present time. He who considers them erroneous might attempt to uncover their errors and replace a useless theory by a more suitable one. If he is unable to do so, he should not criticize the procedure of those who work for the dissemination of the knowledge of modern agricultural technology. It is futile to criticize statements such as "the short-sighted rationalism of the nineteenth century regarded the acts and dispensations of the old ritual . . . simply as superstition and thought it was to be pushed aside by instruction in the public schools." [25] If one goes through the long list of rites—not very commendable from the standpoint of present-day sentiment—that Eduard Hahn has assembled in his writings on the basis of astonishingly extensive research, one finds scarcely any whose elimination would be regretted.[26] For what purpose should the empty forms of a technology whose fruitlessness no one can deny be retained?

In the behavior of men we can distinguish only two basic forms, between which there is a sharp conceptual division: unconscious behavior, or vegetative reaction, and conscious behavior, or action. All action, however, is necessarily in accord with the statements of the a priori theory of human action. Goals change, ideas of technology are transformed, but action always remains action. Action always seeks means to realize ends, and it is in this sense always rational and mindful of utility. It is, in a word, human.

4. INSTINCT SOCIOLOGY AND BEHAVIORISM

If one rejects the method of modern economics and renounces the formal comprehension of action under the eudaemonistic principle that action aims without exception at the enhancement of well-being as judged by the individual according to his subjective standard of values, then the only choice that remains is between the procedure of instinct sociology and that of behaviorism. Instinct sociology seeks to evade the crux of the problem by correlating with every desire an instinct that is supposed to "explain" action. This is the method that explains the effect of opium on the basis of the *virtus dormitiva cuius est natura sensus assupire*. Behaviorism, on the other hand, avoids explanation entirely and is satisfied with the mere recording of individual acts. Neither "coarsely materialistic" behaviorism nor "idealistic" instinct sociology would be at all able, if they were consistent, to refer under one head to two actions that were not perfectly alike. For the principle that leads them to treat both the instinct for bread and the instinct for potatoes as the instinct for food, or to consider the consumption of bread and the consumption of potatoes as eating, would also have to lead them to broader generalizations until they arrived at the most comprehensive category, "want-satisfaction" or "enhancement of well-being." Both are helpless when confronted with the problem of the conflict of different wishes, aims, and desires in the face of limited means for their satisfaction.

What a contrast between the wealth of knowledge that we already owe to economic and sociological theory today, and the poverty and inadequacy of what these two doctrines have to offer!

NOTES

1. Vierkandt, *Gesellschaftslehre* (2nd ed.; Stuttgart, 1928), p. 23.
2. *Ibid.*
3. *Op. cit.*, p. 37.
4. *Kölner Vierteljahrscheften für Soziologie* III, (1923), 179.
5. Vierkandt, *op. cit.*, p. 61.

6. Feuerbach, *Sämtliche Werke* (republished by Bolin and Jodl, Stuttgart, 1907), X, 231. "Happiness," says Feuerbach (*ibid.*), is "nothing but the healthy, normal condition of a being."
7. Vierkandt, *op. cit.,* p. 48.
8. Vierkandt, *op. cit.,* pp. 31 f.
9. Vierkandt, *op. cit.,* p. 47.
10. Vierkandt, *op. cit.,* p. 60.
11. Vierkandt, *op. cit.,* p. 41.
12. Vierkandt, *op. cit.,* p. 63.
13. Cf. also Vierkandt's article "Kultur des 19. Jahrhunderts und Gegenwart," *Handwörterbuch der Soziologie,* pp. 141 ff.
14. Cf. Myrdal, *Das politische Element in der nationalökonomischen Doktrinbildung,* translated by Mackenroth (Berlin, 1932), pp. 299 f. [Translator's note: The quotations are from the German edition of Myrdal's book, published under the title cited. In the English-language edition, which, as the title indicates, was translated from the German by Paul Streeten and published by Routledge and Kegan Paul, Ltd. in London in 1953, the quoted passages, perhaps in consequence of von Mises' critique in this text, have been considerably weakened.]
15. Myrdal, *op. cit.,* p. 299.
16. Myrdal, *op. cit.,* p. 300.
17. Böhm-Bawerk, *Kapital und Kapitalzins* (4th ed.; Jena, 1921), Part II, Vol. I, p. 236, footnote.
18. Hahn, *Die Entstehung der Pflugkultur* (Heidelberg, 1909), pp. 40 ff., 105 ff., 139 ff., 152 ff.; Frobenius, *Paideuma, Umrisse einer Kultur und Seelenlehre* (Munich, 1921), pp. 72 f.
19. Hahn, *Die Entstehung der wirtschaftlichen Arbeit* (Heidelberg, 1908), pp. 102 ff.
20. Hahn, *Die Entstehung der Pflugkultur,* p. 63.
21. *Ibid.,* p. 86.
22. *Ibid.,* p. 87.
23. *Ibid.,* pp. 117 ff.
24. Cf. Frobenius, *Paideuma,* pp. 70 ff.
25. Cf. Hahn, *Die Entstehung der Pflugkultur,* p. 87.
26. A few examples from a compilation by Hahn (*Die Entstehung der Pflugkultur,* pp. 118 ff.): sacred prostitution; lewd jokes, especially on the part of women, at agricultural festivals; the singing of licentious songs by the most eminent women of Bautzen; running around the fields naked by Wendish female flax-workers until as late as 1882.

2

Sociology and History

Rationalism brought about two revolutionary changes in the sciences of human action. Into history, which had hitherto been the only science of human action, it introduced the critical method. It freed that science from its naive attachment to what had been handed down in the chronicles and historical works of the past and taught it not only to draw upon new sources—documents, inscriptions, and the like—but to subject all sources to critical scrutiny. What the science of history thereby gained can never be lost again, nor has its value ever been contested. Even the attempts undertaken in recent times to "intuit" history cannot do without the critical method. History can be investigated only on the basis of sources, and no one will seriously want to question the fact that its subject matter must be approached critically. The only question that can raise uncertainty is not whether, but how sources are to be analyzed and criticized.

The other great accomplishment of rationalism was the construction of a theoretical science of human action, i.e., a science that aims at the ascertainment of universally valid laws of human conduct. All that this science owes to August Comte is its name. Its foundations had been laid in the eighteenth century. What the thinkers of the eighteenth and the early nineteenth centuries strove to develop above all was economics, which is up to the present the best elaborated branch of sociology. However, they also sought to provide the basis for a system of thought extending beyond the relatively narrow sphere of economic theory and embracing the whole of sociology.[1]

The fundamental admissibility and possibility of sociology was

68

challenged in the second half of the nineteenth century. To many the idea was intolerable that there can be laws of human action independent of the historical milieu. Accordingly, they considered history as the only science competent to take human action as its cognitive object. This attack upon sociology's right to exist was leveled almost exclusively against economics. Its critics did not realize that economics is only a branch of a more comprehensive science extending beyond its domain, but exhibiting the same logical character. Later, when sociology became better known in Germany and all its branches came under attack, the fact went unnoticed that it makes the same claim to universal validity for its statements as economics does. For in the meanwhile the treatment of the problem by Windelband, Rickert, and Max Weber had set it in a new light, as a result of which the logical character of sociology had come to be viewed differently.

The rejection of sociology and economics was also motivated, perhaps even above all else, by political considerations. For a goodly number, like Schmoller, Brentano, and Hasbach, for example, these were indeed decisive.[2] Many wished to support political and economic programs which, had they been subjected to examination by the methods of economic theory, would have been shown to be quite senseless, not in terms of a different scale of value, but precisely from the point of view of the goals that their advocates hoped to achieve by means of them. Interventionism could appear as a suitable policy for attaining these goals only to one who ignored all the arguments of economics. To everyone else it had to be evident that such a policy is inexpedient.[3] In the speech of May 2, 1879, before the Reichstag with which Bismarck sought to justify his financial and economic program, he asserted that he set no greater store by science in regard to all these questions than in regard to any other judgment on organic institutions, that the abstract theories of science in this respect left him completely cold, and that he judged "according to the experience familiar to us." [4] The Historical-Realist School, in treating of the economic aspects of political science, proclaimed the same view, with more words, but scarcely with better arguments. In any case, however, there were *also* unbiased objections in the debate over the scientific character of sociology. The following discussions deal only with these.

There are two different ways of setting methodological and epistemological investigations upon a secure foundation. One can attempt to reach solid ground by undertaking to deal directly with the ultimate problems of epistemology. This procedure would no doubt be the best if it offered any promise of success, so that one could hope to find truly firm ground at that deep level. However, one can also take another path, by starting from the definite concepts and propositions of science and verifying their logical character. It is evident that cognition of the ultimate foundations of our knowledge can never be attained in this manner. But neither does the first way offer such a possibility. On the other hand, the second way protects us from the fate that has befallen most investigations that have been concerned with the methodological and epistemological questions of economics in recent years. These investigations became so badly bogged down in the difficulty of the ultimate problems of epistemology that they never reached the point where they could deal with the logical problems of sociology, which are comparatively easier to solve. The ultimate problems pose difficulties that are not to be mastered with the limited means of the human mind.

The scope of the following discussions is, from the outset, much more narrowly circumscribed. We do not propose to treat of the ultimate questions of cognition. All that will be undertaken here is to explain what sociology is and with what claim to validity it constructs its concepts and arrives at its conclusions. The fact that we shall be primarily concerned with economic theory requires no special justification. It is that branch of sociology which has thus far received fullest development and has attained the greatest systematic precision. The logical character of a science is studied to greatest advantage in its most highly developed branches. In the following discussions the starting point will not be, as is regrettably the practice in many works on methodology and epistemology, the formulation given to the problems and their solutions by the classical economists, which is logically unsatisfactory, but, of course, the present state of the theory.[5]

1. THE METHODOLOGICAL AND THE LOGICAL PROBLEM

To begin with, departing from the procedure usually followed, one must distinguish the methodological from the logical problem.

As a rule, methodology is understood to be logic conceived as the theory of the methods of thought. We shall speak of it in the less customary sense as the technique of scientific thought (heuristic) and contrast it, as an art (*ars inveniendi*), to the science of logic.

For a long time, following in the path of Bacon, the inductive method has been held in especially high esteem. The natural sciences, so one heard, particularly from laymen, owed their success primarily to perfect induction. It was said that the general law could be derived only when all individual cases had been compiled. One did not let oneself be disconcerted by the fact that Bacon and most of those who expounded his theory themselves had no successes to show and that precisely the most successful inquirers had taken a different view. No notice was taken of the fact that Galileo, for example, had declared the customary perfect induction uncertain, and that for the comparison of a number of individual cases he substituted the analysis of *one* case, from which he derived the law that was then to be experimentally verified. What was altogether fantastic was that perfect induction was praised as the specific method of the natural sciences, whereas in fact it was not used by scientists at all, but by antiquarians. Because of the scarcity of the sources available to them, the latter set out in principle to draw their conclusions from an exhaustive study of all the accessible data.

What counts is not the data, but the mind that deals with them. The data that Galileo, Newton, Ricardo, Menger, and Freud made use of for their great discoveries lay at the disposal of every one of their contemporaries and of untold previous generations. Galileo was certainly not the first to observe the swinging motion of the chandelier in the cathedral at Pisa. Many doctors before Breuer had gone to the bedside of a person suffering from hysteria. It is merely the routine of scientific procedure that can be taught and presented in textbooks. The power to accomplish feats of scientific achievement can be awakened only in one who already possesses the necessary intellectual gifts and strength of character. To be sure, without the foundations, which mastery of the scientific technique and literature provides, nothing can be accomplished. However, the decisive factor remains the personality of the thinker.

On this point opinions are no longer divided. We need not spend any more time on it.

The situation is altogether different with regard to the logical problem. In the course of the *Methodenstreit* * the question of the logical character of sociology fell into the background until it was finally dropped entirely. But in the early years of the *Methodenstreit* this was not the case. At that time, first Walter Bagehot and then Carl Menger argued against the rejection in principle of every theoretical science of human action by pointing out the character and logical necessity of a theoretical science of social phenomena. It is well known how this dispute ended in Germany. Economics disappeared from the universities, and its place was taken, occasionally even under its name, by the study of the economic aspects of political science, an encyclopedic collection of knowledge from various subjects. Whoever wished to define this study scientifically viewed it as a history of governmental administration, economic conditions, and economic policy continued into the most recent past. From this history one endeavored, by adherence to the standards of value accepted by the authorities and the political parties, to derive practical rules for future economic policy in a way similar to that of the writer on military affairs who seeks to discover rules for the conduct of coming wars from the study of the campaigns of the past. In general, the investigator of the economic aspects of political science differed from the historian in that he was usually more concerned with the most recent past and with problems of internal politics, fi-

---

* A discussion concerning the method and epistemological character of economics carried on in the second half of the eighties and into the nineties of the last century between Carl Menger and his supporters on the side of the Austrian School of economics, and the proponents of the German Historical School, led by Gustav von Schmoller.

nance, and economic policy and was less intent on concealing his political point of view and quicker to draw from the past practical applications for the politics of the future. The logical character of his work scarcely ever became a problem for him. If it did, however, his mind was soon set at rest by the dicta of Schmoller.

The first sign of disquietude is to be seen in the controversy over value judgments that broke out in the second and third lustrums of the twentieth century. The matter-of-factness with which political demands were advanced as postulates of science in lectures, textbooks, and monographs began to give offense. A group of younger professors insisted that the world view of the instructor should not influence the content of his teaching or at least that the instructor, as soon as he does present his personal value judgments, point out the subjective character of what is being taught. However, the discussions connected with this agitation scarcely touched upon the problem of the possibility of a theoretical science of social phenomena.[6]

2. THE LOGICAL CHARACTER OF HISTORY

In the meantime, completely apart from everything connected with the logical problems involved in the relation between sociology and history, an important advance had taken place in the logic of the moral sciences.

The demand had long since been made that history be at last raised to the status of a genuine science by adopting the methods of the natural— i.e., the nomothetic—sciences.[7] Some declared this demand unrealizable because they saw no way by which one could discover historical laws. Imbued with the conviction that only nomothetic science can properly lay claim to the name of science, they regretfully admitted that history is not a science. (For this reason many wanted to call it an art.) Others again credited themselves with the power of formulating "laws of world history." Kurt Breysig proved the most prolific in this respect.

It should be noted that what was at issue was not the problem of a theoretical science of human action. What was sought were laws of historical development, laws of history, not laws of sociology. Breysig's thirty-first law, for example, reads: "Under the rule of the Kaiser and of the people, which developed concomitantly, the national economy had to advance to a hitherto unheard of boom in trade and industry." [8]

In France Bergson and in Germany Windelband, Rickert, and Max Weber combatted the confusion of concepts that underlay this demand for a new science of history. They sought to define logically the character of history and historical investigation and to demonstrate the inapplicability of the concepts and procedures of physics to history. What the Southwest German School of New Criticism thereby accomplished, notwithstanding its shortcomings, deserves the highest recognition and must constitute the foundation and starting point of all further investigations concerning the logic of history. Yet in one respect this accomplishment is completely inadequate: it is not based on any acquaintance with the problem of a theoretical science of social phenomena and for that reason pays no heed to it. Windelband, Rickert, and Max Weber knew only the natural sciences and history; they were strangers to the existence of sociology as a nomothetic science. [9]

This statement, as far as it concerns Max Weber, requires further elaboration. Weber was, to be sure, a professor of economics at two universities and a professor of sociology at two others. Nevertheless, he was neither an economist nor a sociologist, but an historian. [10] He was not acquainted with the system of economic theory. In his view economics and sociology were historical sciences. He considered sociology a kind of more highly generalized and summarized history.

It needs scarcely to be emphasized that in pointing this out we do not mean to belittle Max Weber and his work. Weber was one of the most brilliant figures of German science of the twentieth century. He was a pioneer and trail blazer, and coming generations will have enough to do to make his heritage intellectually their own and to digest and elaborate it. That he was an historian and an investigator into the logical character of history does not mean that he failed with regard to the problems which the period presented and which he undertook to treat. His field was just that of history, and in this field he did far more than his share. And finally, if it is possible today to approach the logical problems of sociology with better conceptual tools, this is primarily due to the work that Max Weber devoted to the logical problems of history.

3. THE IDEAL TYPE AND SOCIOLOGICAL LAW

In Weber's eyes,

the real configuration (i.e., the configuration in the concrete case) of the socio-cultural life which surrounds us, in its universal, but for that reason no less individually framed, context and in its connection with other socio-cultural conditions, likewise individually constituted, out of which it has come into existence

appears as the "starting point of the social sciences." [11] But wherever

the causal explanation of a "cultural phenomenon"—an "historical individual"—comes into question, knowledge of *laws* of causation cannot be the *end,* but only the *means* of investigation. It facilitates and makes possible for us the imputation of the culturally significant components of the phenomena, in their individuality, to their concrete causes. As far and only as far as it accomplishes this is it valuable for the cognition of individual concatenations. And the more "general," i.e., the more abstract, the laws, the less they accomplish for the requirements of the causal imputation of *individual* phenomena and thereby, indirectly, for the understanding of the meaning of cultural events.[12]

Weber places "historian and sociologist" in the same category: the task of both is "cognition of cultural reality." [13] Therefore, for him the logical and methodological problem is the same in sociology and history, viz.,

What is the logical function and structure of the *concepts* with which our science, like every science, deals? Or, more particularly, formulated with regard to the crucial problem: what importance do *theory* and the formation of theoretical concepts have for the cognition of cultural reality? [14]

Max Weber's answer to this question is, in effect, that "abstract economic theory" is but a "special case of a way of forming concepts which is peculiar to the sciences of human culture and, in a certain sphere, indispensable for them"; here we have "before us an example of those syntheses which are generally termed 'ideas' of historical phenomena." [15] It is the production of a "conceptual representation" which coordinates "definite references and events of historical life into a cosmos of interrelationships immanently free of contradiction." We make the characteristic features of this interrelationship clear to ourselves pragmatically by constructing an "ideal type." [16] The ideal type

is arrived at through the one-sided *intensification* of *one* or *several* aspects and through integration into an immanently consistent *conceptual representation* of a multiplicity of scattered and discrete *individual* phenomena, present here in greater number, there in less, and occasionally not at all, which are in congruity with these one-sidedly intensified aspects.[17]

Consequently, "abstract economic theory," which, in Weber's view, presents "an ideal representation of proceedings on the commodity market in the social organization of an exchange economy, free competition, and strictly rational action," [18] has the same logical character as the "idea of the 'town economy' of the Middle Ages" or as the "idea of handicraft" [19] or as ideas "like individualism, imperialism, mercantilism, and innumerable conventional ideas formed in a similar way by means of which we seek to grasp reality in thought and understanding." [20] These concepts cannot be defined "according to their content through a 'presuppositionless' *description* of *any one* concrete phenomenon or through an abstracting and lumping together of that which is *common* to *several* concrete phenomena." [21] They are specimens, says Weber, of the "ideal type," a concept peculiar to history and sociology—in short, to all cultural sciences.

Yet even for Weber sociology and history are not identical. "Sociology constructs *type* concepts and seeks the *general* principles of events," while history

strives for causal analysis and imputation of *individual culturally important* actions, institutions, and personalities . . . As is the case with every generalizing science, the character of its abstractions postulates that its concepts must be relatively free of content. What it offers instead is increased *clarity* of concepts. This increased clarity is obtained through the greatest possible *adequacy to meaning* [*Sinnadäquanz*], which is what sociology strives to attain in forming its concepts.[22]

Hence, the difference between sociology and history is considered as only one of degree. In both, the object of cognition is identical. Both make use of the same logical method of forming concepts. They are different merely in the extent of their proximity to reality, their fullness of content, and the purity of their ideal-typical constructions. Thus Max Weber has implicitly answered the question that had once constituted the substance of the *Methodenstreit* entirely in the sense of those who denied the logical legitimacy of a theoretical science of social phenomena. According to him, social science is logically conceivable only as a special, qualified kind of historical investigation.

However, the theory with which he is acquainted and which he rejects is not the theory that Walter Bagehot and Carl Menger had in mind when they attacked the epistemology of the Historical School. What Max Weber is thinking of is something entirely different. He wants to prove to us

the senselessness of the idea, which at times even dominates the historians of our subject, that the goal of cultural science, even if a long way off, should be to construct a logically complete system of concepts in which reality would be comprehended in an arrangement in some sense *definitive* and from which it could again be deduced.[23]

Nothing appears to him more hazardous than

the intermingling of history and theory arising from "naturalistic" prejudices, whether one believes that the "real" substance, the "essence," of historical reality has been fixed in those theoretical, conceptual representations,[24] or one uses them as a Procrustean bed into which history is to be squeezed, or one hypostatizes the "concepts" as a "genuine" reality standing behind the flux of phenomena as real "forces" which work themselves out in history.[25]

As far as Max Weber seeks to define the logical character of historical investigation, as far as he rejects the endeavors to construct "historical laws," and as far as he demonstrates, following in the footsteps of Windelband and Rickert, the inapplicability to history of the methods used by the natural sciences in forming their concepts, one can agree with him without hesitation. In all these respects he continues and perfects the work of his predecessors, and his contributions to epistemology are imperishable.[26] But where he went beyond this and attempted to determine the character of sociological investigation, he failed and had to fail because by sociology he understood something entirely different from the nomothetic science of human action, the possibility of which had constituted the subject of the *Methodenstreit*. The reason why Weber fell into this misconception can be easily understood and explained from his personal history and from the state in which the knowledge of the findings of sociological investigation existed in his day in the German Reich, and especially at the universities. Historians of the subject may concern themselves with this aspect of the question. All that is of importance to us here is the rectification of the misunderstandings which, while they certainly do not owe their origin to Max Weber, received wide dissemination through his having made them the foundation of his epistemology.[27]

The basis of Weber's misconceptions can be exposed only by consideration of the question whether the concepts of economic theory do in fact have the logical character of the "ideal type." This question is plainly to be answered in the negative. It is quite true also of the concepts of economics that they are "never empirically identifiable in reality" in their "conceptual purity." [28] Concepts are never and nowhere to be found in reality; they belong rather to the province of thought. They are the intellectual means by which we seek to grasp reality in thought. Yet it cannot be contended that these concepts of economic theory are obtained through "one-sided *intensification* of *one* or *several* aspects and through integration into an immanently consistent *conceptual* representation of a multiplicity of scattered and discrete *individual* phenomena, present here in greater number, there in less, and occasionally not at all, which are in congruity with these one-sidedly intensified aspects." On the contrary, they are obtained through reflections having in view the comprehension of what is contained in *each* of the individual phenomena taken into consideration. To determine whether the construction of this or that concept or proposition really succeeds in this intention in a way that is logically unobjectionable and correctly grasps reality is one of the tasks of the science whose logical character is the subject of dispute. What interests us here is not the question of the material truth of individual concepts and propositions and of the theoretical structure connecting them into a system, but the logical permissibility and expedience of formulating such propositions, not to mention their necessity for the attainment of the goals set for that science.

Human action, which constitutes the subject matter of all investigation in the social sciences, both historical and theoretical, presupposes a state of affairs that we shall express in Gottl's formulation, since Max Weber opposed it with what we regard as defective reasoning. Gottl considers "privation" (by which he understands the fact that "an aspiration can never be realized without in some way impairing the fulfillment of other aspirations") as one of the two "fundamental conditions" that govern our action.[29] Now Weber maintains that there are exceptions to this fundamental situation in which man finds himself. It is not true that "the conflict of several *ends,* and therefore the necessity of *choosing* among them, is a state of affairs which holds absolutely."[30] However, this objection of Weber's is correct only insofar as there are also "free goods"; but as far as it is correct, "action" does not take place. If all goods were "free goods," man would economize only with his personal activity, i.e., with the application of his personal powers and his passing life. He would disregard the things of the external world.[31] Only in a Cockaigne populated by men who were immortal and indifferent to the passage of time, in which every man is always and everywhere perfectly satisfied and fully sated, or in a world in which an improvement in satisfaction and further satiation cannot be attained, would the state of affairs that Gottl calls "privation" not exist. Only as far as it does exist does action take place; as far as it is lacking, action is also lacking.

Once one has realized this, one also implicitly realizes that every action involves choice among various possibilities. All action is economizing with the means available for the realization of attainable ends. The fundamental law of action is the economic principle. Every action is under its sway. He who wants to deny the possibility of economic science must begin by calling into question the universal validity of the economic principle, i.e., that the necessity to economize is characteristic of all action by its very nature. But only one who has completely misunderstood the principle can do this.

The most common misunderstanding consists in seeing in the economic principle a statement about the material and the content of action. One reaches into psychology, constructs the concept of want, and then searches for the bridge between want, the presentation of a feeling of uneasiness, and the concrete decision in action. Thus the want becomes a judge over action: it is thought that the correct action, the one corresponding to the want, can be contrasted to the incorrect action. However, we can never identify the want otherwise than in the action.[32] The action is always in accord with the want because we can infer the want only from the action. Whatever anyone *says* about his own wants is always only discussion and criticism of past and future behavior; the want first becomes manifest in action and only in action. It is, of course, clear to everyone that with regard to what we say about the wants of other—not to mention all—men, there can be only two possibilities: either we state how they have acted or presumably will act, or we state how they should have acted or how they should act in the future.

For this reason no misunderstanding can be more fundamental than that of historicism when it sees in the "desire for economy a part of a later development" and adds that the "man in the state of nature does not act with the fullest purposiveness";[33] or when it explains the economic principle as a specific feature of production in a money economy.[34] Max Scheler correctly refuted this idea, although he himself was prevented, by his desire to find an absolute determination of the rank of values, from drawing the conclusions from his answer that are crucial for ethics.

That the pleasant is, *ceteris paribus,* preferred to the unpleasant is not a proposition based on observation and induction; it lies in the nature of these values and in the nature of sentient feeling. If, for example, a traveler, an historian, or a zoologist were to describe a type of man or animal to us in which the opposite were the case, we would "a priori" neither believe him nor need to believe him. We would say: This is out of the question.

At most these beings feel different *things* to be pleasant and unpleasant from what we do; or else, it is not that they prefer the unpleasant to the pleasant, but that for them there must exist a value (perhaps unknown to us) of a *modality* which is "higher" than the modality of this stage and that they can bear the unpleasant only because they "prefer" this value. Or we are confronted by a case of perversion of *desires,* in consequence of which they experience things injurious to life as "pleasant." Like all these relations, what our proposition expresses is also at the same time a *law of insight* into alien expressions of life and concrete historical valuations (indeed, even into one's *own* remembered valuations). Therefore, it is already *presupposed* in all observations and inductions. For example, it is "a priori" as concerns all ethnological experience. Not even the adoption of the point of view of the theory of evolution can further "explain" this proposition and the facts it denotes.[35]

What Scheler says here about the pleasant and the unpleasant is the fundamental law of action, which is valid independently of place, time, race, and the like. If we substitute in Scheler's remarks "subjectively considered more important" for "pleasant," and "subjectively considered less important" for "unpleasant," this becomes even clearer.

Historicism does not take its task seriously enough in being satisfied with the simple statement that the quality of human action is not supertemporal and has changed in the course of evolution. In undertaking to defend such statements, one at least has the obligation to point out in what respects the action of the allegedly prerational era differed from that of the rational era; how, for example, action other than rational could take place or would have been able to take place. Max Weber alone felt this obligation. We owe to him the only attempt ever made to raise this basic thesis of historicism from the level of a journalistic *aperçu* to that of scientific investigation.

Within the realm of "meaningful action" Weber distinguishes four types. Action can

be (1) purposive-rational, i.e., guided by anticipations of the behavior of the objects of the external world and of other men, and using these anticipations as "conditions" or as "means" for the attainment of the *ends* rationally considered and sought by the actor himself; (2) valuational, i.e., guided by conscious belief in the unqualified *intrinsic* value of a definite mode of conduct—ethical, aesthetic, religious, or any other—purely for its own sake and independently of its consequences; (3) affective, especially *emotional*, when it is guided by burning passions and moods; and (4) traditional, when it is guided by the familiarity of custom.[36]

Beyond every kind of meaningful action there is "a merely reactive mode of behavior which is not attendant on a subjectively intended meaning." The boundaries between meaningful and merely reactive action are in a state of flux.[37]

First, let us consider what Max Weber calls "merely reactive" behavior. Biology and the natural sciences in general are able to approach the behavior of the objects of their examination only from without. For that reason they can establish no more than the existence of a relationship of stimulus and response. Beyond this they must say: *ignorabimus*. The natural scientist may dimly suspect that somehow the behavior of the object stimulated has to be explained in a way similar to that of rational human action, but it is not given for him to see more deeply into these matters. With regard to human behavior, however, our position is entirely different. Here we grasp meaning, i.e., as Max Weber says, "the meaning subjectively intended by the actor," which is "not an objectively 'correct' or a metaphysically determined 'real' meaning." [38] Where we observe among animals, which we are unable to credit with human reason, a mode of behavior that we would be in a position to grasp if we had observed it in a human being, we speak of instinctive behavior.

The response of a human being to stimuli can be either reactive or meaningful, or both reactive and meaningful at the same time.

The body responds reactively to poisons, but, in addition, action can also respond meaningfully by taking an antidote. Only meaningful action, on the other hand, responds to an increase in market prices. From the point of view of psychology, the boundary between meaningful and reactive behavior is indeterminate, as is the boundary between consciousness and unconsciousness. However, it may be that only the imperfection of our thinking prevents us from discovering that action and reaction to stimuli are essentially alike and that the difference between them is merely one of degree.

When we say that an instance of human behavior is merely reactive, instinctive, or conative, we mean that it takes place unconsciously. It must be noted, however, that where we deem it inexpedient to conduct ourselves in such a way, we meaningfully set about to eliminate merely reactive, instinctive, or conative behavior. If my hand is touched by a sharp knife, I instinctively draw it back; but if, for example, a surgical operation is intended, I will endeavor to overcome reactive behavior through conscious action. Conscious volition controls all spheres of our behavior that are at all accessible to it by tolerating only that reactive, instinctive, or conative conduct which it sanctions as expedient and would itself have carried out. Consequently, from the point of view of the investigation proper to the science of human action, which aims at something quite different from that proper to psychology, the boundary between meaningful and merely reactive behavior is not at all indeterminate. As far as the will has the power to become efficacious, there is only meaningful action.

This leads us to an examination of the types of behavior that Weber contrasts with rational behavior. To begin with, it is quite clear that what Weber calls "valuational" behavior cannot be fundamentally distinguished from "rational" behavior. The results that rational conduct aims at are also values and, as such, they are beyond rationality. To use Weber's expression, they have "unqualified *intrinsic* value." Rational action is " 'rational' only in its means." [39] What Weber calls "valuational" conduct differs from rational conduct only in that it regards a definite mode of behavior also as a value and accordingly arranges it in the rank order of values. If someone not only wants to earn his livelihood in general, but also in a way which is "respectable" and "in accordance with his station in life"—let us say as a Prussian Junker of the older stamp, who preferred a government career to the bar—or if someone forgoes the advantages that a Civil Service career offers because he does not want to renounce his political convictions, this is in no way an action that could be termed non-rational. Adherence to received views of life or to political convictions is an end like any other, and like any other it enters into the rank order of values.

Weber here falls into the old misunderstanding which the basic idea of utilitarianism repeatedly encounters, namely, that of regarding as an "end" only values that are material and can be expressed in money. When Weber holds that "whoever acts, without consideration of the consequences to be anticipated, in the service of his conviction of what duty, honor, beauty, religious instruction, filial love, or the importance of an 'issue,' no matter of what kind, seem to dictate to him" acts "in a purely valuational manner," [40] he employs an inappropriate mode of expression to describe this state of affairs. It would be more accurate to say that there are men who place the value of duty, honor, beauty, and the like so high that they set aside other goals and ends for their sake. Then one sees rather easily that what is involved here are ends, different, to be sure, from those at which the masses aim, but ends nevertheless, and that therefore an action directed at their realization must likewise be termed rational.

The situation is no different with regard to traditional behavior. A farmer replies to an agricultural chemist who recommends to him the use of artificial fertilizers that he does not allow any city man to interfere in his farming. He wants to continue to proceed in the same way that has been customary in his village for generations, as his father and grandfather, all able farmers, have taught him, a way that has up to now always proved itself successful. This attitude on his part merely signifies that the farmer wants to keep to the received method because he regards it as the better method. When an aristocratic landowner rejects the proposal of his steward to use his name, title, and coat of arms as a trade mark on the packages of butter going to the retail market from his estate, basing his refusal on the argument that such a practice does not conform to aristocratic tradition, he means: I will forgo an increase in my income that I could attain only by the sacrifice of a part of my dignity. In the one case, the custom of the family is retained because—whether it is warranted or not is of no importance for us—it is considered more "rational"; in the other case, because a value is attached to it which is placed above the value that could be realized through its sacrifice.

Finally, there remains "affective" action. Under the impulse of passion, the rank order of ends shifts, and one more easily yields to an emotional impulse that demands immediate satisfaction. Later, on cooler consideration, one judges matters differently. He who endangers his own life in rushing to the aid of a drowning man is able to do so because he yields to the momentary impulse to help, or because he feels the duty to prove himself a hero under such circumstances, or because he wants to earn a reward for saving the man's life. In each case, his action is contingent upon the fact that he momentarily places the value of coming to the man's aid so high that other considerations—his own life, the fate of his own family—fall into the background. It may be that subsequent reconsideration will lead him to a different judgment. But at the moment—and this is the only thing that matters—even this action was "rational."

Consequently, the distinction Max Weber draws within the sphere of meaningful action when he seeks to contrast rational and nonrational action cannot be maintained. Everything that we can regard as human action, because it goes beyond the merely reactive behavior of the organs of the human body, is rational: it chooses between given possibilities in order to attain the most ardently desired goal. No other view is needed for a science that wants to consider action as such, aside from the character of its goals.

Weber's basic error lies in his misunderstanding of the claim to universal validity made by the propositions of sociology. The economic principle, the fundamental law of the formation of exchange ratios, the law of returns, the law of population, and all other like propositions are valid always and everywhere if the conditions assumed by them are given.

Max Weber repeatedly cites Gresham's law as an example of a proposition of economics. However, he does not neglect to place the word "law" in quotation marks in order to show that in this case, as well as in the case of the other propositions of sociology, understood as a discipline involving the method of historical understanding, all that is at issue is a question of "typical *chances,* confirmed by observation, of a course of social action to be *expected* in the presence of certain states of affairs which can be understood from the typical motives and typical meaning intended by the actors." [41] This "so-called 'Gresham's law,' " is, he says,

a rationally evident anticipation of human action under given conditions and under the ideal-typical assumption of purely rational action. Only experience (which ultimately can in some way be expressed "statistically") concerning the actual disappearance from circulation of specie undervalued in the official statutes can teach us how far action really does take place in accordance with it. This experience does in fact demonstrate that the proposition has a very far-reaching validity.[42]

Gresham's law—which, incidentally, was referred to by Aristophanes in the *Frogs,* and clearly enunciated by Nicolaus Oresmius (1364), and not until 1858 named after Sir Thomas Gresham by Macleod—is a special application of the general theory of price controls to monetary relations.[43] The essential element here is not the "disappearance" of "good" money, but the fact that payments that can be made with the same legal effect in "good" or in "bad" money, as suits the debtor, are made in money undervalued by the authorities. It will not do to assert that this is always the case "under the ideal-typical assumption of purely rational action," not even when one uses the word "rational" as a synonym for "aiming at the greatest monetary gain," which is apparently what Max Weber has in mind.

A short while ago a case was reported in which Gresham's law was "set aside." A number of Austrian entrepreneurs visited Moscow and were made acquainted by the Russian rulers (who wanted to induce them to grant long-term commodity credits to the

Soviet Union) with the situation of Russia by means of the old method that Prince Potemkin employed in dealing with his sovereign. The gentlemen were led into a department store where they made use of the opportunity to purchase small mementos of their trip and presents for their friends back in Austria. When one of the travelers paid with a large banknote, he received a gold piece in his change. Amazed, he remarked that he had not known gold coins effectively circulated in Russia. To this the cashier replied that customers occasionally paid in gold and that in such a case he treated the gold pieces like every other kind of money and likewise gave them out again in change. The Austrian, who was apparently not one to believe in "miracles," was not satisfied with this reply and looked into the matter further. Finally, he succeeded in learning that an hour before the visit of his party a government official had appeared in the department store, handed over a gold piece to the cashier, and ordered him to conspicuously hand this one gold piece *al pari* to one of the foreigners in giving him his change. If the incident really took place in this way, the "pure purposive-rationality" (in Weber's sense) of the behavior of the Soviet authorities can certainly not be denied. The costs arising for them from it—which are determined by the premium on gold—appeared warranted in their eyes by the end—obtaining long-term commodity credits. If such conduct is not "rational," I wonder what else would be.

If the conditions that Gresham's law assumes are not given, then action such as the law describes does not take place. If the actor does not know the market value differing from the legally controlled value, or if he does not know that he may make his payments in money that is valued lower by the market, or if he has another reason for giving the creditor more than is due him —for example, because he wants to give him a present, or because he fears violent acts on the part of the creditor—then the assumptions of the law do not apply. Experience teaches that for the mass of debtor-creditor relationships these assumptions do apply. But even if experience were to show that the assumed conditions are not given in the majority of cases, this could in no way weaken the chain of reasoning that has led to the construction of the law or deprive the law of the importance that is its due. However, whether or not the conditions assumed by the law are given, and whether or not action such as the law describes takes place, "purely purposive-rational" action occurs in any case. Even one who gives the creditor a present or who avoids the threat of an extortionist acts rationally and purposively, as does one who acts differently, out of ignorance, from the way he would act if he were better informed.

Gresham's law represents the application to a particular case of laws of catallactics that are valid without exception always and everywhere, provided acts of exchange are assumed. If they are conceived imperfectly and inexactly as referring only to direct and immediate monetary gain—if, for example, they are interpreted to mean that one seeks to purchase and to pay one's debts as cheaply as possible and to sell as dearly as possible—then, of course, they must still be supplemented by a series of further propositions if one wants to explain, let us say, the particularly cheap prices of advertised articles offered by department stores in order to attract customers. No one, however, can deny that in this case too the department stores proceed "purely rationally" and purposively on the basis of cool consideration.

If I simply want to buy soap, I will inquire about the price in many stores and then buy in the cheapest one. If I consider the trouble and loss of time which such shopping requires so bothersome that I would rather pay a few cents more, then I will go into the nearest store without making any further inquiries. If I also want to combine the support of a poor disabled veteran with the purchase of soap, then I will buy from the invalid peddler, though this may be more expensive. In these cases, if I wanted to enter my expenditures accurately in my household account book, I should have to set down the cost of the soap at its common selling price and make a separate entry of the overpayment, in the one instance as "for my convenience," and in the other as "for charity." [44]

The laws of catallactics are not inexact, as the formulation that many authors have given them would lead us to believe. When we ascribe the character of universal validity and objectivity to the propositions of catallactics, objectivity is not only to be understood in the usual and literal epistemological sense, but also in the sense of freedom from the taint of value judgment, in accordance with the demand made—with, of course, complete justification—for the social sciences in the most recent dispute over this question. Only the subjective theory of value, which treats every value judgment, i.e., every subjective valuation, in the same way in order to explain the formation of exchange ratios and which makes no attempt whatever to separate "normal" action from "abnormal" action, lives up to this demand. The discussion of value judgments would have been more fruitful if those who took part in it had been familiar with modern economics and had understood how it solves the problem of objectivity.

The refusal to admit that the theorems of economics have the character of scientific laws and the proposal to speak rather of "tendencies" can be explained only by the unfamiliarity with which the Historical-Realist School combats modern economics. Whenever economics is spoken of, it thinks only of classical economics. Thus, Karl Muhs, to cite the most recent representative of this school, maintains that

chains of causal connection, pure and self-contained, of such a kind that a given fact everlastingly and unconditionally has another as a consequence, appear at no time in economic life. In reality, every causal connection is usually combined with other facts, likewise operating with a certain intensity as causes. The latter as a rule influence to some extent the effects of the former. The result, therefore, comes into being as the effect of a causal *complex*. Reduction of the entire process to a simple formula, in which *one* effect is attributed to *one* cause, is impossible because it is incompatible with the multifarious causal complexity of the process. Where definite facts do causally govern an occurrence to a great extent . . . it is more suitable to speak of regularities or conformities to law or tendencies, but always with the reservation that the operation of such tendencies can be hampered or modified by other causal factors.

This is

the realization of the conditional and relative nature of all regularity in the phenomena of the economic and social spheres,

which has long since established itself in economics.[45]

One can understand the wide dissemination of these and related views when one considers, on the one hand, how obvious they must seem to everyone who has in mind the distinction between economic and noneconomic principles of price determination that has come down to us from classical economics and was at first retained in the terminology—though it is certainly not in accordance with the purport—even of the founders of the Austrian School;[46] and when one considers, on the other hand, that we are confronted here with the basic error of the Historical-Realist School.

Every law of causation—no matter in what science—gives us information about a relationship of cause and effect. This information, in its theoretical value for our knowledge as well as in its practical importance for the understanding of concrete events and for the orientation of our action, is in no way influenced by the fact that at the same time another causal relationship can lead to the opposite result, so that the effect of one is entirely or in part counterbalanced by the effect of the other. Occasionally one endeavors to take this into account by qualifying the law with the addition *ceteris paribus,* but this, after all, is self-evident. The law of returns does not lose its character as a law because changes in technology, for example, take place that compensate for its effects. The appeal to the multiplicity and complexity of "life" is logically untenable. The human body also lives, and its processes are subject to a "multifarious causal complexity." Yet surely no one would want to deny the character of a law to the proposition that eating protein, carbohydrates, and fat is beneficial to the functions of the body simply because eating cyanide at the same time must prove fatal.[47]

To summarize: The laws of sociology are neither ideal types nor average types. Rather, they are the expression of what is to be singled out of the fullness and diversity of phenomena from the point of view of the science that aims at the cognition of what is essential and necessary in every instance of human action. Sociological concepts are not derived "through one-sided *intensification of one* or *several* aspects and through integration into an immanently consistent *conceptual representation* of a multiplicity of scattered and discrete individual phenomena, present here in greater number, there in less, and occasionally not at all, which are in congruity with these one-sidedly intensified aspects." They are rather a generalization of the features to be found in the same way in every single instance to which they refer. The causal propositions of sociology are not expressions of what happens as a rule, but by no means must always happen. They express that which necessarily must always happen as far as the conditions they assume are given.

4. THE BASIS OF THE MISCONCEPTIONS CONCERNING THE LOGICAL CHARACTER OF ECONOMICS

Economic theory, like every theory and every science, is rationalistic in the sense that it makes use of the methods of reason—*ratio*. What, indeed, could science be without reason? Nevertheless, one may seek to pit metaphysical poetry, masquerading as philosophy, against discursive reasoning. However, to do this is to reject science as such.

The rejection of science, of scientific reasoning, and, consequently, of rationalism is in no way a requirement of life, as some would have us believe. It is rather a postulate fabricated by eccentrics and snobs, full of resentment against life. The average man may not trouble his head about the teachings of "gray theory," yet he avidly seizes upon all the findings of science that lend themselves to the improvement of man's technical equipment in the battle for the increase of his material wealth. The fact that many of those who make their living by scientific work are unable to find inner satisfaction in this employment is not an argument for the abolition of science.

However, those who rally round the standard of antirationalism in the theory of social phenomena, especially in economics and in the historical sciences, do not in the least want to do away with science. Indeed, they want to do something altogether different. They want, on the one hand, to smuggle into particular scientific chains of reasoning arguments and statements that are unable to withstand the test of a rational critique, and, on the other hand, to dispose, without relevant criticism, of propositions to which they are at a loss to raise any tenable objections. What is usually involved in such cases is a concession to the designs and ideas of political parties, though often it is simply the desire of a less gifted person—who would somehow like to be noticed at any cost—for scientific achievement. Not everyone is so honest as to admit openly what his real motive is; it is no pleasure to spend one's whole life in the shadow of a greater man.[48]

If someone advocates national autarky, wants to shut his country off from trade with other countries, and is prepared to bear all the material and spiritual consequences of such a policy in order to reach this goal, then this is a value judgment, which, as such, cannot be refuted by argumentation. However, this is not really the case. The masses could be induced to make certain small sacrifices in favor of autarky, but they are scarcely ever to be moved to favor making large sacrifices for such an ideal. Only the literati are enthusiastic about poverty, i.e., the poverty of others. The rest of mankind, however, prefer prosperity to misery. Inasmuch as one can scarcely appear before the public with the argument that the attainment of this or that ideal of the literati is not too dearly bought even at the price of a considerable reduction in general prosperity, and at the same time entertain any hopes of success, one must seek to prove that its attainment imposes only an inconsiderable or no material sacrifice; indeed, that it even brings a distinct material gain. In order to prove this, in order to demonstrate that the restriction of trade and commerce with foreign countries, nationalization and municipalization, and even wars are "besides, ever so much a good business," one must strive to insert irrational links into the chain of reasoning, because it is impossible to prove things of this kind with the rational, sober arguments of science. It is obvious that the employment of irrational elements in the train of an argument is impermissible. Ends are irrational, i.e., they neither require nor are capable of a rational justification. But what is merely the means to given ends must always be subject to rational examination.

The misunderstanding—excusable in the light of the development of the doctrines, though for that reason all the more serious —that identifies "rational" action with "correct" action is universally propagated. Max Weber expressly combatted this confusion,[49] although, as we have seen, he repeatedly fell into it in other passages of his writings.

"The theory of marginal utility," says Weber, "treats . . . human action as if it took place from A to Z under the control of a businesslike calculation: calculation based on knowledge of all the relevant conditions." [50] This is precisely the procedure of classical economics, but in no way that of modern economics. Because it had not succeeded in overcoming the apparent antinomy of value, no other way remained open for classical economics than to start with the action of the businessman. Since it could not deal with the concept of use value, which it did not know how to divide into objective and subjective use value, it was unable to revert to what lies behind and, in the last analysis, governs and directs the conduct of the businessman and entrepreneur, viz., the conduct of the consumers. Whatever did not pass through a businessman's calculations and account books was outside the orbit of classical economics. However, if one limits one's consideration to the conduct of the businessman, then, of course, one must distinguish between the correct and the incorrect conduct of business. For as a businessman—though not also in his capacity as a consumer—the entrepreneur has as his given goal the greatest possible monetary profit of the undertaking.

Modern economics, however, does not start from the action of the businessman, but from that of the consumers, that is to say, from the action of everybody. In its view, therefore—and herein lies its "subjectivism," in contrast to the "objectivism" of the classical economists, and, at the same time, its "objectivity," in contrast to the normative position of the older school—action on the part of the economizing individual is neither correct nor incorrect. Modern economics is not and cannot be concerned with whether someone prefers healthful food or narcotic poisons; no matter how perverted may be the ethical or other ideas that govern his conduct, its "correctness" is not a matter to be judged by economics. Economics has to explain the formation of prices on the market, which means how prices are really arrived at, not how they ought to be arrived at. Prohibitionists see a serious failing of mankind in the consumption of alcoholic beverages, which they attribute to misunderstanding, weakness of character, and immorality. But in the view of catallactics there is only the fact that there is a demand for alcohol. He who has to explain the price of brandy is not concerned with the question whether it is "rational" or moral to drink brandy. I may think what I will about motion picture dramas, but as an economist I have to explain the formation of the market prices for the cinema, actors, and theater seats, not sit in judgment on the films. Catallactics does not ask whether or not the consumers are right, noble, generous, wise, moral, patriotic, or church-going. It is concerned not with why they act, but only with how they act.

Modern subjectivist economics—the theory of marginal utility —again takes up the old theory of supply and demand, which once had to be given up on account of the inability of the classical economists to resolve the paradox of value, and develops it further. If one sees the significance of the movements of market prices, as the modern theory does, in the fact that a state of rest is not reached until total demand and total supply coincide, it is clear that *all* factors that influence the conduct of the parties on the market—and consequently also "noneconomic" and "irrational" factors, like misunderstanding, love, hate, custom, habit, and magnanimity—are included.

Therefore, Schelting's statement that economic theory "assumes a society that arose only through the operation of economic factors" [51] does not apply to modern economics if one understands the term "economic factors" in Schelting's sense. In another section,[52] I point out that even Menger and Böhm-Bawerk did not completely grasp this logical fundamental of the theory they founded and that not until later was the significance of the transition from the objective to the subjective theory of value appreciated.

No less inaccurate is the assertion, made in accordance with the view universally prevailing among the supporters of the His-torical-Realist School, that "the other chief fictions of abstract theory are 'free competition' and the absolute insignificance of governmental and other acknowledged regulations for the develop-ment of the cooperative economic action of economic subjects." [53] This does not even apply to classical economics. Scarcely anyone would want to maintain that the modern theory has bestowed too little attention on the problem of monopoly prices. The case of limited competition on the buyers' or sellers' side offers the theory no special problem: it always has to deal only with the subjects appearing and acting on the market. Nothing else is to be predicated of those who may still enter the market if no factors hold them back than that their supervention would change the market situation. Nor does the theory—and this is true of both the classical and the modern—assume the "absolute insignificance of governmental and other acknowledged regulations." It devotes very searching investigations to these "interferences" and con-structs a special theory of price controls and interventionism.

Mitscherlich too maintains that the theory of marginal utility is "best tailored for the free economy." For that reason, the Middle Ages would "not at all have been able to think of it." There it would have been "pointless." "What, indeed," he asks, "would the Middle Ages have said to the statement of a Carl Menger when he argues: 'That final degree of intensity of the want which can still be satisfied by the given supply—i.e., the marginal utility—serves as the measure of valuation'?" [54]

It may be presumed that the Middle Ages would have under-stood no more of the modern theory of price formation than of Newtonian mechanics or of the modern notions of the functions of the heart. Nevertheless, rain drops fell no differently in the Middle Ages than they do today, and hearts did not beat other-wise than they do now. Though the men of the Middle Ages would not have understood the law of marginal utility, they nevertheless did not and could not act otherwise than as the law of marginal utility describes. Even the man of the Middle Ages sought to ap-portion the means at his disposal in such a way that he attained the same level of satisfaction in every single kind of want. Even in the Middle Ages the wealthier man did not differ from the poorer man only in that he ate more. Even in the Middle Ages no one voluntarily exchanged a horse for a cow unless he valued the cow more highly than the horse. Even at that time the interventionist acts of the government and other institutions of compulsion brought about effects no different from those which the modern theory of price controls and intervention points out.

The objection is urged against modern economic theory that "the economy of free competition necessarily" constitutes "its basic schema" and that it is unable to "comprehend theoretically the organized economy of the present, the economy of regulated competition" and the "entire phenomenon of imperialism." [55] When this objection is raised, it suffices to point out that what historically started the battle against the theory and has given that battle its pertinacity and its popularity is the fact that precisely on the basis of the theory, and only on this basis, is an accurate judgment possible of the effects both of every individual interventionist measure and of the total phenomenon of interventionism in all of its historical forms. One simply turns the facts of history upside down when one maintains that the Historical School rejected economic theory because the latter was incapable of explaining the historical phenomenon of interventionism. In fact, the theory was rejected precisely because one had to arrive at an explanation on the basis of it. This explanation, however, was not politically acceptable to the adherents of the Historical School, but, on the other hand, they were at a loss to refute it. Only by equating "theoretically comprehend" with "uncritically glorify" can one assert that modern economics has not theoretically comprehended the phenomenon of imperialism.

And certainly no one who has followed the political and economic discussions of recent years with even the slightest attentiveness will want to deny that everything that has been done for the elucidation of the problems presented by the "regulated" economy was accomplished exclusively by theorists with the methods of "pure" theory. Not to mention currency problems and monopoly prices, let us remind ourselves only of the discussions concerning the cause of unemployment as a permanent phenomenon and those concerning the problems of protectionism.[56]

Three assumptions, Max Weber thinks, underlie abstract economic theory: the social organization of an exchange economy, free competition, and strictly rational action.[57] We have already discussed free competition and strictly rational—i.e., purposive—action. For the third assumption the reader is referred, on the one hand, to the starting point of all investigations of the modern school, viz., the isolated, exchangeless economy, which some sought to ridicule as the Robinson Crusoe economy; and, on the other hand, to the investigations concerning the economy of an imaginary socialist community.

5. HISTORY WITHOUT SOCIOLOGY

One can completely agree with Max Weber when he declares:

Wherever the causal explanation of a "cultural phenomenon"—an "historical individual"—comes into question, knowledge of *laws* of causation cannot be the *end,* but only the *means* of investigation. It facilitates and makes possible for us the imputation of the culturally significant components of the phenomena, in their individuality, to their concrete causes. As far and only as far as it accomplishes this is it valuable for the cognition of concatenations in individual cases.[58]

Weber is wrong, however, when he adds:

The more "general," i.e., the more abstract, the laws, the less they accomplish for the requirements of the causal imputation of *individual* phenomena and thereby, indirectly, for the understanding of the meaning of cultural events . . . From the point of view of exact natural science, "laws" are all the more important and valuable the *more general* they are; from the point of view of the cognition of historical phenomena in their concrete setting, the *most general* laws are also always the least valuable because they are the most empty of content. For the more comprehensive is the validity of a generic concept—i.e., its scope—the more it leads us *away* from the fullness of reality; because, in order to contain the most common element possible of many phenomena, to be as abstract as possible, it must consequently be *devoid* of content.[59]

Although Weber even goes so far as to speak of "all so-called 'economic laws' without exception" in the arguments by which he arrives at these conclusions, he could, nevertheless, only have had in mind the well-known attempts to discover laws of historical development. If one recalls Hegel's famous proposition: "World history . . . depicts the development of the spirit's consciousness of its freedom, and the material realization brought about by this consciousness," [60] or one of Breysig's propositions, then Weber's statements at once become understandable. Applied to the propositions of sociology, they appear inconceivable.

Whoever undertakes to write the history of the last decade will not be able to ignore the problem of reparations. [61] At the center of this problem, however, stands that of the transfer of the funds involved. Its essence is the question whether or not the stability of the gold value of German money can be affected by the payment of sums for reparations, and particularly by their transfer to foreign countries. This question can be examined only by the methods of economic theory. Any other way of examining it would simply be nonsensical. It is worthy of note that not just some of those who have participated in this discussion, but all without exception, from first to last resort to the universally valid propositions of economic theory. Even one who starts from the balance-of-payments theory, which science has decisively rejected, adheres to a doctrine that makes the same logical claim to universal validity as the theory that modern science acknowledges as correct. Without recourse to such propositions, a discussion of the consequences that must follow on certain assumptions could never be carried on. In the absence of a universally valid theory, the historian will be unable to make any statements connected with the transfer of funds, no matter whether the payments are actually made according to the Dawes Plan or whether they cease for some reason not yet given. Let us assume that the payments are made and that the gold value of the mark does not change. Without recourse to the principle of the theory of purchasing-power parity, one could still not infer from this that Germany's payment had not affected its currency. It could be that another causal chain, acting at the same time, did not permit the effect on currency anticipated by the balance-of-payments theory to become visible. And if this were so, the historian would either completely overlook this second causal chain or would not be able to understand its effect.

History cannot be imagined without theory. The naive belief that, unprejudiced by any theory, one can derive history directly from the sources is quite untenable. Rickert has argued in an irrefutable way that the task of history does not consist in the duplication of reality, but in its reconstitution and simplification by means of concepts.[62] If one renounces the construction and use of theories concerning the connections among phenomena, on no account does one arrive at a solution of the problems that is free of theory and therefore in closer conformity with reality. We cannot think without making use of the category of causality. All thinking, even that of the historian, postulates this principle. The only question is whether one wants to have recourse to causal explanations that have been elaborated and critically examined by scientific thought or to uncritical, popular, prescientific "dogmas." No explanations reveal themselves directly from the facts. Even if one wanted to draw conclusions uncritically—*post hoc, ergo propter hoc*—one would be completely at a loss in view of the confusing plethora and diversity of phenomena. It is precisely the "multifarious causal complexity" of processes of which Muhs speaks,[63] i.e., the concurrence in them of a multiplicity of causal factors, that makes theory necessary.

For ages historians have made use of theories provided by nonscientific thought and laying claim to universal validity. Consider to what an extent such a theory is contained in the simple sentence, "The defeated king found himself forced to conclude peace under unfavorable conditions." What is involved here are simple and scarcely disputed theories, which, by their very character, are nonscientific, but this does not change the fact that they are still theories, i.e., statements understood as universally valid. In addition, the historian employs theories taken from all the other sciences, and it goes without saying that one is justified in demanding, in such cases, that the theories used conform to the present state of science, i.e., they must, in our view, be correct theories. The old Chinese historian could trace extraordinarily dry weather back to moral lapses on the part of the emperor and report that after the monarch's expiation rain fell again. The ancient historian could ascribe the early death of the king's son to the jealousy of the gods. Today, in the present state of meteorology and pathology, we look for a different explanation. Even though the sources were to inform us unequivocally that Numa Pompilius was acquainted with Camena Egeria, we would be unable to believe it and would disregard them. The intercourse of witches with the devil has been established as proved according to the rules of legal evidence; yet, on the strength of our theory, we deny this possibility, all documents to the contrary notwithstanding.[64] The historian must regard all other sciences as auxiliary to his own and must be thoroughly familiar with as much of them as is required by the particular tasks he has set for himself. Whoever treats of the history of the Julian-Claudian dynasty will scarcely be able to do without a knowledge of the theory of heredity and psychiatry. Whoever writes a history of bridge-building will need a thorough knowledge of bridge-building; whoever writes a history of strategy will need a thorough knowledge of strategy.

Now the proponents of historicism, of course, admit all this as far as all other sciences are concerned, but they deny it with reference to sociology. Here the matter seems to them to be different. No substantial reason for this difference is to be discovered, but, psychologically, the resistance of many historians is easily understood. As far as the other sciences are relevant to history, the alternative is either that the historian needs to acquire a moderate degree of knowledge, which does not exceed the amount possessed as a matter of course by every educated person, or that special fields of historical knowledge not closely connected with the sphere proper to history become autonomous disciplines. One does not have to be a meteorologist to know that no matter how serious the failings of the monarch, they cannot influence the weather. And even one who understands only very little of the theory of heredity will know what weight to attach to the divine extraction that historical sources attribute to many dynasties.

Making the history of medicine and similar disciplines autonomous affects but slightly the sphere proper to history. The claims of sociology, however, even if only as a result of the failure to recognize the boundaries between sociological and historical investigations, are felt by many historians as an infringement on their very own domain.

Each and every proposition of history implicitly contains theorems of sociology. No statement concerning the effect of political measures is conceivable that could forgo recourse to universally valid propositions about human action. Whether the topic under discussion is the "social question," mercantilist policy, imperialism, power politics, or wars and revolutions, we again and again encounter in the historian's discussions statements that are inferences from universally valid propositions of sociology. Just as Monsieur Jourdain was astonished to learn that what he had always been speaking was prose, so historians too show surprise when one points out to them that they make use of the theorems of sociology from first to last.

It is regrettable, however, that these theorems, which they unhesitatingly employ, occasionally belong to prescientific thought. One who disregards the results of modern sociology does not therefore work "free of theory." He employs the naive, obsolete theory of an epoch of scientific thought long since superseded or else the still more naive theory of prescientific thought. The effect this has on economic history is nothing short of grotesque. Economic history did not become possible until classical economics had produced a scientific apparatus for political and economic thought. Previous attempts—for example, those dealing with the history of trade—were nothing but a compilation of memoranda. Nowadays the economic historian seeks to emancipate himself from theory altogether. He disdains to approach his task with the logical tools of a developed scientific theory and prefers to content himself with the small measure of theoretical knowledge that today reaches everyone through the newspapers and daily conversation. The presuppositionlessness of which these historians boast consists, in reality, in the uncritical repetition of eclectic, contradictory, and logically untenable popular misconceptions, which have been a hundred times refuted by modern science.[65] Thus, the diligent work performed by entire generations of scholars has remained unproductive. The Historical School failed precisely in the province of social and economic history, which it claimed as its proper domain.

Now the champions of history "devoid of theory" maintain, of course, that their concepts and theorems must be derived from the historical data, inasmuch as there are no universally valid, supertemporal laws of human action. As we have seen, the thesis that there can also be irrational action and that rational action is generally only the result of a long historical development rests on a gross misunderstanding. Historicism, however, goes still further. It dismisses the doctrine of the supertemporality of reason as a prejudice of the Enlightenment. The logical structure of human reason, we are informed, has changed in the course of the ages, in the same way as, for example, technical knowledge and skills.[66]

We shall not enter here into what is to be said in principle, from the standpoint of sociology, against this postulate of historicism.[67] In any case, such reasoning would prove unacceptable to the proponents of historicism, who deny the possibility of any supertemporal theory in contradistinction to historical experience. Therefore, we must confine ourselves to what even historicism must acknowledge as an immanent critique of its thesis. The first point to be established, however, is that none of the sources of historical information accessible to us contains anything that could shake the assumption of the immutability of reason. Never has even an attempt been made to state concretely in what respects the logical structure of reason could have changed in the course of the ages. The champions of historicism would be greatly embarrassed if one were to require of them that they illustrate their thesis by pointing out an example.

In this respect, the failure of ethnology has been no less conspicuous than that of history. Wilhelm Jerusalem to be sure, has emphatically stated: "Kant's firm belief in the timeless, completely immutable logical structure of our reason . . . has not only not been confirmed by the findings of modern ethnology, but has been proved completely incorrect." [68] But even Jerusalem has not undertaken in a single instance to show us in what way the logic of primitive peoples is structurally different from our logic. A general appeal to the writings of ethnologists is not sufficient here. Ethnology shows only that the conclusions arrived at by the reasoning of primitive peoples are different from those which we arrive at and that the range of things primitive peoples are accustomed to think about is different from the circle of our intellectual interests. When primitive man assumes magical and mystical connections where we assume connections of a different kind, or where we find no connection at all, or when he sees no connection where we do see one, this shows only that the content of his reasoning differs from that of our own, but not that his reasoning is of a different logical structure from ours.

In support of his statement, Jerusalem refers repeatedly to the works of Lévy-Bruhl. However, nothing that Lévy-Bruhl sets forth in his admirable writings on this topic says anything more than that members of primitive races have no understanding of the problems with which, in the civilized countries, a narrow circle of intellectually distinguished men concern themselves. "An African," says Lévy-Bruhl, borrowing from Bentley's narrative,

never thinks a matter out if he can help it. . . . They never recognized any similarity between their own trading and the coast factory. They considered that when the white man wanted cloth, he opened a bale and got it. Whence the bales came and why and how—that they never thought of.

The primitive man has a habit of mind which makes him

stop short at his earliest perception of things and never reason if he can in any way avoid it.[69]

Lévy-Bruhl and Bentley seem to have confined their association to the members of primitive races. Had they also looked about in Europe—and, one might add, among European economists and politicians—they would certainly not have considered the practice of never thinking matters out and never reasoning as peculiarities of primitive peoples alone. As Lévy-Bruhl says, citing a report by

Mangin, the Mossi on the Niger river are lacking in reflection. For that reason they are also wanting in ideas.

Conversation with them turns only upon women, food, and (in the rainy season) the crops.[70]

What other subjects did many contemporaries of Newton, Kant, and Lévy-Bruhl prefer?

It must be pointed out, moreover, that from the data he compiled, Lévy-Bruhl never draws the conclusions that Jerusalem wants to infer from them. For example, expressly summing up his observations about the causal reasoning of primitive races, Lévy-Bruhl remarks:

The primitive mind, like our own, is anxious to find the reasons for what happens, but it does not seek these in the same direction as we do. It moves in a world where innumerable occult powers are everywhere present, and always in action or ready to act.[71]

And, on the basis of searching investigations, Cassirer arrives at the conclusion:

When one compares the empirical-scientific and the mythical conceptions of the world, it becomes immediately obvious that the contrast between them is not based on their employing totally different categories in the study and explanation of reality. It is not in the nature, the quality of these categories, that myth and empirical-scientific cognition differ, but in their *modality*. The methods of connecting things that both employ in order to give the perceptibly diverse the form of unity so as to fit the manifold into a framework demonstrates a thoroughgoing analogy and correspondence. They exhibit the same most general "forms" of perception and reasoning which constitute the unity of consciousness as such and which, therefore, constitute the unity of mythical consciousness in the same way as that of pure cognitive consciousness.[72]

What the proponents of historicism fail to see is that even propositions like: "The theorems of classical economics possessed relative truth for the age in which they were constructed" can be enunciated only if one has already adopted a supertemporal, universally valid theory. Without such a theory the historian could not consider his task anything more than the compilation and publication of source materials. Thus, it has been no fortuitous coincidence, but inner necessity, that the age in which historicism has held sway has been characterized by a progressive decline in historical research and historical writing. With a few laudable exceptions, for history the upshot of historicism has been, on the one hand, the publication of sources, and, on the other hand, dilettantist constructions, such as those of Chamberlain and Spengler.

If history is not to be a meaningless absurdity, then every statement that it makes about a causal relationship must be thought through to its conclusion and examined for its compatibility with the entire structure of our knowledge. However, this cannot be done without sociological theory.

One must agree completely with Max Weber when he says that for the causal explanation of cultural phenomena "knowledge of laws of causation cannot be the *end,* but only the *means* of investigation." Sociology is an auxiliary—though, to be sure, an indispensable auxiliary—of history. Sociological—and especially economic—theory stands in the same relationship to politics. Every science is an end in itself only for him who thirsts after the knowledge of it.

6. UNIVERSAL HISTORY AND SOCIOLOGY

Max Weber did not want merely to outline a program and methodology for a science of social phenomena. In addition to excellent treatises on history, he himself published extensive works that he termed sociological. We, of course, cannot recognize their claim to this designation. This is not meant as an unfavorable criticism. The investigations collected in Weber's posthumously published major work, *Wirtschaft und Gesellschaft,* belong to the best that German scientific literature of the last decades has produced. Yet in their most important parts they are not sociological theory in our sense. Nor are they history in the customary meaning of the term. History deals with one town or with German towns or with European towns in the Middle Ages. Until Weber's time it knew nothing like the brilliant chapter in his book that deals simply with the "town" in general, a universal theory of town settlement for all times and among all peoples, the ideal type of the town in itself.

Weber, who did not realize that there is a science that aims at universally valid propositions, considered this sociology. If we were to acquiesce in this usage and to seek another name for what we understand by sociology, we should cause hopeless confusion. Therefore, we must maintain our distinction and attempt to give another name to what Weber regarded as sociology. Perhaps the most suitable would be: *universal teachings of history,* or more briefly, *universal history.*

The fact that one usually designates by this name attempts at presenting comprehensively the history of all ages and nations need not prevent us from employing it to denote what Weber undertook to do. For such presentations are unable to proceed otherwise than by joining to the history of the development of one culture or of one people the history of the development of another. Consequently, universal history in this sense signifies only a series of works that do not lose their original character and independence in being thus subsumed under a common category. Universal history in our sense—sociology in Weber's sense—would consist in bringing into relief and treating individually the ideal-typical constructions employed by history. It would correspond approximately, but only approximately, to what Bernheim, in his thematic division of the province of history, designates as universal history, or cultural history in the wider sense. To specialized history he contrasts universal history, within which he differentiates two subdivisions:

1. Universal history, or cultural history in the wider sense; also called world history: the history of men in their activities as social beings at all times and in all places, in consistent continuity of development.
2. Universal political history (*Allgemeine Staatengeschichte*); also called world history, and previously universal history as well: a compendium-like joining together of the history of all imporant nations.[73]

It need certainly not be especially emphasized that the point in question is, of course, not the terminology, but only the logical and conceptual distinction.

The situation is analogous in the treatment of economic problems. Between economic theory, on the one hand, and economic history and descriptive economics—which must also be economic history—on the other, lies universal descriptive economics, which serves for the special treatment of the ideal-typical constructions employed by economic history.

The boundaries between these domains are not always observed in actual scientific work and in its presentation for the public, and, indeed, there is no necessity for such a separation. The creative mind yields what it has to offer, and for this we are indebted to it. Nevertheless, even one who would never think of overstepping the boundaries that separate the individual domains of subject matter must be acquainted with what is happening on the other side of the boundaries. No sociologist can do without history, and no historian can do without sociology.

Historicism declared the historical method the only one permissible and appropriate for the treatment of the problems posed by the sciences of human action. One group of the proponents of historicism considered a theoretical science of human action altogether impossible. Others did not want to deny completely the possibility of such a science in the distant future, which would have at its disposal the fruits of more ample spadework on the part of historians. The opponents of historicism, of course, never challenged the justification, the logical admissibility, or the usefulness of historical investigation. What was called into question in the *Methodenstreit* was never history, but always only theory. From the point of view of economics and political science the fateful error of historicism lay precisely in its rejection of theory. Indeed, the tenor of the attack upon theory was essentially political and was directed toward protecting from disagreeable criticism economic policies that could not withstand scientific examination. From the point of view of science, the failure to recognize the truth that all historical investigation and every description of social conditions presuppose theoretical concepts and propositions was more serious than the misconception that history and descriptive economics could be pursued without theory. The most pressing task of the logic of historical science is to combat this error.

7. SOCIOLOGICAL LAWS AND HISTORICAL LAWS

We call the method of scientific work that examines the effect, *ceteris paribus*, of change in one factor, the static method.[74] Nearly everything that sociology and its hitherto best developed branch, economics, have thus far accomplished is due to the use of the static method. The assumption it makes, viz., that all other conditions remain perfectly unchanged, is an indispensable fiction for reasoning and science. In life everything is continually in flux, but for thought we must construct an imaginary state of rest.[75] In this manner we conceptually isolate the individual factors in order to be able to study the effect of changes in them. The word "static" should not prevent us from seeing that the method in question is one whose goal is precisely the investigation of change.[76]

In the present state of the science, it is not yet possible to determine whether dynamic laws are feasible within the system of catallactics. A dynamic law would need to be able to show how changes would have to occur on the basis of forces acting within the static system even though no change in the data took place from without. It is well known that Ricardo and many epigones of the classical school—even Marx, for example—undertook such attempts, and that similar efforts have been made on the basis of modern science as well. We need not go into this more deeply at this time. Nor need we be concerned here with the question whether laws of sociological dynamics could be demonstrated to hold outside the narrow frame of economic theory. We must adhere to the notion of the dynamic law only in order to contrast it to the notion of the historical law.

The formulation of historical laws, i.e., laws of historical change, has repeatedly been designated as the task of history. Many even set out to formulate such laws. Of course, these laws did not meet the demands one must make of a scientific law. They lacked universal validity.

In all these "laws," as, for example, in Breysig's, of which we have given an example above,[77] the basis of this deficiency lies in the fact that ideal types were used in the construction of the law. Inasmuch as ideal types do not possess universal validity, propositions involving them must be similarly deficient. All the concepts encountered in the thirty-first law of Breysig, which has already been quoted, are to be viewed as ideal types. Not only are "rule of the Kaiser," "rule of the people," and "boom in trade and industry" to be understood in this way, but also "national economy" in the sense in which this term is employed by Breysig.

Laws of historical stages occupy a special position. Stages of historical development arranged in a series are delineated as ideal types, and then the statement is made that history consists in the progression from one stage to the next, and thence on to the third, and so on. It is obvious that as long as the necessity of such a progression cannot be established, this does not yet signify the demonstration of a conformity to law.[78] If, however, the progression is maintained to be necessary, then this pronouncement, but not the ideal-typical constructions of the stages, would have to be regarded as a law, although only if its content were free of every reference to ideal types.

The laws of progress seek to satisfy this requirement. They trace the operation of one or several forces to whose permanent action they unequivocally attribute the direction in which social changes take place. Whether this development leads to good or evil, whether it signifies improvement or decline, is immaterial. Progress means here: progression on the necessary path. Now, it is, of course, true that all laws of progress hitherto formulated, in so far as they are not to be rejected from the outset as fictions in no way corresponding to reality, lose the strict character of law through their connection with ideal-typical constructions. Yet it would not be difficult to enucleate clearly the sociological law underlying each of them and to verify it. Even if we were then to deny that the historical law is a law, we should nevertheless find in it a law of sociological dynamics.

Work performed under the division of labor is more productive than isolated work. The same expenditure of labor and of goods of higher order produces a greater quantity of output and enables feats to be accomplished that an isolated worker would never be in a position to achieve. Whether or not this proposition of empirical technology and the physiology of labor is valid without exception—as far as we are at all warranted in speaking of absolute validity in the case of an empirical law—is of no importance for us, since, in any case, it is certain that only one or two instances, if any, can be cited, and then only with difficulty, for which it would not be valid. The increase in productivity brought about by the division of labor is what gives impetus to the formation of society and to the progressive intensification of social cooperation. We owe the origin and development of human society and, consequently, of culture and civilization, to the fact that work performed under the division of labor is more productive than when performed in isolation. The history of sociology as a science began with the realization of the importance for the formation of society of the increase in productivity achieved under the division of labor. However, sociology in general, and economics in particular, have viewed the law of the division of labor not as a constituent part of their own structure of thought, but as a datum, though one which is almost always—or, for all practical purposes, always—present. It is instructive to see how the Historical School sought to arrive at a "historical law" in this case.

Bücher's theory of stages wants to comprehend "all economic development, at least that of the Central and Western European nations, where it can be historically traced with sufficient accuracy" under a "principle of central significance for understanding the essential phenomena of the economy." The theory finds this principle in the relation in which the production of goods stands to their consumption. Specifically, it is discernible in the length of the route that goods must travel in passing from producers to consumers. Hence follows his division into the three stages of the self-sufficient household economy, the town economy, and the national economy.[79]

We shall not dwell on the fact that each one of the three stages is delineated, and can be delineated, only as an ideal type. This is a shortcoming characteristic of all these "laws." What is noteworthy is only that the freedom with which the historian may construct ideal types enables Bücher to reject the obvious idea, apparently displeasing to him for political reasons, that "mankind is on the point of rising to a new stage of development, which would have to be contrasted to the three previous stages under the name of world economy." [80] However, it cannot be our task to point out all the minor weaknesses and flaws in Bücher's schematization. What concerns us is exclusively the logical form, and not the concrete content, of the theory. All that Bücher is in a position to state is that in the course of historical development up to the present three stages are to be distinguished. He is unable to give us any information about the *causa movens* of the changes that have occurred hitherto or about future developments. One cannot understand how Bücher, on the basis of his theory, comes to call every succeeding stage the "next higher" in relation to the preceding one, or why he assumes without hesitation that "the transition from the national economy to the next higher stage . . . will come," while expressly adding that one cannot know how "the economic future will look in detail." [81] The metaphorical use of the term "stage" need not have led him to say "higher" stage instead of merely "succeeding" stage; and on the basis of his theory nothing can warrant his predicting that any further change will take place, much less his confident assurance that such a change could not consist in a regression to one of the previous stages. Consequently, it is impossible to see a "law" in a theory of this kind; and Bücher rightly avoids designating it as such.[82]

A question, however, which is in any case much more important than whether or not one is dealing with a "law" here is whether the construction of such schemata is useful for the enlargement and deepening of our knowledge of reality.

We must answer this question in the negative. The attempt to force economic history into a concise schema is not only without value for cognition, as we see from the remarks above; it has an effect nothing short of detrimental. It was responsible for Bücher's failure to see that a shortening of the route that goods traveled in passing from producers to consumers occurred in the later Roman Empire precisely as a result of the decline in the division of labor. The dispute about whether or not the economy of the ancients is to be viewed as a self-sufficient household economy may appear idle to us when we reject Bücher's, as we do every similar, schematization. Yet if one does not wish to close one's mind to the possibility of understanding one of the greatest changes in history, the decline of ancient civilization, one must not fail to appreciate the fact that antiquity had gone further in the division of labor—or, to use Bücher's own words, in "the length of the route that goods travel in passing from the producers to the consumers" —than the first centuries of the Middle Ages. The realization of the higher productivity of work performed under the division of labor places at our disposal the indispensable means for the construction of the ideal types necessary for the intellectual comprehension of this event. In this respect, the concepts of the self-sufficient household economy (production solely for one's own consumption, the exchangeless economy), the town economy (production for a clientele), and the national economy (commodity production) may prove their usefulness as ideal types appropriate to the subject matter. The decisive and fateful error lies not in their construction, but in the attempt to connect them with a schema of stages and to base this schema on the law of the division of labor.

It was therefore with good reason that Bücher refrained from any attempt to base his theory of stages on the law of the higher productivity of work performed under the division of labor. This law makes only one statement about the objective result that can be attained through the division of labor. It does not say that the tendency toward further intensification of the division of labor is always operative. Whenever and wherever an economic subject is confronted with the choice between a procedure employing a more intensive and one employing a less intensive division of labor, he will adopt the former, provided that he has also recognized the objectively greater output that he can thereby attain and provided also that he values this difference in output more highly than the other consequences which, perhaps, are bound up with the transition to a more intensive division of labor. However, the law as such can make no statement about whether or to what extent this recognition does in fact take place. It can teach us to comprehend and explain causally a change that has already taken place, whether it be in the direction of a more intensive or of a less intensive development of the division of labor, but the law cannot show us why or even that the division of labor must always be more intensively cultivated. We are able to arrive at this conclusion only on the basis of an historical judgment—that is, one formed with the conceptual means at the disposal of history— of what peoples, groups, and individuals want under the influence of the factors determining their existence: their inborn qualities (racial inheritance) and their natural, social, and intellectual environment.

However, we do not know how these external factors are transformed within the human mind to produce thoughts and volitions directed and operating upon the outer world. We are able to ascertain this only *post factum,* but in no way can we deduce it in advance from a known regularity formulated as a law. Hence, we cannot infer from the law of the division of labor that the division of labor must always make further progress. The division of labor may again be set back temporarily or even permanently. A government may be dominated by an ideology that sees its social ideal in the reversion to autarky. One may consider this quite improbable, but one cannot make a clear and definite prediction about it, for the reasons which have already been given. In any case, one must not overlook the fact that today an ideology hostile to the international division of labor is beginning to exercise a great influence upon the foreign economic policy of many nations.

The law of the division of labor does not belong to the universally valid system of a priori laws of human action. It is a datum, not an economic law. For that reason it appears impossible to formulate on its basis an exact law of progress, i.e., a law free of ideal-typical constructions. On this point the optimists among the liberal sociologists of the Enlightenment, who were confident of progress and who were always reproached with "defective historical intelligence," were logically much more correct than their critics. They never denied that they based their firm belief in continual social progress not on "laws," but on the assumption that the "good" and the "reasonable" must ultimately prevail. The same shortcomings can be shown in every attempt to construct a theory of historical stages. Underlying all such theories are generally, though not always, observations and discoveries that are correct in themselves. But the use that these theories make of them is impermissible. Even where the experience to which they refer does not exhibit merely a nonrepeatable succession of phenomena, these theories go far beyond what is logically legitimate. Before the beginnings of an independent social science, historians were aware of the importance of proper location for productivity. Since the conditions that make locations appear more or less favorable undergo change, one acquires a means of historically explaining shifts of location and migratory movements. On the other hand, the theories of geographical stages, entirely apart from the fact that they present the law of location in the most crudely oversimplified and inadequate way, render access to the understanding of these problems only more difficult. Hegel maintained:

World history goes from East to West; for Europe is obviously the end of world history, and Asia, the beginning. While the "East" in itself is something quite relative, there exists for world history an East κατ᾽ ἐξοχήν; for, although the earth is a sphere, history, nevertheless, does not travel in a circle around it, but has, on the contrary, a determinate East, viz., Asia. Here rises the external, physical sun, and in the West it sinks down; in compensation for which, however, the inner sun of self-consciousness, which diffuses a nobler splendor, rises here.[83]

And according to Mougeolle, there is a "law of altitudes," namely, that in the course of history the city is increasingly forced down into flat land by the mountains; and a "law of latitudes," to the effect that civilization has always moved from the tropics toward the poles.[84] In these laws too we find all the shortcomings that attach to every theory of historical stages. The *causa movens* of the changes is not shown, and the accuracy of the geographical concepts that they contain cannot conceal the fact that for the rest they are based on ideal-typical constructions, and indeed on such as are uncertain and therefore unusable, like "world history" and "civilization." But still more serious by far is the fact that without any hesitation they leap from the statement of the law of location to a volition uniquely determined by it.

Becher accounts as follows for his opinion that the possibility of historical laws cannot be denied in principle:

One did not want to admit historical laws as such because they are of a secondary, reducible, and derivative nature. This rejection rests upon an unsuitable, narrowly conceived notion of law, which, if applied consistently to the natural sciences, would compel us to deny the title of natural laws to many relationships that everyone designates as such. For most of the laws of natural science—e.g., the laws of Kepler, the laws of wave theory concerning resonance, interference, and so on, and the geometric-optical laws of the effect of concave mirrors and lenses—are of a secondary and derivative character. They can be traced back to more fundamental laws. The laws of nature are no more all ultimate, irreducible, or fundamental than they are all elementary, i.e., laws of elementary, not complex phenomena. . . . However, if this designation is quite generally conferred on numerous "laws" of natural science which are neither fundamental nor elementary, then it will not do to deny it to historical laws simply because they are not fundamental or elementary in character.[85]

In my opinion, this argument does not get to the heart of the matter. The question is not whether the designation "law" is to be applied only to fundamental or elementary regularities. This, after all, is an unimportant question of terminology. In and of itself, it would not be impossible, although inexpedient in the greatest measure and disregardful of all economy of thought, to formulate the laws of acoustics as statements about concerts rather than sound waves. However, it would certainly not be possible to include in these laws, if they are to retain the character of laws of natural science, statements about the quality and expression of the musical performance. They would have to confine themselves to what can be described by the methods of physics. We are unable to include the entire course of historical phenomena in laws, not because they are complicated and numerous or because factors and conditions independent of one another are involved in them, but because they include also factors whose role we are unable to determine precisely. The concepts of sociology extend as far as exactness is possible in principle. On the other side of these boundaries lies the domain of history, which, by means of ideal types, fills with the data of historical life the frame provided by sociology.

8. QUALITATIVE AND QUANTITATIVE ANALYSIS IN ECONOMICS

Sociology cannot grasp human action in its fullness. It must take the actions of individuals as ultimately given. The predictions it makes about them can be only qualitative, not quantitative. Accordingly, it can say nothing about the magnitude of their effects. This is rougly what is meant by the statement that the characteristic feature of history is concern with the individual, the irrational, life, and the domain of freedom.[86] For sociology, which is unable to determine in advance what they will be, the value judgments that are made in human action are ultimate data. This is the reason why history cannot predict things to come and why it is an illusion to believe that qualitative economics can be replaced or supplemented by quantitative economics.[87] Economics as a theoretical science can impart no knowledge other than qualitative. And economic history can furnish us with quantitative knowledge only *post factum*.

Social science is exact in the sense that it strives with conceptual rigor for an unequivocally defined and provable system. It is idle to dispute over whether one should make use of mathematical forms of presentation in sociology, and particularly in economics. The problems confronting sociology in all its branches, including economics, present such extraordinary difficulties that, in the eyes of many, even the most perplexing mathematical problems possess the advantage of being more easily visualized. Whoever believes that he cannot do without the help that the reasoning and terminology of mathematics affords him in the mastery of economic problems is welcome to make use of them. *Vestigia terrent!* Those theorists who are usually designated as the great masters of mathematical economics accomplished what they did without mathematics. Only afterwards did they seek to present their ideas in mathematical form. Thus far, the use of mathematical formulations in economics has done more harm than good. The metaphorical character of the relatively more easily visualized concepts and ideas imported into economics from mechanics, which may be warranted as a didactic and occasionally as a heuristic expedient as well, has been the occasion of much misunderstanding. Only too often the criticism to which every analogy must be subjected has been neglected in this case. Of primary importance is what is set forth in words in the preliminary statement that has to serve as the starting point for further mathematical elaboration. This statement, however, is always nonmathematical.[88] Whether or not its further elaboration in mathematical terms can be useful depends on the correctness of this initial nonmathematical statement. To be sure, if the mathematical elaboration is itself incorrect, it will arrive at incorrect results even though it may start from a correct statement; but mathematical analysis can never expose an error made in an incorrect statement.

Even the mathematical sciences of nature owe their theories not to mathematical, but to nonmathematical reasoning. Mathematics has a significance in the natural sciences altogether different from what it has in sociology and economics. This is because physics is able to discover empirically constant relationships, which it describes in its equations.[89] The scientific technology based on physics is thereby rendered capable of solving given problems with quantitative definiteness. The engineer is able to calculate how a bridge must be constructed in order to bear a given load. These constant relationships cannot be demonstrated in economics. The quantity theory of money, for example, shows that, *ceteris paribus,* an increase in the quantity of money leads to a decrease in the purchasing power of the monetary unit, but the doubling of the quantity of money does not bring about a fifty-percent decline in its purchasing power. The relationship between the quantity of money and its purchasing power is not constant. It is a mistake to think that, from statistical investigations concerning the relationship of the supply of and the demand for definite commodities, quantitative conclusions can be drawn that would be applicable to the future configuration of this relationship. Whatever can be established in this way has only historical significance, whereas the ascertainment of the specific gravity of different substances, for example, has universal validity.[90]

Economics too can make predictions in the sense in which this ability is attributed to the natural sciences. The economist can and does know in advance what effect an increase in the quantity of money will have upon its purchasing power or what consequences price controls must have. Therefore, the inflations of the age of war and revolution, and the controls enacted in connection with them, brought about no results unforseen by economics. However, this knowledge is not quantitatively definite. For example, economics is not in a position to say just how great the reduction in demand will be with which consumption will react to a definite quantitative increase in price. For economics, the concrete value judgments of individuals appear only as data. But no other science—not even psychology—can do any more here.

To be sure, even the valuations of individuals are causally determined. We also understand how they come about. That we are unable to foretell their concrete configuration is due to the fact that we here come up against a boundary beyond which all scientific cognition is denied to us. Whoever wants to predict valuations and volitions would have to know the relationship of the world within us to the world outside us. Laplace was unmindful of this when he dreamed of his cosmic formula.

9. THE UNIVERSAL VALIDITY OF SOCIOLOGICAL KNOWLEDGE

If one conceives of "nature" as Kant did, as "the existence of things as far as it is determined according to universal laws," [91] and if one says, in agreement with Rickert, "Empirical reality becomes nature when we view it with respect to the universal; it becomes history when we view it with respect to the particular and the individual," [92] then one must necessarily arrive at the conclusion that sociology—supposing such a discipline at all feasible—is to be regarded as a natural science, that is, as one making use of the methods of the sciences of nature. On the other hand, one must, in that case, deny the possibility of historical laws. Of course, in many instances the idea that natural science and nomothetic science are identical concepts lay at the root of the contention that history had only to adopt the methods of the sciences of nature in order to become a nomothetic science of human action. Terminological misunderstandings of all kinds have enveloped discussion of these questions in the greatest confusion.

Kant's and Rickert's terminology is no doubt to be accounted for by the fact that sociology remained unknown to both and even the very possibility of a theoretical science of social phenomena never seriously became a problem for them. As regards Kant, this requires no further proof.[93] As for Rickert, one need only note the sparse and altogether inadequate comments he devoted to sociology. Though Rickert must admit that there can be no objection to "a natural science or a generalized presentation of social reality," [94] it does not occur to him to become familiar with sociology itself in order to find some way toward the solution of its logical problems. He disregards the principle that "occupation with the philosophy of science presupposes knowledge of the sciences themselves." [95] It would be a mistake to reproach Rickert for this, especially as his own contributions to the logic of history are not to be disputed. Nevertheless, it must be pointed out with regret that Rickert remains far behind Menger as regards the recognition of the distinction—set forth at the very beginning of the latter's work—which appears within the social sciences themselves, between the historical sciences, directed toward the comprehension of phenomena in their particularity, and the theoretical sciences, which are directed toward the comprehension of the universal characteristics of phenomena.[96]

The last position still held in the dogged battle against the recognition of sociology is that of those who would limit the validity of sociological laws to a definite historical period. It was Marxism that first fell back upon this expedient. In the view of interventionism, whose triumph in the sphere of practical politics the adherents of the Historical School wanted to aid in achieving, every attempt to demonstrate a regularity in the sequence of social phenomena had to appear as a dangerous challenge to the dogma of the omnipotence of government interference. Interventionism simply rejected every theory. The case was different with Marxism, at least in the province of theory. In practical politics, of course, the attitude of Marxism gradually underwent a change: step by step the Marxist parties proceeded to adopt the slogans of interventionism. But it did not occur to the Marxist theoreticians to call into question the demonstration by classical economics that all forms of government interference with the market are senseless because the goals aimed at cannot be attained by means of them. The Marxists adopted this view all the more readily because it enabled them to point out the futility of every attempt to reform the existing social order and to refer all the discontented to the coming regime of socialism.

What Marxism needed was a theory that enabled it to quash the extremely embarrassing economic discussion of the possibility of realizing the socialist community—a discussion to which it was unable to contribute any relevant arguments. The theory of economic systems offered it this opportunity. According to this theory, in the course of history one economic system succeeds another, and in this succession—as is the case in all theories of historical stages—the later system is to be regarded as the "higher" system. The basic metaphysical and teleological orientation, which the scientific theories of historical stages presented by List, Hildebrand, Schmoller, and Bücher seek to disguise, is quite naively adopted by Marxism, although it insistently claims for itself the title of "scientific" socialism. The end and goal of all history is the socialist Kingdom of Promise. However, inasmuch as socialism is a new economic system and has not yet been achieved, it would be "utopian"—and, in the language of Marxism, this means unscientific—to attempt today to discover the laws by which the economy and society of this future system will be governed. The only function of science, on this view, is to investigate the laws of present and past economic systems. In *Kapital* Marx wanted to undertake this task in regard to the present, capitalist economic system. Later, attempts were made to distinguish within the era of capitalism several subsidiary periods, each with its peculiar economic system (early capitalism, high capitalism, late capitalism, and the transition period) and to delineate the economy of each.

We can disregard here the inadequacy of the efforts that Sombart, Rosa Luxemburg, Hilferding, Bucharin, and others devoted to these tasks.[97] The only question that concerns us here is: Would a theory valid for only one historical era still be a theory in the sense in which we differentiate theory from history? If we recall what we have said above concerning the logical character of laws of historical stages, the answer cannot be difficult to find. The division of the entire course of history into periods can be undertaken only on the basis of ideal types. Consequently, the idea of an individual economic period lacks universal validity from the very outset, since the characteristics that define it need not be exhibited in every individual case comprised by it. Thus, a "theoretical" proposition that is supposed to be valid only for the conditions of that economic period can likewise be conceived only in ideal-typical terms.

If one assumes, for example, the predominance of the "capitalist spirit" as the criterion of the capitalist era of history, one, of course, does not assert that this spirit, no matter how narrowly circumscribed, straightway seized all men living in that era. The idea that still other "spirits" were operative as well is quite compatible with the ideal type; for it is certainly never maintained that the capitalist spirit prevailed *without exception,* but only that it predominated, in the era of capitalism. However, if one then formulates, let us say, laws of price determination in the capitalist economy, these laws can surely not be intended as having no exception. At least where different mentalities are to be found alongside the otherwise predominant capitalist spirit, other laws of price determination can, and indeed must, be valid. For this reason, whoever is willing to grant recognition solely to theories that are dependent on history disputes in fact the legitimacy of every universally valid theory. The only science he accepts in the sphere of human action is history, with the logical structure of the ideal type peculiar to it.

However, for this school, as well as for all other proponents of historicism, the rejection of the possibility of a universally valid theory is of merely academic significance. In effect, it is programmatic and nothing more. In actual practice, use is unhesitatingly made of concepts and propositions that, from the logical point of view, can be understood only as having universal validity. Every particular "spirit" that is supposed to be peculiar to each of the individual periods reveals itself on closer examination as an ideal dominating the majority of individuals in a given period, and the particular form of the economy proves to be a technique of social cooperation imposed by the distinctiveness of this ideal and by the prevailing views about the best way of realizing it.

The objection may be made that the species *homo sapiens* is but a temporal phenomenon and that, accordingly, a science of human action pure and simple could differ merely in degree, but not in logical character, from a science of human action valid within a limited historical period. However, this objection misunderstands the sole meaning that can be attached to the concept of universal validity in the realm of the science of human action, viz., valid wherever the assumed conditions, which are to be strictly defined, are given. The determination of the subject matter of the science of human action is not based on the empirical distinction between man and his prehuman ancestors, but on the conceptual difference between action and the merely reactive behavior of cells.

CONCLUSION

The battle of the proponents of historicism against the nomothetic science of human action was absurd and preposterous, and the rejection of the demand of naturalism that historical investigations, pursued with the methods of the natural sciences, should seek for "historical laws" was necessary and fully justified.

History cannot fulfill its task if it does not employ the most precise logic. At every step of the way it must make use of universally valid concepts and propositions; it must use reason—*ratio*—; it must, whether it wants to or not, theorize. If this is the case, then it is obvious that nothing but the best theory is good enough for it. The historian is not warranted in uncritically accepting any concept or proposition from the stock of naive popular habits of thought. He must first subject all concepts and propositions to a sharp, critical examination. He must think every idea through to its consequences, and again and again question and examine it. He must connect the individual ideas into a coherent system. In short, he must either practice theorizing himself or accept theory where it is developed in a scientific way with all the resources available to the human mind.

It is evident that the mere elaboration of a theory is not yet a contribution to history. Yet history can get on with the task proper to it only when the resources that theory provides are completely exhausted. Only there does the realm of history—the realm of the individual, of that which happens but once, of the historical whole—begin. It cannot cross the threshold of this realm until it has been brought there by the power of rational thinking.

Rothacker maintains that the specific "understanding" made use of in the moral sciences proceeds along the two paths of conception and explanation up to the point at which a leap "into an irrational relationship" paves the way for it.

If a work is *conceived,* no understanding in the strict sense is involved. If it is *explained,* there is likewise no understanding. But where we find ourselves compelled to look for something that is individually vital in a work, something that is not completely analyzable in conception nor completely explicable, we expect to encounter attempts at pure understanding, *at understanding in the pregnant sense.*

However, "rational measures" which have first been "exploited to the full" must precede this understanding.[98]

At the start of the *Methodenstreit,* Walter Bagehot, who, in 1876, was the first to object to the rejection of theory by the Historical School, declared that an historical presentation of economics is

no substitute for a preliminary theory. You might as well try to substitute a corollary for the proposition on which it depends. The history of . . . is the history of a confused conflict of many causes; and unless you know what sort of effect each cause is likely to produce,

124 *Epistemological Problems of Economics*

you cannot explain any part of what happens. It is like trying to explain the bursting of a boiler without knowing the theory of steam. Any history . . . could not be usefully told, unless there was a considerable accumulation of applicable doctrine before existing. You might as well try to write the "life" of a ship, making up as you went along the theory of naval construction. Clumsy dissertations would run over the narrative; and the result would be a perfect puzzle.[99]

The champions of historicism forgot this. They wanted to compile data "devoid of theory." This made the work of even the best of them fruitless. History can never really be history without the intellectual tools provided by the theory of human action. History must rest on theory, not to alienate itself from its proper tasks, but on the contrary, in order more than ever to discharge them in the true sense of history.

And Bagehot's words should never be forgotten:

Rightly conceived, the historical method is no rival to the abstract method rightly conceived.[100]

NOTES

1. Kracauer, *Soziologie als Wissenschaft* (Dresden, 1922), pp. 20 ff.
2. Cf. Pohle, *Die gegenwärtige Krisis in der deutschen Volkswirtschaftslehre* (2nd ed.; Leipzig, 1921), pp. 86 ff., 116 ff.
3. Cf. my *Kritik des Interventionismus*, pp. 2 ff., 57 ff.
4. *Fürst Bismarcks Reden,* ed. by Stein, VII, 202.
5. Even Menger does not start from the modern statements of subjectivist economics in his famous *Untersuchungen über die Methode der Sozialwissenschaften,* but from the system, the methodology, and the logic of classical economics. The transition from the classical to the modern system did not take place all at once, but gradually. It took a long time until its effects were felt in all branches of economic thought, and still a longer time before the significance of the revolution that had taken place was fully appreciated. Only to the retrospective gaze of the historian of economic thought do the years in which Menger, Jevons, and Walras brought forth their theories appear as the beginning of a new era in the history of our science.
6. The point in question in the dispute about the freedom of the social sciences from all valuations had long since been resolved. It had never in any way consituted a problem whose solution could have caused any difficulties. Cf. Cantillon, *Essai sur la nature du commerce en general,* ed. with an English translation by Higgs (London, 1931), pp. 84-85; Ricardo, *Notes on Malthus' "Principles of Political Economy,"* ed. by Hollander and Gregory (Baltimore, 1928), p. 180; Mill, J. S., *System of*

Logic Ratiocinative and Inductive (8th ed.; London, 1872), Book VI, chapter 12, §6; Cairnes, *Essays in Political Economy, Theoretical and Applied* (London, 1873), pp. 256 ff.; Sidgwick, *The Principles of Political Economy* (2nd ed.; London, 1887), pp. 12 ff.

7. On this point cf. Bernheim, *Lehrbuch der historischen Methode* (6th ed.; Leipzig, 1908), pp. 101 ff.; Rothacker, *Einleitung in die Geisteswissenschaften* (Tübingen, 1920), p. 195.

8. Breysig, *Der Stufenbau und die Gesetze der Weltgeschichte* (2nd ed.; Berlin, 1927), p. 165.

9. Cf. above p. 119 concerning Rickert's observations, in which he admits the possibility of "a presentation according to the methods of the natural sciences and by means of generalization" of the "vicissitudes of civilized mankind."

10. Jaspers (*Max Weber* [Oldenburg, 1932], p. 43) calls Weber a "universal historian" and adds: "His sociology is universal history." On Weber as an economist, cf. my *Kritik des Interventionismus,* pp. 85 ff.

11. Max Weber, *Gesammelte Aufsätze zur Wissenschaftslehre* (Tübingen, 1922), pp. 172 f.

12. *Ibid.,* p. 178.

13. *Ibid.,* p. 181.

14. *Ibid.,* p. 185.

15. *Ibid.,* pp. 189 f.

16. *Ibid.,* p. 190.

17. *Ibid.,* p. 191.

18. *Ibid.,* p. 190.

19. *Ibid.,* p. 191.

20. *Ibid.,* p. 193.

21. *Ibid.,* p. 193.

22. *Ibid.,* pp. 520 f.

23. *Ibid.,* p. 184.

24. Namely, in the ideal types.

25. *Ibid.,* p. 195.

26. Schelting aptly says: "With the concept of the 'ideal type' Max Weber for the first time clearly and plainly recognized a specific mode of forming concepts. The 'ideal type' is a logical discovery. It is not an 'invention.' In no way did Max Weber want to urge anything upon science that it had not already accomplished. He wanted to clarify a logical state of affairs already existing because it is of the essence of cognition in the cultural sciences." Cf. Schelting, "Die logische Theorie der historischen Kulturwissenschaft von Max Weber und im besonderen sein Begriff des Idealtypus," *Archiv für Sozialwissenschaft,* XLIX, 174. Cf. further Pfister, *Die Entwicklung zum Idealtypus* (Tübingen, 1928), pp. 131 ff.

27. Max Weber's epistemology has been continued and revised by Alfred Schütz (*Der sinnhafte Aufbau der sozialen Welt* (Vienna, 1932) in a way which also seeks to dispose of the judgment of the logical character of economic propositions to which I objected. (Cf. pp. 277 ff. especially.) Schütz's penetrating investigations, based on Husserl's system, lead to

findings whose importance and fruitfulness, both for epistemology and historical science itself, must be valued very highly. However, an evaluation of the concept of the ideal type, as it is newly conceived by Schütz, would exceed the scope of this treatise. I must reserve dealing with his ideas for another work.

28. Max Weber, *Wissenschaftslehre,* p. 191.
29. Gottl, *Die Herrschaft des Wortes* (1901), now in *Wirtschaft als Leben* (Jena, 1925) pp. 165 f.
30. Weber, *Wissenschaftslehre,* p. 117, footnote 2. Compare with this Weber's paraphrase: "the fundamental state of affairs to which are connected all those phenomena which we term 'socio-economic' in the broadest sense." *Ibid.,* p. 161.
31. Cf. my *Socialism,* trans. by J. Kahane (2nd ed.; New Haven, 1951), p. 113. Cf. further Heckscher, "A Plea for Theory in Economic History," *Economic History,* I, 527.
32. Concerning the hypostatization involved in the concept of "want," cf. Felix Kaufmann, "Logik und Wirtschaftswissenschaft," *Archiv für Sozialwissenschaft,* LIV, 620 ff.
33. Halberstädter, *Die Problematik des wirtschaftlichen Prinzips* (Berlin and Leipzig, 1925), p. 61.
34. Cf. Lexis, *op. cit.,* p. 14.
35. Scheler, *Der Formalismus in der Ethik und die formale Wertethik* (2nd ed.; Halle, 1921), p. 104.
36. Max Weber, "Wirtschaft und Gesellschaft," *Grundriss der Sozialökonomik* (Tübingen, 1922), Part III, p. 12.
37. *Ibid.,* p. 2.
38. *Ibid.,* p. 1.
39. *Ibid.,* p. 13.
40. *Ibid.,* p. 12.
41. *Ibid.,* p. 9.
42. *Ibid.,* p. 5.
43. Cf. my *Kritik des Interventionismus,* pp. 123 ff.
44. Cf. further below pp. 177 f.
45. Karl Muhs, "Die 'wertlose' Nationalökonomie," *Jahrbücher für Nationalökonomie und Statistik,* CXXIX, 808.
46. On this point cf. below pp. 174 ff.
47. I have intentionally not chosen as an example here a proposition of a natural science involving mathematics, but a statement of biology. The statement is imprecise in the form in which I present it and cannot assume the strict character of a law in any conceivable form. I have done this because it was incumbent upon me to show that, with the argument of the joint operation of a multiplicity of causal factors, the character of the strictest conformity to law cannot be denied even to a statement of this kind.
48. Freud reports a case in which this was openly admitted. Freud, "Zur Geschichte der psychoanalytischen Bewegung," *Sammlung Kleiner Schriften zur Neurosenlehre,* 4th Series (2nd ed.; Vienna, 1922), p. 57.
49. Cf. Max Weber, *Wissenschaftslehre,* p. 503.

50. *Ibid.*, p. 370.
51. Schelting, *op. cit.*, p. 721.
52. Cf. below pp. 171 ff.
53. Schelting, *loc. cit.*, p. 721.
54. Mitscherlich, "Wirtschaftswissenschaft als Wissenschaft," *Schmollers Jahrbuch*, L, 397.
55. Salin, *Geschichte der Volkswirtschaftslehre* (2nd ed.; Berlin, 1929), pp. 97 f.
56. Cf. Heckscher, *op. cit.*, p. 525.
57. Weber, *Wissenschaftslehre*, p. 190.
58. Weber, *Wissenschaftslehre*, p. 178.
59. *Ibid.*, pp. 178 ff.
60. Hegel, *Vorlesungen über die Philosophie der Weltgeschichte*, ed. by Lasson (Leipzig, 1917), Vol. I (*Philosophische Bibliothek*, Vol. 171a), p. 148.
61. In judging this example it should be noted that it has been carried over unchanged from the first publication of this article, which appeared in 1929.
62. Cf. Rickert, *Kulturwissenschaft und Naturwissenschaft*, pp. 28 ff. Cf. further, Sombart, "Zur Methode der exakten und historischen National-ökonomie," *Schmollers Jahrbuch*, LII, 647.
63. Cf. Muhs, *op. cit.*, p. 808.
64. "*Historiquement, le diable est beaucoup plus solidement prouvé que Pisistrate: nous n'avons pas un seul mot d'un contemporain qui dise avoir vu Pisistrate; des milliers des 'temoins oculaires' déclarent avoir vu le diable, il y a peu de faits historiques établis sur un pareil nombre de témoignages indépendants. Pourtant nous n'hesitons plus à rejeter le diable et à admettre Pisistrate. C'est que l'existence du diable serait inconciliable avec les lois de toutes les sciences constituées.*" Langlois-Seignobos, *Introduction aux études historiques* (3rd ed.; Paris, 1905), pp. 177 f.
65. Cf. Bouglé, *Qu'est-ce que la sociologie?* (5th ed.; Paris, 1925), pp. 54 ff.
66. Cf. Mannheim, "Historismus," *Archiv für Sozialwissenschaft*, LII, 9.
67. Cf. Husserl, *Logische Untersuchungen*, I, 136 ff.
68. Jerusalem, "Die soziologische Bedingtheit des Denkens und der Denkformen," *Versuche zu einer Soziologie des Wissens*, edited by Max Scheler (Munich and Leipzig, 1924), p. 183.
69. Cf. Lévy-Bruhl, *Primitive Mentality*, trans. by Lilian Clare (New York, 1923), pp. 27 f.
70. *Ibid.*, p. 27.
71. *Ibid.*, p. 437.
72. Cassirer, *Philosophie der symbolischen Formen* (Berlin, 1925), II, 78.
73. Bernheim, *op. cit.*, p. 53. Kracauer (*op. cit.*, pp. 24 ff.) speaks of comparative social history and comparative cultural history.
74. The distinction between statics and dynamics as I conceive it differs from the distinction as Amonn conceives it. This difference cannot be gone into more thoroughly here. However, I must, of course, call particular attention to what Amonn says regarding the entirely different

meaning that attaches to these conceptual correlates in mechanics and in economics. The concepts of statics and dynamics in economics do not involve the application of an analogy drawn from mechanics, but represent a mode of thinking appropriate to the character of economic science, for which only the name employed by mechanics was borrowed. Cf. Amonn, *Grundzüge der Volkswohlstandslehre* (Jena, 1926), Part I, pp. 275 ff.

75. Cf. J. B. Clark, *Essentials of Economic Theory* (New York, 1907), pp. 130 ff.

76. It is a serious misunderstanding to believe, as Flügge does ("Institutionalismus in der Nationalökonomie der Vereinigten Staaten," *Jahrbüchern für Nationalökonomie und Statistik,* New Series, LXXI, 339) that the construction of a static state would not be suited to lead to the understanding of economic changes.

77. Cf. above pp. 73 f.

78. Cf. Simmel, *Die Probleme der Geschichtsphilosophie* (4th ed.; Munich and Leipzig, 1922), pp. 107 ff.

79. Cf. Bücher, *Die Entstehung der Volkswirtschaft,* Series I, (10th ed.; Tübingen, 1917), p. 91. Bücher's theory of historical stages is taken here as representative of an entire class of such theories, among which, for example, we may number that of Schmoller. The dispute over precedence connected with Bücher's theory is without importance from our point of view.

80. *Ibid.,* p. 149.

81. *Ibid.,* p. 150.

82. On the other hand, Becher, *Geisteswissenschaften und Naturwissenschaften* (Munich and Leipzig, 1921), pp. 131, 171 f. is inclined to see in these theories of historical stages "universal laws, or, if one wishes to speak more reservedly, principles of historical economic development."

83. Hegel, *op. cit.,* pp. 232 f.

84. Cf. Mougeolle, *Les problèmes de l'histoire,* pp. 98 ff., 121 ff.

85. Cf. Becher, *op. cit.,* p. 175.

86. Simmel seeks in an ingenious way to express this singularity of the historical in his discussion of individual causality. Cf. Simmel, *op. cit.,* pp. 100 ff.

87. Mitchell shares this illusion with many others. Cf. Mitchell, "Quantitative Analysis in Economic Theory," *American Economic Review,* XV, 1 ff.

88. Cf. Dingler, *Der Zusammenbruch der Wissenschaft* (Munich, 1926), pp. 63 ff.; Schams, "Die Casselschen Gleichungen und die mathematische Wirtschaftstheorie," *Jahrbücher für Nationalökonomie und Statistik,* Series III, Vol. LXXII, pp. 386 ff. Painlevé aptly states the objection to the mathematical treatment of economics in his preface to the French edition of Jevons' *Principles* (Paris, 1909), pp. v ff.

89. Cairnes, *The Character and Logical Method of Political Economy,* pp. 118 ff.; Eulenburg, "Sind historische Gesetze möglich?" *Hauptprobleme der Soziologie* (Munich, 1923), I, 43.

90. Therefore, it would also be a mistake to attempt to attack the statement

in the text by referring to the fact that the natural sciences borrowed the statistical method from sociology and now seek to make it serve their own purposes.

91. Kant, *Prolegomena zu einer jeden künftigen Metaphysik,* ed. by Insel, IV, 417, §14.
92. Rickert, *Die Grenzen der naturwissenschaftlichen Begriffsbildung* (2nd ed.; Tübingen, 1913), p. 224; Rickert, *Kulturwissenschaft und Naturwissenschaft,* p. 60.
93. Concerning Kant's fundamental social views, cf. my *Socialism,* pp. 298, 434.
94. Rickert, *Die Grenzen der naturwissenschaftlichen Begriffsbildung,* pp. 196 f.; similarly, p. 174. The conclusion at which Rickert finally arrives —that sociology can never take the place of history—is, of course, to be concurred with.
95. Weyl, "Philosophie der Mathematik und Naturwissenschaft," *Handbuch der Philosophie* (Munich and Berlin, 1927), p. 3. Wundt has endeavored to base his investigations on a more thoroughgoing study of the social sciences. Cf. Wundt, *Logik* (3rd ed.; Stuttgart, 1908), III, 458 ff. The period and milieu in which he worked explain the fact that he misunderstood modern subjectivist economics in his study. He could not be made aware of this deficiency even, as we have already seen, by Menger's book on methodology.
96. Cf. Menger, *Untersuchungen über die Methode der Sozialwissenschaften und der politischen Ökonomie insbesondere* (Leipzig, 1883), pp. 3 ff.
97. One could not arrive at such a theory by any of the procedures of thought available to us. Cf. above pp. 9 ff., 25 ff.
98. Rothacker, "Logik und Systematik der Geisteswissenschaften," *Handbuch der Philosophie* (Munich and Berlin, 1927), pp. 123 f.
99. Bagehot, "The Postulates of English Political Economy," *Works,* edited by Russel Barrington (London, 1915), VII, pp. 103-104. The fact that Bagehot in the following pages of his treatise makes untenable concessions to the arguments of historicism and supports the idea of laws which are to be valid only for a definite period need not be considered here. On this point, cf. John Neville Keynes, *The Scope and Method of Political Economy* (London, 1891), pp. 289 ff.
100. Bagehot, *op. cit.,* p. 104.

3

Conception and Understanding

1. COGNITION FROM WITHOUT AND COGNITION FROM WITHIN

We explain a phenomenon when we trace it back to general principles. Any other mode of explanation is denied to us. Explanation in this sense in no way means the elucidation of the final cause, the ontological basis, of the being and becoming of a phenomenon. Sooner or later we must always reach a point beyond which we cannot advance.

Thus far we have been unable to succeed in grasping in any way the relationship that exists between the psychical and the physical. We are not at present in a position to provide any explanation of it in terms of general principles. Hence, in spite of the unity of the logical structure of our thought, we are compelled to have recourse to two separate spheres of scientific cognition: the science of nature and the science of human action.

We approach the subject matter of the natural sciences from without. The result of our observations is the establishment of functional relations of dependence. The propositions concerning these relationships constitute the general principles by which we explain the phenomena of nature. Once we have constructed the system of these principles, we have done all that we can do. In the sciences of human action, on the other hand, we comprehend phenomena from within. Because we are human beings, we are in a position to grasp the meaning of human action, that is, the meaning that the actor has attached to his action. It is this comprehension of meaning that enables us to formulate the general principles by means of which we explain the phenomena of action.

One will best appreciate what is accomplished by this approach to human action, which comprehends its meaning, if one contrasts to it the attempt of behaviorism to view the behavior of men from without, in accordance with the methods of animal psychology. The behaviorists want to abandon the endeavor to grasp the conduct of man on the basis of its meaning. They want to see in him nothing but reactions to definite stimuli. If they were to carry out their program rigorously, they could do nothing but record the occurrences that have taken place at a particular time. And it would be impermissible for them to infer from what has occurred at a particular time anything concerning what might have occurred in other previous cases or what will take place in the future.

As a rule, the situation to which man consciously reacts can be analyzed only with concepts that make reference to meaning. If one chooses to analyze the situation without entering into the meaning that acting man sees in it, the analysis will not be successful in bringing into relief what is essential in the situation and decisive of the nature of the reaction to it. The conduct of a man whom another wants to cut with a knife will be entirely different depending on whether he beholds in the intended operation a mutilation or a surgical incision. And without recourse to meaning, there is no art by which one can succeed in analyzing a situation like that arising in the production of a supply of consumers' goods. The reaction of conscious conduct is, without exception, meaningful, and it is to be comprehended only by entering into its meaning. It is always an outgrowth of a theory, that is, a doctrine that connects cause and effect, and of the desire to attain a definite end.

Only by deceiving itself could behaviorism reach the point where it would be in a position to say anything about action. If, true to its resolve, behaviorism were completely to renounce the attempt to grasp meaning, it could not even succeed in singling out what it declares to be the subject matter of its research from all that the senses observe of human and animal behavior.[1] It would not succeed in marking off its function from that of physiology. Physiology, Watson maintains, is concerned in particular with the behavior of the parts of the animal; behaviorism, with the behavior of the whole animal.[2] Yet surely neither the reaction of the body to an infection nor the phenomena of growth and age are to be classified as "behavior of the parts." If, on the other hand, one chooses to regard a movement of the hand as an instance of behavior on the part of the "whole animal," one can, of course, do so only on the view that in this movement of the hand something becomes operative that cannot be attributed to any particular part of the body. This something, however, can be nothing else than "meaning" or that which begets "meaning."

Whatever results behaviorism has attained in the observation of the behavior of animals and children it owes to the—of course, concealed and denied—smuggling in of teleology. Without it, all that behaviorism would have been able to accomplish would have remained nothing more than an enormous compilation of cases occurring in a given place and at a given time.

2. CONCEPTION AND UNDERSTANDING

In German logic and philosophy the term "understanding" (*Verstehen*) has been adopted to signify the procedure of the sciences of human action, the essence of which lies in grasping the meaning of action.[3] To take this term in the sense accepted by the majority of those who have employed it, one must, above all, bear in mind that in Germany the development and refinement of a theoretical science having in view the attainment of universally valid principles of human action had either not been considered at all or else had been vehemently opposed. Historicism did not want to admit that, in addition to the disciplines that make use of the methods of history and philology, there is still another, a science that aims at universally valid cognition. The champions of historicism wanted to approve only of history (in the broadest sense) and challenged the very possibility and legitimacy of sociology in general and of economic theory in particular. They did not see that without recourse to propositions accepted as universally valid, even history cannot be understood and that the theory of human action is logically *prior* to history. It is to the merit of historicism that it rejected the endeavors of naturalism, which—no less mistakenly than historicism, though in another regard—for its part condemned all historical disciplines and wanted to replace history with a science of the laws of human development that was to be modeled on the prototype of Newtonian mechanics or on that of the Darwinian theory of evolution. The concept of understanding as the specific methodological tool of the sciences of human action was developed by historicism to serve it no less in the struggle against naturalism than in that against the nomothetic science of human action.

Today, when understanding is discussed in German scientific literature, it is, as a rule, made clear that what is meant by the term is the method of the "moral sciences," which comprehends meaning, in contrast to the method of cognition from without employed by the natural sciences. But since, as we have mentioned, this literature is almost completely lacking in any realization that a theoretical science of human action is also possible, it has generally sought to define understanding as the specific comprehension of the unique and the irrational, as the intuitive grasp of the historically nonrepeatable, in contrast to conception, which is attainable by rational methods of thought.[4] In and of itself, it would have been possible to include in the definition of understanding every procedure that is directed toward the comprehension of meaning. However, as things stand today, we must accommodate ourselves to the prevailing usage. Therefore, within the procedures employed by the sciences of human action for the comprehension of meaning we shall differentiate between conception and understanding. Conception seeks to grasp the meaning of action through discursive reasoning. Understanding seeks the meaning of action in empathic intuition of a whole.

Where conception is at all applicable, it takes precedence over understanding in every respect. That which results from discursive reasoning can never be refuted or even affected by intuitive comprehension of a context of meaning. The province of understanding lies only where conception and the concept are unable to penetrate: in the apprehension of the quality of values. In the domain open to conception, strict logic rules: one is able to prove and disprove; there is a point to conversing with others about what is "true" and what is "false" and to posing problems and discussing their solution. What has been arrived at by means of conception must be acknowledged as established, or else must be shown to be either unproved or confuted. It cannot be avoided and it cannot be circumvented. On the other hand, where understanding enters, the realm of subjectivity begins. We are unable to impart to others any certain knowledge of what is intuitively foreknown and apprehended, of what has not been hardened in the forge of conceptual thought. The words in which we express it bid others to follow us and to re-experience the complex whole that we have experienced. But whether and how we are followed depends on the personality and the inclination of the one bidden. We cannot even determine with certainty whether we have been understood as we wanted to be understood, for only the sharp imprint of the concept ensures unequivocalness; it is to a concept alone that words can be made to fit precisely.

In this respect, understanding suffers from the same insufficiency as all other efforts—artistic, metaphysical, or mystical—to reproduce the intuition of a whole. What we are confronted with in these attempts are words that can be understood in different senses, from which a person takes out what he himself puts in. As far as the historian describes the political and military deeds of Caesar, no misunderstanding can arise between him and his readers. But where he speaks of Caesar's greatness, his personality, his charism, then the words of the historian can be understood in different ways. There can be no discussion concerning understanding because it is always subjectively conditioned. Conception is reasoning; understanding is beholding.

"Conception" of rational behavior does not set goals for itself as ambitious as those that "understanding" pursues. Nevertheless, in its own domain, it is able to accomplish all that it undertakes to do. For we grasp and conceive rational behavior by means of the immutable logical structure of our reason, which is the basis of all rationality. The a priori of reasoning is at the same time the a priori of rational action. Conception of human behavior is the γνῶσις τοῦ ὁμοίου τῷ ὁμοίῳ of Empedocles.

3. THE IRRATIONAL AS AN OBJECT OF COGNITION

All attempts at scientific explanation can at best succeed only in explaining the changes in something given. The given itself is inexplicable. It simply is. Why it is remains hidden from us. It is the irrational—that which reasoning cannot exhaust, that which concepts are unable to grasp without leaving something still unexplained.

For the science of human action, the valuations and goals of the final order at which men aim constitute the ultimate given, which it is unable to explain any further. Science can record and classify values, but it can no more "explain" them than it can prescribe the values that are to be acknowledged as correct or condemned as perverted. The intuitive apprehension of values by means of understanding is still not an "explanation." All that it attempts to do is to see and determine what the values in a given case are, and nothing more. Where the historian tries to go beyond this, he becomes an apologist or a judge, an agitator or a politician. He leaves the sphere of reflective, inquiring, theoretical science and himself enters the arena of human action.

Science belongs completely to the domain of rationality. There can no more be a science of the irrational than there can be irrational science. The irrational lies outside the domain of human reasoning and science. When confronted with the irrational, reasoning and science can only record and classify. They are unable to penetrate more "deeply," not even with the aid of the "understanding." Indeed, the criterion of the irrational is precisely that it cannot be fully comprehended by reasoning. That which we are able to master completely by reasoning is no longer irrational.

The purest example of the irrational as an object of scientific activity is to be found in what is called *Kunstwissenschaft.* *
Kunstwissenschaft can never be more than the history of the arts and of artists, of art techniques, of the subjects and themes treated

* Translator's note: The German term *Kunstwissenschaft*, which is used in the original, means a discipline that deals both with the history of art and with aesthetic evaluations of it.

by art, and of the ideas governing it. There is no universally valid theory of the artistic, of aesthetic values, or of artistic individuality. What writers on art say about it, whether in commendation or in condemnation, expresses only their own personal experience of the work of art. This may be called "understanding," but, as far as it goes beyond the ascertainment of the irrational facts of the case, it is definitely not science. One who analyzes a work of art breaks it up in the strict sense of the word. Its specific aesthetic quality, however, is effective only in the whole of the work, not in its parts. A work of art is an attempt to experience the universe as a whole. One cannot analyze or dissect it into parts and comment on it without destroying its intrinsic character. *Kunstwissenschaft,* therefore, can never do more than skirt the fringes of art and works of art. It can never grasp art as such. This discipline may nevertheless appear indispensable to many because it provides access to the enjoyment of works of art. In the eyes of others it may be clothed with a special dignity reflected from the splendor of the objects of art themselves. Still others say that it cannot ever approach the specifically artistic. This too is true, although one is not therefore justified in looking down upon art historians and art history.

The position of science toward the other values of acting men is no different from that which it adopts toward aesthetic values. Here too science can do no more with respect to the values themselves than to record them and, at most, classify them as well. All that it can accomplish with the aid of "conception" relates to the means that are to lead to the realization of values, in short, to the rational behavior of men aiming at ends. History and sociology are not fundamentally different in this respect. The only distinction between them is that sociology, as a theoretical science, strives for universally valid laws of rational behavior, whereas history, employing these laws, presents the temporal course of human action. The subject matter of history is the historically given in its individuality. It must treat this with the means provided by theory, but as long as it does not overstep its bounds and attempt to prescribe values, history cannot exhaust the individuality of the given even with the help of "understanding." History may, if one insists, be called a science of the irrational, but one must not forget that it is able to gain access to the irrational only by means of rational science. At the point where these means fail, history can succeed in nothing beyond the ascertainment of the irrational facts of the case through empathic understanding.

Understanding does not explain the individual, the personal, or the values given in experience, because it does not grasp their meaning by way of conception. It merely beholds them. Hence, as far as understanding is involved, there can be no progress in the historical sciences in the sense in which there is progress in the natural sciences or in sociology. There is progress in the historical sciences only as far as conception is involved; i.e., as far as improvement in the treatment of sources and more penetrating sociological cognition enable us to grasp the meaning of events better than was previously possible. Today, for instance, with the help of economic theory we are capable of comprehending the events of economic history in a way that was not available to the older historians. However, history must be repeatedly rewritten because the subjective element in the passing of time and the change in personalities again and again open up new vistas for the understanding.

This subjective element, which is always mixed in with understanding, is responsible for the fact that history can be written from a variety of points of view. There is a history of the Reformation from the Catholic standpoint and another from the Protestant standpoint. Only one who fails to recognize the fundamental differences that exist between conception and understanding, between sociology and history, will be prone to assume that these differences exist in the sphere of sociology as well and to contrast, for example, a German sociology to English sociology or a proletarian economics to bourgeois economics.

4. SOMBART'S CRITIQUE OF ECONOMICS

It is completely erroneous to believe that the theories of catallactics can in any way be called into question by the assertion that they are merely "rational schemata." [5] I have already attempted elsewhere to set forth in detail the misunderstandings in regard to the logical character of modern economics that Max Weber fell into.[6] As far as Sombart follows in his footsteps, all further comment is unnecessary.

Sombart, however, goes much further than Weber.

The concept of "exchange," for example, says nothing whatever. It derives its "meaning" exclusively through its relation with the historical context in which the "exchange" takes place. "Exchange" in the primitive economy (silent barter), "exchange" in the handicraft economy, and "exchange" in the capitalist economy are things enormously different from one another.[7] Price and price are completely different things from market to market. Price formation in the fair at Vera Cruz in the seventeenth century and in the wheat market on the Chicago Exchange in the year 1930 are two altogether incomparable occurrences.[8]

Yet even Sombart does not deny that there are universally valid concepts in economics. He distinguishes

three different kinds of economic concepts: 1. The universal-economic primary concepts . . . which are valid for all economic systems; 2. the historical-economic primary concepts . . . which . . . are valid only for a definite economic system; and 3. the subsidiary concepts . . . which are constructed with regard to a definite working idea.[9]

We need not consider this division in detail here. All that concerns us is the question whether the assignment of the concepts of exchange and price formation to the second group can be justified. Sombart gives no reason for it, unless one wants to see a reason in remarks like the following:

It would be absurd to assign the same tasks to chess-playing and to playing fox and geese. It is equally absurd to construct the same schemata for the self-sufficient household economy of a peasant and the economy of high capitalism.[10]

Even Sombart did not go so far as to assert that the word "exchange" when used in reference to primitive economy is nothing more than a homonym of the word "exchange" when used in reference to the capitalist economy, or that the word "price" when used in reference to the fair in Vera Cruz in the seventeenth century is nothing more than a homonym of the word "price" when used in reference to the Chicago Exchange in the year 1930; like, for example, "sole" in the sense of a fish and "sole" in the sense of the bottom part of a shoe. He speaks repeatedly of exchange, price, and price formation without further qualification, which would be completely absurd if they required to be distinguished from their homonyms. When he says, "A theory of the formation of markets must precede a theory of price formation," [11] this is itself a proposition valid for all price formation and thus contradicts his assertion: "The concept of 'exchange,' for example, says nothing whatever." If price formation and price formation really were "two altogether incomparable occurrences," it would be just as absurd to assert this proposition as, for example, to assert a proposition supposedly valid for all soles—i.e., for all of a certain species of fish and for all bottom parts of shoes. Something, therefore, must be common to both occurrences. In fact, we even learn that there are "requirements of price formation" that arise "from the essential, the mathematical, and the rational conformity to law to which, of course, price formation is also subject." [12]

If, however, it is established that unequivocal concepts are connoted by the terms "exchange," "price," and "price formation," then it is of little avail to say that the concept itself involves "things enormously different from one another" and "altogether incomparable occurrences." Such vague phrases are satisfactory only when their purpose is to point out that identically sounding *words* are used to express different concepts. But if we have *one* concept before us, we can proceed in no other way than by first precisely defining that concept and then seeing how far it reaches, what it includes, and what it does not comprehend. Sombart, however, is evidently a stranger to this procedure. He does not ask what exchange and price are. He unconcernedly employs these terms as everyday, unscientific usage presents them.

Fully imbued with the bitter resentment of the school of thought that was worsted in the *Methodenstreit* and, indeed, in all other scientific respects, Sombart speaks only in terms of contempt of the economic theory of marginal utility. This theory seeks to provide precise definitions for the concepts that he simply picks up as he finds them and makes use of without hesitation. It analyzes them and thereby explicates everything contained in them, purging them of all the unessential elements that imprecise reasoning may have mixed in with them. One cannot think about the concept of exchange without implicitly also thinking about everything that is taught by the economic theory of exchange. There is no exchange that conforms "more" to the law of marginal utility, and none that conforms "less." There is "exchange," and there is "nonexchange," but there are no differences in degrees of exchange. Whoever misunderstands this has not taken the trouble to become acquainted with the work of the economic theory of the last thirty years.

If a traveler from the Germany of "high capitalism," driven off his course to an island inhabited by primitive tribes, observes the strange behavior of the natives, which is at first incomprehensible and unintelligible to him, and suddenly realizes that they are "exchanging," then he has "conceived" what is going on there, even though he may be familiar only with the exchange of "high capitalism." When Sombart calls an occurrence in Vera Cruz in the seventeenth century an "exchange" and speaks of "price formation" in this exchange, he has employed the concepts of exchange and price formation to comprehend the meaning of this occurrence. In both cases the "rational schema" serves to make possible the comprehension of an event that otherwise cannot be grasped at all, either in conception or in understanding. Sombart must make use of this rational schema because otherwise he would be completely at a loss to deal with this event by reasoning. However, he wants to employ the rational schema only up to a certain point, so that he may avoid the inescapable logical consequences of using it, and does not see the significance of his procedure. Yet the "rational schema" is either to be employed or not to be employed. If one has decided to use it, one must accept all the consequences of this step. One must avail oneself of all that is contained in the concept.

Sombart alleges that only he—and, of course, his supporters— should be considered theorists "in the true sense." The others—the "manufacturers of rational schemata"—can be styled "theorists" only in quotation marks.[13] He reproaches these "theorists" with three deficiencies. In the first place, the majority of them have not "correctly grasped the meaning of the schemata they have developed, owing to their own lack of real theoretical education." They "considered them natural laws and, using them as a basis, constructed a system after the pattern of the natural sciences." [14] Inasmuch as in German philosophy, following Kant's precedent, nomothetic science was equated with natural science, those who maintained the feasibility of a science of human action aiming at universally valid cognition had to classify this science as a natural science.[15] But this did not influence the character and content of the scientific investigations they carried on.

The second fault that Sombart finds with the "theorists" is that they have produced "much too many and often much too complicated means of production"—Sombart labels "schemata" as "means of production"—the use of which is "impossible, and which are more of a hindrance than a help to the process of production (like, for example, a tractor on a farm for which it is not suited)." [16] The metaphorical language that Sombart uses here diverts attention from the only important point at issue: either the theory is correct or it is incorrect. There cannot be too much of a correct theory. If the theory is correct, then neither can it also be "too complicated." Whoever finds it so has only to replace it with a correct, yet simpler, theory. But Sombart does not attempt this at all. On the contrary. In another passage he reproaches the "theory" with being too simple: "Actual relationships can be so involved, and frequently are so involved, that a schema affords but little help." [17]

Sombart's third criticism of the "theorists" is that they have "frequently constructed inappropriate schemata, that is to say, means of production with which nothing can be done, machines that do not operate." In this category he classes "in great part the theory of marginal utility, the very modest cognitive value of which has already been realized. However, this is not the place to substantiate this view more thoroughly." [18] Thus, the "theory" is incorrect because it is incorrect, and because one has already realized this fact. Sombart has yet to produce the substantiation of this assertion. He makes a value judgment concerning the theory of marginal utility. He himself has aptly pointed out what is to be thought of such value judgments.[19]

I have so often explained what political and economic ideals motivated the hostile view of theory taken by the interventionists and the socialists that I need not repeat my observations on this point.[20] Moreover, an historical explanation enables us to understand the error involved here exclusively from an aspect that must appear as accidental when viewed from the standpoint of theoretical investigation. We can grasp Sombart's misconception only on the basis of a strict logical examination of his reasoning.

In the case of no other opponent of catallactics are the political motives of this hostility so clearly evident as they are in that of Sombart. The frank acceptance of modern economic theory would fit much better than its rejection into the system of philosophy that he expounds in his most recent work. Nevertheless, a fiery temperament and a feeling of obligation to his own past convictions again and again make him unfaithful to his intention of conducting an investigation neutral with regard to value judgments. Sombart believes he has understood our "economic epoch" with its "economic system"—"modern capitalism"—from within. Can one who styles the age "whose culmination we are first experiencing" as the age "of means that are employed without sense and whose abundant and elaborate use finally imperceptibly becomes an end in itself" [21] really make such a claim? Does not the fact that Sombart himself again and again calls rationalization the essence of this age stand in the most radical contradiction with it? Rationalism means the precise weighing of means and ends.

Sombart, of course, is enthusiastic about the Middle Ages. He holds the values that, in his opinion, were current during that era in particularly high esteem. Men, he thinks, have since then shifted their field of vision from the "eternal values to the things of this world." [22] Sombart finds this reprehensible. But can one say that, for this reason, means are employed "without sense"? They are—we do not wish to examine the matter further—employed perhaps in a different sense, but certainly not "without sense." Even if it were true that their "abundant and elaborate use" has become an "end in itself," a science neutral with regard to value judgments, which understands, but does not prescribe, would not be warranted in denying the "sense" of this end. It can judge the employment of means in the light of their expediency, i.e., from the point of view of their suitability for attaining the end that those who employ them want to attain; but it can never sit in judgment on the ends themselves.

In spite of the best of intentions, the inquirer who scorns the intellectual help that the "rational schemata" of economic theory can give him is all too prone to make valuations and to assume the role of a judge.

5. LOGIC AND THE SOCIAL SCIENCES

In the last generation the distinctive logic of the social sciences was confronted with two tasks. On the one hand, it had to show the distinctive peculiarity, the feasibility, and the necessity of history. On the other hand, it had to show not only that there is, but also how there can be, a science of human action that aims at universally valid cognition. There can be no doubt that a great deal has been accomplished for the solution of these two problems. That these solutions are not "final" or "definitive" is evident, for as long as the human mind does not stop thinking, striving, and inquiring, there is no such thing as "finality" and "definitiveness."

The demand is repeatedly made by those who champion political ideals that cannot be defended by logical argumentation that thinking in the field of the social sciences be exempted from the regulative principles necessary to all other thinking. This is a matter with which scientific thought, which considers itself bound by these logical principles, is unable to concern itself.

When, more than a century ago, Sismondi appeared on the scene against Ricardo, he declared that political economy is no *"science de calcul,"* but a *"science morale,"* for which he enunciated the proposition: *toute abstraction est toujours une déception.*[23] Neither Sismondi nor the many who have taken over this cliché have divulged to us the secret of how science could be pursued without abstract concepts. Today, the "living concept," which has the power to take on new content, is recommended to us as the most recent product of the logic of the social sciences. In the programmatic declarations that introduce a new *Zeitschrift für geistige und politische Gestaltung,* issued by a circle of German university professors, we read:

Concepts are living only so long as they have the power to take on new content. Taking on new content does not mean shedding the old, nor does it mean breaking away from the sources that gave rise to the concept. Taking on new content means, on the contrary, the power of a concept, and through it the power of its source, to prove that it is able to overcome every threat of rigidity.[24]

That, using concepts of changeable content, one can argue excellently and can even concoct a system is certainly to be conceded. We "understand" very well the need of certain political parties for such makeshifts. However, the only thing that it concerns us to establish here is that this is not a need of scientific thought engaged in the cognition of social phenomena, but the need of political parties that are unable to justify their programs logically. Today these parties are striving for world dominion with good prospect of success. The masses follow them, the state has handed over all the schools to them, and the literati praise them to the skies. These facts make it all the more necessary to repeat the truism that there is only *one* logic and that all concepts are distinguished by the unequivocalness and immutability of their content.

NOTES

1. Cf. Bühler, *Die Krise der Psychologie* (Jena, 1927), p. 46.
2. Cf. Watson, *Behaviorism* (New York, 1924), p. 11.
3. Wach undertakes far-reaching historical and exegetical investigations concerning the development of the theory of understanding in German science in his work, *Das Verstehen, Grundzüge einer Geschichte der hermeneutischen Theorie im 19. Jahrhundert* (3 volumes, Tübingen, 1926-1933). If one also wanted to sketch the history of "conception" in the sense in which this term is used in the present text, one would have to go back, above all, to the literature of utilitarianism.
4. Cf. Rothacker, *Logik und Systematik der Geisteswissenschaften,* pp. 119 ff.

5. Cf. Sombart, *Die drei Nationalökonomien,* p. 259.
6. Cf. above pp. 75 ff. What has been said concerning the erroneous identification of "rational" and "correct" action (above all, on pp. 93 ff.) also contains the reply to Sombart's arguments, *op. cit.,* p. 261.
7. Cf. Sombart, *op. cit.,* p. 211.
8. *Op. cit.,* p. 305.
9. *Op. cit.,* p. 247.
10. *Op. cit.,* p. 301.
11. *Op. cit.,* p. 305.
12. *Ibid.*
13. Sombart, *op. cit.,* p. 303.
14. *Ibid.*
15. Cf. above p. 118.
16. Cf. Sombart, *loc. cit.,* p. 303.
17. *Op. cit.,* p. 301.
18. *Op. cit.,* p. 304.
19. *Op. cit.,* pp. 289 f.
20. Cf. above, p. 69; further, my *Kritik des Interventionismus,* pp. 24 ff., 68 ff.
21. Cf. Sombart, p. 87.
22. *Op. cit.,* p. 85.
23. Sismondi, *Nouveaux principes d'économie politique* (Paris, 1819), I, 288.
24. Cf. Tillich, "Sozialismus," *Neue Blätter für Sozialismus,* (1930), I, 1.

4

On the Development of the Subjective Theory of Value

1. THE DELIMITATION OF THE "ECONOMIC"

Investigations concerning the money prices of goods and services constituted the historical starting point of the reflections that led to the development of economic theory. What first opened the way to success in these inquiries was the observation that money plays "merely" an intermediary role and that through its interposition goods and services are, in the last analysis, exchanged against goods and services. This discovery led to the further realization that the theory of direct exchange, which makes use of the fiction that all acts of exchange are conducted without the intervention of any medium, must be given logical priority over the theory of money and credit, i.e., the theory of indirect exchange, which is effected by means of money.

Still further possibilities were disclosed when it was realized that acts of interpersonal exchange are not essentially different from those which the individual makes within his own household without reaching beyond it into the social sphere. Hence, every allocation of goods—even those in the processes of production—is an exchange, and consequently the basic law of economic action can be comprehended also in the conduct of the isolated farmer. Thus, the foundation was laid for the first correct formulation and satisfactory solution of the problem of the delimitation of "economic" action from "noneconomic" action.

This problem had been approached previously in two different

146

ways, each of which necessarily rendered its solution considerably more difficult. Classical economics had not succeeded in overcoming the difficulties posed by the apparent paradox of value. It had to construct its theory of value and price formation on the basis of exchange value and to start from the action of the businessman, because it was not able to base its system on the valuations of the marginal consumers. The specific conduct of the businessman is directed toward the attainment of the greatest possible monetary profit. Since the classical economists beheld in this phenomenon the essence of economic conduct, they had to distinguish accordingly between "economic" and "noneconomic" action. As soon as the transition was made to the subjective theory of value, this distinction, because it contradicts the basic thought of the whole system, could not but prove totally unserviceable and indeed nothing short of absurd. Of course, it took a long time before it was recognized as such.

If the distinction between the "economic" and the "noneconomic" proved untenable when formulated in terms of the motives and immediate goals of the actor, the attempt to base it on differences among the objects of action fared no better. Material things of the external world are exchanged not only against other things of this kind; they are exchanged also against other—"immaterial"—goods like honor, fame, and recognition. If one wishes to remove these actions from the province of the "economic," then a new difficulty arises. For a great many of the acts in which material goods are exchanged serve one or both parties to the transaction merely as a preliminary means for the attainment of such "immaterial" satisfactions. However, every attempt to draw a sharp distinction here necessarily led to barren scholastic discussions which entangled themselves in immanent contradictions—discussions such as the successors of the classical economists devoted to the related endeavors to delimit the concepts of a "good" and "productivity." But even if one wished to disregard this problem completely, one could not ignore the fact that human action exhibits an indissoluble homogeneity and that action involving the exchange of material goods against immaterial goods differs in no significant respect from action involving the exchange of material goods alone.

Two propositions follow from the subjective theory of value that make a precise separation between the "economic" and the "noneconomic," such as the older economics sought, appear impracticable. First, there is the realization that the economic principle is the fundamental principle of all rational action, and not just a particular feature of a certain kind of rational action. All rational action is therefore an act of economizing. Secondly, there is the realization that every conscious, i.e., meaningful, action is rational. Only the ultimate goals—the values or ends— at which action aims are beyond rationality and, indeed, always and without exception must be. It was no longer compatible with subjectivism to equate "rational" and "irrational" with "objectively practical" and "objectively impractical." It was no longer permissible to contrast "correct" action as "rational" to "incorrect" action, i.e., action diverted through misunderstanding, ignorance, or negligence from employing the best means available to attain the ends sought. Nor was it henceforth possible to call an action irrational in which values like honor, piety, or political goals are taken into consideration. Max Weber's attempt to separate rational action from other action on the basis of such distinctions was the last of its kind. It was necessarily doomed to failure.[1]

If, however, all conscious conduct is an act of rational economizing, then one must be able to exhibit the fundamental economic categories involved in every action, even in action that is called "noneconomic" in popular usage. And, in fact, it is not difficult to point out in every conceivable human—that is, conscious—action the fundamental categories of catallactics, namely, value, good, exchange, price, and costs. Not only does the science of ethics show this, but even everyday popular usage gives us ample demonstrations of it. One has only to consider, for example, how, outside the domain customarily designated as that of science, terms and phrases are used that have these categories as their specific denotation.

2. PREFERRING AS THE BASIC ELEMENT IN HUMAN CONDUCT

All conscious conduct on the part of men involves preferring an A to a B. It is an act of choice between two alternative possibilities that offer themselves. Only these acts of choice, these inner decisions that operate upon the external world, are our data. We comprehend their meaning by constructing the concept of importance. If an individual prefers A to B, we say that, at the moment of the act of choice, A appeared more important to him (more valuable, more desirable) than B.

We are also wont to say that the need for A was more urgent than the need for B. This is a mode of expression that, under certain circumstances, may be quite expedient. But as an hypostatization of what was to be explained, it became a source of serious misunderstandings. It was forgotten that we are able to infer the need only from the action. Hence, the idea of an action not in conformity with needs is absurd. As soon as one attempts to distinguish between the need and the action and makes the need the criterion for judging the action, one leaves the domain of theoretical science, with its neutrality in regard to value judgments. It is necessary to recall here that we are dealing with the theory of action, not with psychology, and certainly not with a system of norms, which has the task of differentiating between good and evil or between value and worthlessness. Our data are actions and conduct. It may be left undecided how far and in what way our science needs to concern itself with what lies behind them, that is, with actual valuations and volitions. For there can be no doubt that its subject matter is given action and only given action. Action that ought to be, but is not, does not come within its purview.

This best becomes clear to us if we consider the task of catallactics. Catallactics has to explain how market prices arise from the action of parties to the exchange of goods. It has to explain market prices as they are, not as they should be. If one wishes to do justice to this task, then in no way may one distinguish between "economic" and "noneconomic" grounds of price determination or limit oneself to constructing a theory that would apply only to a world that does not exist. In Böhm-Bawerk's famous example of the planter's five sacks of grain, there is no question of a rank order of objective correctness, but of a rank order of subjective desires.

The boundary that separates the economic from the non-economic is not to be sought within the compass of rational action. It coincides with the line that separates action from nonaction. Action takes place only where decisions are to be made, where the necessity exists of choosing between possible goals, because all goals either cannot be achieved at all or not at the same time. Men act because they are affected by the flux of time. They are therefore not indifferent to the passage of time. They act because they are not fully satisfied and satiated and because by acting they are able to enhance the degree of their satisfaction. Where these conditions are not present—as in the case of "free" goods, for example—action does not take place.

3. EUDAEMONISM AND THE THEORY OF VALUE

The most troublesome misunderstandings with which the history of philosophical thought has been plagued concern the terms "pleasure" and "pain." These misconceptions have been carried over into the literature of sociology and economics and have caused harm there too.

Before the introduction of this pair of concepts, ethics was a doctrine of what ought to be. It sought to establish the goals that man should adopt. The realization that man seeks satisfaction by acts both of commission and of omission opened the only path that can lead to a science of human action. If Epicurus sees in ἀταραξία the final goal of action, we can behold in it, if we wish, the state of complete satisfaction and freedom from desire at which human action aims without ever being able to attain it. Crude materialistic thinking seeks to circumscribe it in visions of Paradise and Cockaigne. Whether this construction may, in fact, be placed on Epicurus' words remains, of course, uncertain, in view of the paucity of what has been handed down of his writings.

Doubtless it did not happen altogether without the fault of

Epicurus and his school that the concepts of pleasure and pain were taken in the narrowest and coarsely materialistic sense when one wanted to misconstrue the ideas of hedonism and eudaemonism. And they were not only misconstrued; they were deliberately misrepresented, caricatured, derided, and ridiculed. Not until the seventeenth century did appreciation of the teachings of Epicurus again begin to be shown. On the foundations provided by it arose modern utilitarianism, which for its part soon had to contend anew with the same misrepresentations on the part of its opponents that had confronted its ancient forerunner. Hedonism, eudaemonism, and utilitarianism were condemned and outlawed, and whoever did not wish to run the risk of making the whole world his enemy had to be scrupulously intent upon avoiding the suspicion that he inclined toward these heretical doctrines. This must be kept in mind if one wants to understand why many economists went to great pains to deny the connection between their teachings and those of utilitarianism.

Even Böhm-Bawerk thought that he had to defend himself against the reproach of hedonism. The heart of this defense consists in his statement that he had expressly called attention already in the first exposition of his theory of value to his use of the word "well-being" in its broadest sense, in which it "embraces not only the self-centered interests of a subject, but everything that seems to him worth aiming at." [2] Böhm-Bawerk did not see that in saying this he was adopting the same purely formal view of the character of the basic eudaemonistic concepts of pleasure and pain—treating them as indifferent to content—that all advanced utilitarians have held. One need only compare with the words quoted from Böhm-Bawerk the following dictum of Jacobi:

We originally want or desire an object not because it is agreeable or good, but we call it agreeable or good because we want or desire it; and we do this because our sensuous or supersensuous nature so requires. There is, thus, no basis for recognizing what is good and worth wishing for outside of the faculty of desiring—i.e., the original desire and the wish themselves.[3]

We need not go further into the fact that every ethic, no matter how strict an opponent of eudaemonism it may at first appear to be, must somehow clandestinely smuggle the idea of happiness into its system. As Böhm-Bawerk has shown, the case is no different with "ethical" economics.[4] That the concepts of pleasure and pain contain no reference to the content of what is aimed at, ought, indeed, scarcely to be still open to misunderstanding.

Once this fact is established, the ground is removed from all the objections advanced by "ethical" economics and related schools. There may be men who aim at different ends from those of the men we know, but as long as there are men—that is, as long as they do not merely graze like animals or vegetate like plants, but act because they seek to attain goals—they will necessarily always be subject to the logic of action, the investigation of which is the task of our science. In this sense that science is universally human, and not limited by nationality, bound to a particular time, or contingent upon any social class. In this sense too it is logically prior to all historical and descriptive research.

4. ECONOMICS AND PSYCHOLOGY

The expression "Psychological School" is frequently employed as a designation of modern subjectivist economics. Occasionally too the difference in method that exists between the School of Lausanne and the Austrian School is indicated by attributing to the latter the "psychological" method. It is not surprising that the idea of economics as almost a branch of psychology or applied psychology should have arisen from such a habit of speech. Today, neither these misunderstandings nor their employment in the struggle carried on over the Austrian School are of anything more than historical and literary interest.

Nevertheless, the relationship of economics to psychology is still problematical. The position due Gossen's law of the satiation of wants yet remains to be clarified.

Perhaps it will be useful first to look at the route that had to be traversed in order to arrive at the modern treatment of the problem of price formation. In this way we shall best succeed in assigning Gossen's first law its position in the system, which is different from the one it occupied when it was first discovered.

The earlier attempts to investigate the laws of price determination foundered on the principle of universalism, which was accepted under the controlling influence of conceptual realism. The importance of nominalistic thought in antiquity, in the Middle Ages, and at the beginning of the modern era should not, of course, be underestimated. Nevertheless, it is certain that almost all attempts to comprehend social phenomena were at first undertaken on the basis of the principle of universalism. And on this basis they could not but fail hopelessly. Whoever wanted to explain prices saw, on the one hand, mankind, the state, and the corporative unit, and, on the other, classes of goods here and money there. There were also nominalistic attempts to solve these problems, and to them we owe the beginnings of the subjective theory of value. However, they were repeatedly stifled by the prestige of the prevailing conceptual realism.

Only the disintegration of the universalistic mentality brought about by the methodological individualism of the seventeenth and eighteenth centuries cleared the way for the development of a scientific catallactics. It was seen that on the market it is not mankind, the state, or the corporative unit that acts, but individual men and groups of men, and that *their* valuations and *their* action are decisive, not those of abstract collectivities. To recognize the relationship between valuation and use value and thus cope with the paradox of value, one had to realize that not classes of goods are involved in exchange, but concrete units of goods. This discovery signalized nothing less than a Copernican revolution in social science. Yet it required more than another hundred years for the step to be taken. This is a short span of time if we view the matter from the standpoint of world history and if we adequately appreciate the difficulties involved. But in the history of our science precisely this period acquired a special importance, inasmuch as it was during this time that the marvelous structure of Ricardo's system was first elaborated. In spite of the serious misunderstanding on which it was constructed, it became so fruitful that it rightly bears the designation "classical."

The step that leads from classical to modern economics is the realization that classes of goods in the abstract are never exchanged and valued, but always only concrete units of a class of goods.

If I want to buy or sell *one* loaf of bread, I do not take into consideration what "bread" is worth to mankind, or what all the bread currently available is worth, or what 10,000 loaves of bread are worth, but only the worth of the *one* loaf in question. This realization is not a deduction from Gossen's first law. It is attained through reflection on the essence of our action; or, expressed differently, the experience of our action makes any other supposition impossible for our thought.

We derive the law of the satiation of wants from this proposition and from the further realization, which is obtained by reflecting upon our action, that, in our scales of importance, we order individual units of goods not according to the classes of goods to which they belong or the classes of wants which they satisfy, but according to the concrete emergence of wants; that is to say, before one class of wants is fully satisfied we already proceed to the satisfaction of individual wants of other classes that we would not satisfy if one or several wants of the first class had not previously been satisfied.

Therefore, from our standpoint, Gossen's law has nothing to do with psychology. It is deduced by economics from reflections that are not of a psychological nature. The psychological law of satiation is independent of our law, though understandably in harmony with it, inasmuch as both refer to the same state of affairs. What distinguishes the two is the difference of method by which they have been arrived at. Psychology and economics are differentiated by their methods of viewing man.

To be sure, Bentham, who may be numbered among the greatest theorists of social science, and who stood at the peak of the economics of his time, arrived at our law by way of psychology and was unable to make any application of it to economics; and in Gossen's exposition it appeared as a psychological law, on which economic theory was then constructed. But these facts in no way invalidate the distinction that we have drawn between the laws of economics and those of psychology. Bentham's great intellect did not serve one science only. We do not know how Gossen arrived at his cognition, and it is a matter of indifference as far as answering our question is concerned. The investigation of the way in which this or that truth was first discovered is important only for history, not for a theoretical science. It is, of course, obvious that the position that Gossen then assigned the law in his system can have no authoritative standing in our view. And everyone knows that Menger, Jevons, and Walras did not arrive at the resolution of the paradox of value by way of Gossen's law.

5. ECONOMICS AND TECHNOLOGY

The system of economic theory is independent of all other sciences as well as of psychology. This is true also of its relationship to technology. By way of illustration we shall demonstrate this in the case of the law of returns.

Even historically the law of returns did not originate in technology, but in reflections on economics. One interpreted the fact that the farmer who wants to produce more also wants to extend the area under cultivation and that in doing so he even makes use of poorer soil. If the law of returns did not hold true, it could not be explained how there can be such a thing as "land hunger." Land would have to be a free good. The natural sciences, in developing a theory of agriculture, were unable either to substantiate or to confute these reflections "empirically." The experience that it took as its starting point was the fact that arable land is treated as an economic good.[5] It is obvious that here too economics and the natural sciences must meet on common ground.

One could not help finally expanding the law of diminishing returns on the cultivation of land into a general law of returns. If a good of higher order is treated as an economic good, then the law of returns—increasing returns up to a certain point, and beyond that point diminishing returns—must hold true of this good. Simple reflection shows that a good of higher order of which the law of returns did not hold true could never be regarded as an economic good: it would be indifferent to us whether larger or smaller quantities of this good were available.

The law of population is a special case of the law of returns. If the increase in the number of workers were always to bring about a proportional increase in returns, then the increase in the means of support would keep pace with the increase in population.

Whoever maintains, like Henry George, Franz Oppenheimer, and others, that the law of population is without practical importance assumes that hand in hand with every increase in population beyond the optimum necessarily go changes in technology or in the social division of labor such that at least no decrease in returns takes place per capita of the total population and perhaps even an increase in returns is thereby brought about. There is no proof for this assumption.

6. MONETARY CALCULATION AND THE "ECONOMIC IN THE NARROWER SENSE"

All action aims at results and takes on meaning only in relation to results. The preferring and setting aside that are involved in action take as their standard the importance of the anticipated result for the well-being of the actor. Whatever directly serves well-being is, without difficulty, given a rank in accordance with its importance, and this provides the rank order in which the goals of action stand at any given moment. How far it is possible to bring the relatively remote prerequisites of well-being into this rank order without resorting to more complicated processes of thought depends on the intelligence of the individual. It is certain, however, that even for the most gifted person the difficulties of weighing means and ends become insurmountable as soon as one goes beyond the simplest processes of production involving only a short period of time and few intermediary steps. Capitalistic production—in Böhm-Bawerk's sense, not in that of the Marxists—requires above all else the tool of economic calculation, through which expenditures of goods and of labor of different kinds become comparable. Those who act must be capable of recognizing which path leads to the goal aimed at with the least expenditure of means. This is the function of monetary calculation.

Money—that is, the generally used medium of exchange—thus becomes an indispensable mental prerequisite of any action that undertakes to conduct relatively long-range processes of production. Without the aid of monetary calculation, bookkeeping, and the computation of profit and loss in terms of money, technology would have had to confine itself to the simplest, and therefore the least productive, methods. If today economic calculation were again to disappear from production—as the result, for example, of the attainment of full socialization—then the whole structure of capitalistic production would be transformed within the shortest time into a desolate chaos, from which there could be no other way out than reversion to the economic condition of the most primitive cultures. Inasmuch as money prices of the means of production can be determined only in a social order in which they are privately owned, the proof of the impracticability of socialism necessarily follows.

From the standpoint of both politics and history, this proof is certainly the most important discovery made by economic theory. Its practical significance can scarcely be overestimated. It alone gives us the basis for pronouncing a final political judgment on all kinds of socialism, communism, and planned economies; and it alone will enable future historians to understand how it came about that the victory of the socialist movement did not lead to the creation of the socialist order of society. Here we need not go into this further. We must consider the problem of monetary calculation in another respect, namely, in its importance for the separation of action "economic in the narrower sense" from other action.

The characteristic feature of the mental tool provided by monetary calculation is responsible for the fact that the sphere in which it is employed appears to us as a special province within the wider domain of all action. In everyday, popular usage the sphere of the economic extends as far as monetary calculations are possible. Whatever goes beyond this is called the noneconomic sphere. We cannot acquiesce in this usage when it treats economic and noneconomic action as heterogeneous. We have seen that such a separation is misleading. However, the very fact that we see in economic calculation in terms of money the most important and, indeed, the indispensable mental tool of long-range production makes a terminological separation between these two

spheres appear expedient to us. In the light of the comments
above, we must reject the terms "economic" and "noneconomic"
or "uneconomic," but we can accept the terms "economic in the
narrower sense" and "economic in the broader sense," provided
one does not want to interpret them as indicating a difference in
the scope of rational and economic action.

(We may remark incidentally that monetary calculation is no
more a "function" of money than astronomical navigation is
a "function" of the stars.)

Economic calculation is either the calculation of future possibilities as the basis for the decisions that guide action, or the
subsequent ascertainment of the results, i.e., the computation of
profit and loss. In no respect can it be called "perfect." One of
the tasks of the theory of indirect exchange (the theory of money
and credit) consists precisely in showing the imperfection—or,
more correctly, the limits—of what this method is capable of.
Nevertheless, it is the only method available to a society based on
the division of labor when it wants to compare the input and the
output of its production processes. All attempts on the part of
the apologists of socialism to concoct a scheme for a "socialist
economic calculation" must, therefore, necessarily fail.

7. EXCHANGE RATIOS AND THE LIMITS
   OF MONETARY CALCULATION

The money prices of goods and services that we are able to
ascertain are the ratios in which these goods and services were
exchanged against money at a given moment of the relatively
recent or remote past. These ratios are always past; they always
belong to history. They correspond to a market situation that is
not the market situation of today.

Economic calculation is able to utilize to a certain extent
the prices of the market because, as a rule, they do not shift so
rapidly that such calculation could be essentially falsified by it.
Moreover, certain deviations and changes can be appraised with
so close an approximation to what really takes place later that

action—or "practice"—is able to manage quite well with monetary calculation notwithstanding all its deficiencies.

It cannot be emphasized strongly enough, however, that this practice is always the practice of the acting individual who wants to discover the result of his particular action (as far as it does not go beyond the orbit of the economic in the narrower sense). It always occurs within the framework of a social order based on private ownership of the means of production. It is the entrepreneur's calculation of profitability. It can never become anything more.

Therefore, it is absurd to want to apply the elements of this calculation to problems other than those confronting the individual actor. One may not extend them to *res extra commercium*. One may not attempt by means of them to include more than the sphere of the economic in the narrower sense. However, this is precisely what is attempted by those who undertake to ascertain the monetary value of human life, social institutions, national wealth, cultural ideals, or the like, or who enter upon highly sophisticated investigations to determine how exchange ratios of the relatively recent, not to mention the remote, past could be expressed in terms of "our money."

It is no less absurd to fall back upon monetary calculation when one seeks to contrast the productivity of action to its profitability. In comparing the profitability and the productivity of action, one compares the result as it appears to the individual acting within the social order of capitalism with the result as it would appear to the central director of an imaginary socialist community. (We may ignore for the sake of argument the fact that he would be completely unable to carry out such calculations.)

The height of conceptual confusion is reached when one tries to bring calculation to bear upon the problem of what is called the "social maximization of profit." Here the connection with the individual's calculation of profitability is intentionally abandoned in order to go beyond the "individualistic" and "atomistic" and arrive at "social" findings. And again one fails to see and will not see that the system of calculation is inseparably connected with the individual's calculation of profitability.

Monetary calculation is not the calculation, and certainly not the measurement, of value. Its basis is the comparison of the more important and the less important. It is an ordering according to rank, an act of grading (Čuhel), and not an act of measuring. It was a mistake to search for a measure of the value of goods. In the last analysis, economic calculation does not rest on the measurement of values, but on their arrangement in an order of rank.

8. CHANGES IN THE DATA

The universally valid theory of economic action is necessarily formal. Its material content consists of the data of human circumstances, which evoke action in the individual case: the goals at which men aim and the means by which they seek to attain them.[6]

The equilibrium position of the market corresponds to the specific configuration of the data. If the data change, then the equilibrium position also shifts. We grasp the effect of changes in the data by means of our theory. With its help we can also predict the quality—or, rather, the direction—of the changes that, *ceteris paribus*, must follow definite changes in the data. From the known extent of changes in the latter, we are unable to predetermine quantitatively what these consequent changes will be. For changes in external conditions must, in order to influence action, be translated into volitions that move men from within. We know nothing about this process. Even materialism, which professes to have solved the problem of the relation between the psychical and the physical by means of the famous simple formula that thinking stands in the same relationship to the brain as gall does to the bladder, has not even undertaken the attempt to establish a constant relationship between definite external events, which are quantitatively and qualitatively discernible, and thoughts and volitions.

All the endeavors that have been and are being devoted to the construction of a quantitative theory of catallactics must, therefore, come to grief. All that can be accomplished in this area is economic history. It can never go beyond the unique and the nonrepeatable; it can never acquire universal validity.[7]

9. THE ROLE OF TIME IN THE ECONOMY

Classical economics distinguished three factors of production: land, labor, and capital. Inasmuch as capital can be resolved into land and labor, two factors remain: labor and the "conditions of well-being" made available by nature. If consumption goods are disregarded, these alone, according to the view to be found in the older literature, are the objects of economizing.

The classical economists, whose attention was directed above all to the conduct of the businessman, could not observe that time too is economized. An account for "time" does not appear in the businessman's books. No price is paid for it on markets. That it is, nevertheless, taken into consideration in every exchange could not be seen from the standpoint of an objectivistic theory of value, nor could one be led to this realization by reflection on the popular precept contained in the saying, "Time is money." It was one of the great achievements of Jevons and Böhm-Bawerk that, in carrying on the work of Bentham and Rae, they assigned the element of time its proper place in the system of economic theory.

The classical economists failed to recognize the essential importance of time, which manifests its effect directly or indirectly in every exchange. They did not see that action always distinguishes between the present and the future—between present goods and future goods. Yet the time differential is important for the economy in still another respect. All changes in the data can make themselves felt only over a period of time. A longer or a shorter period must elapse before the new state of equilibrium, in accordance with the emergence of the new datum, can be reached. The static—or, as the classical economists called it, the natural—price is not reached immediately, but only after some time has passed. In the interim, deviations ensue that become the source of special profits and losses. The classical economists and their epigones not only did not fail to recognize this fact; on the contrary, they occasionally overestimated its importance. The modern theory too has paid special attention to it. This is true above all of the theory of indirect exchange. The theory of changes in the purchasing power of money and of their concomitant social consequences is based entirely on this fact. A short while ago, in a spirit of remarkable terminological and scholastic conscientiousness, an attempt was made to deny to the circulation credit theory of the trade cycle its customary name, viz., the monetary theory of crises, on the ground that it is constructed on the basis of a "time lag." [8]

As has been stated, economic theory has failed to see the importance of the fact that a shorter or a longer period of time must go by before the equilibrium of the market, once it has been disturbed by emergence of new data, can again be established. This assertion would never have been made if, for political reasons, repeated attempts had not been made to embarrass the discussion of economic questions with irrelevant objections. The defenders of interventionism have occasionally attempted to confront the arguments of the critics of this policy—arguments supported by the irrefutable deductions of economics—with the alleged fact that the propositions of economics hold true only in the long run. Therefore, it was maintained, the ineluctable conclusion that interventionist measures are senseless and inexpedient cannot yet be drawn. It would exceed the scope of this treatise to examine what force this argument has in the dispute over interventionism. It is sufficient here to point out that the liberal doctrine provides a direct, and not merely an indirect, demonstration of the senselessness and inexpediency of interventionism and that its arguments can be refuted only by pointing to interventionist measures that do not, in fact, bring about effects that run counter to the intentions of those who have recourse to them.

10. "RESISTANCES"

The economist is often prone to look to mechanics as a model for his own work. Instead of treating the problems posed by his science with the means appropriate to them, he fetches a metaphor from mechanics, which he puts in place of a solution. In this way the idea arose that the laws of catallactics hold true only ideally, i.e., on the assumption that men act in a vacuum, as it were. But, of course, in life everything happens quite differently. In life there are "frictional resistances" of all kinds, which are responsible for the fact that the outcome of our action is different from what the laws would lead one to expect. From the very outset no way was seen in which these resistances could be exactly measured or, indeed, fully comprehended even qualitatively. So one had to resign oneself to admitting that economics has but slight value both for the cognition of the relationships of our life in society and for actual practice. And, of course, all those who rejected economic science for political and related reasons—all the etatists, the socialists, and the interventionists—joyfully agreed.

Once the distinction between economic and noneconomic action is abandoned, it is not difficult to see that in all cases of "resistance" what is involved is the concrete data of economizing, which the theory comprehends fully.

For example, we deduce from our theory that when the price of a commodity rises, its production will be increased. However, if the expansion of production necessitates new investment of capital, which requires considerable time, a certain period of time will elapse before the price rise brings about an increase in supply. And if the new investment required to expand production would commit capital in such a way that conversion of invested capital goods in another branch of production is altogether impossible or, if possible, is so only at the cost of heavy losses, and if one is of the opinion that the price of the commodity will soon drop again, then the expansion of production does not take place at all. In the whole process there is nothing that the theory could not immediately explain to us.

Therefore, it is also incorrect to make the assertion that the propositions of the theory hold true only in the case of perfectly free competition. This objection must appear all the more remarkable as one could sooner assert that the modern theory of price determination has devoted too much attention to the problem of monopoly price. It certainly stands to reason that the propositions of the theory should first be examined with respect to the simplest case. Hence, it is not a legitimate criticism of economic theory that, in the investigation of competitive prices, it generally starts from the assumption that all goods are indefi-nitely divisible, that no obstacles stand in the way of the mobility of capital and labor, that no errors are made, etc. The subsequent dropping of these elementary assumptions one by one then affords no difficulty.

It is true that the classical economists inferred from their in-quiry into the problems of catallactics that, as far as practical eco-nomic policy is concerned, all the obstacles that interventionism places in the path of competition not only diminish the quantity and value of the total production, but cannot lead to the goals that one seeks to attain by such measures. The investigations that modern economics has devoted to the same problem lead to the identical conclusion. The fact that the politician must draw from the teachings of economic theory the inference that no obstacles should be placed in the way of competition unless one has the intention of lowering productivity does not imply that the theory is unable to cope with the "fettered" economy and "frictional resistances."

11. COSTS

By costs classical economics understood a quantity of goods and labor. From the standpoint of the modern theory, cost is the importance of the next most urgent want that can now no longer be satisfied. This conception of cost is clearly expressed outside the orbit of the economic in the narrower sense in a statement like the following, for example: The work involved in preparing for the examination cost me (i.e., prevented) the trip to Italy. Had I not had to study for the examination, I should have taken a trip to Italy.

Only if one employs this concept of cost does one realize the importance that attaches to profitability. The fact that production is discontinued beyond the point at which it ceases to be profitable means that production takes place only as far as the goods of higher order and the labor required to produce one commodity are not more urgently needed to produce other commodities. This observation shows how unwarranted is the popular practice of objecting to the limitation of production to profitable undertakings without also mentioning those enterprises that would have to be discontinued if others were maintained beyond the point of profitability.

The same observation also disposes of the assertion, made repeatedly, that the subjective theory of value does justice only to the private aspect of price formation and not to its economic implications for society as well. On the contrary, one could turn this objection around and argue that whoever traces the determination of prices to the costs of production alone does not go beyond the outlook of the individual businessman or producer. Only the reduction of the concept of cost to its ultimate basis, as carried out by the theory of marginal utility, brings the social aspect of economic action entirely into view.

Within the field of modern economics the Austrian School has shown its superiority to the School of Lausanne and the schools related to the latter, which favor mathematical formulations, by clarifying the causal relationship between value and cost, while at the same time eschewing the concept of function, which in our science is misleading. The Austrian School must also be credited with not having stopped at the concept of cost, but, on the contrary, with carrying on its investigations to the point where it is able to trace back even this concept to subjective value judgments.

Once one has correctly grasped the position of the concept of cost within the framework of modern science, one will have no difficulty in seeing that economics exhibits a continuity of development no less definite than that presented by the history of other sciences. The popular assertion that there are various schools of economics whose theories have nothing in common and that every economist begins by destroying the work of his predecessors in order to construct his own theory on its ruins is no more true than the other legends that the proponents of historicism, socialism, and interventionism have spread about economics. In fact, a straight line leads from the system of the classical economists to the subjectivist economics of the present. The latter is erected not on the ruins, but on the foundations, of the classical system. Modern economics has taken from its predecessor the best that it was able to offer. Without the work that the classical economists accomplished, it would not have been possible to advance to the discoveries of the modern school. Indeed, it was the uncertainties of the objectivistic school itself that necessarily led to the solutions offered by subjectivism. No work that had been devoted to the problem was done in vain. Everything that appears to those who have come afterward as a blind alley or at least as a wrong turning on the way toward a solution was necessary in order to exhaust all possibilities and to explore and think through to its logical conclusion every consideration to which the problems might lead.

NOTES

1. Cf. above pp. 82 ff.
2. Cf. Böhm-Bawerk, *Kapital und Kapitalzins,* Part II, Vol. I, p. 236, footnote.
3. According to Fr. A. Schmid, quoted by Jodl, *Geschichte der Ethik* (2nd ed.), II, 661.
4. Cf. Böhm-Bawerk's comments on Schmoller, *op. cit.,* p. 239, footnote; on Vierkandt, cf. above p. 55.
5. Cf. Böhm-Bawerk, *Gesammelte Schriften,* ed. by F. X. Weiss (Vienna, 1924), I, 193 ff.
6. Cf. the fruitful investigations of Strigl: *Die ökonomischen Kategorien und die Organisation der Wirtschaft* (Jena, 1923).
7. This is also true, for example, of the attempts of Moore in particular. (*Synthetic Economics,* New York, 1929.) Cf. the critique by Ricci, *Zeitschrift für Nationalökonomie,* I, 694 ff.
8. Cf. Burchardt, "Entwicklungsgeschichte der monetären Konjunkturtheorie," *Weltwirtschaftliches Archiv* XXVIII, 140; Löwe, "Über den Einfluss monetärer Faktoren auf den Konjunkturzylus," *Schriften des Vereins für Sozialpolitik,* CLXXIII, 362.

5

Remarks on the Fundamental Problem of the Subjective Theory of Value

The following essay makes no claim to originality. It presents nothing that was not already contained at least implicitly in the writings of the founders of the modern theory and explicitly in the works of present-day theorists and in my own writings. Nevertheless, I believe that what I am about to present here must be said once again, and precisely in this form, in order to put an end to the serious misunderstandings that modern economic theory repeatedly encounters.

What needs to be especially emphasized is that, above all others, Menger and Böhm-Bawerk are the ones responsible for this misunderstanding of the theory. Neither understood it in all its ramifications, and both in turn were themselves misunderstood. The writings of Menger and Böhm-Bawerk include propositions and concepts carried over from the objective theory of value and therefore utterly incompatible with the subjectivism of the modern school. The problem arises not so much from imperfections of theory, because there can be no doubt about the fundamental ideas of their system, as from stylistic faults in the presentation of it, which do not detract from the thought, but only from the writings in which it was expounded. It was not difficult for those who came afterward to find the right way and to present the ideas of the masters in logically developed form. But it may be conceded that it is not easy for everyone to avoid error here.

167

The great many who want to study the system, but who are not professional economists and turn only to the works of its masters, or who view subjectivist economics merely from the factional standpoint of its opponents, cannot help being led astray.

1.

The subjective theory of value traces the exchange ratios of the market back to the consumers' subjective valuations of economic goods. For catallactics the ultimate relevant cause of the exchange ratios of the market is the fact that the individual, in the act of exchange, prefers a definite quantity of good A to a definite quantity of good B. The reasons he may have for acting exactly thus and not otherwise—for example, the reasons why someone buys bread, and not milk, at a given moment—are of absolutely no importance for the determination of a market price. What is alone decisive is that the parties on the market are prepared to pay or to accept this price for bread and that price for milk. Individuals as consumers value goods exactly so much and no more or less at a given moment because of the operation of the social and the natural forces that determine their lives. The investigation of these determining factors is the task of other sciences, not that of economics. Economics, the science of catallactics, does not concern itself with them and, from its standpoint, cannot concern itself with them. Psychology, physiology, cultural history, and many other disciplines may make it their business to investigate why men like to drink alcohol; for catallactics what is alone of importance is that a demand for alcoholic beverages exists in a definite volume and strength. One person may buy Kant's works out of a thirst for knowledge; another, for reasons of snobbery. For the market, the motivation of the buyers' actions is indifferent. All that counts is that they are prepared to spend a definite sum.

This and nothing else is the essential element of the economic theory of wants. Only the historical development of economics as a science can explain why the meaning of this theory could be so much misunderstood that many even wanted to assign it entirely to psychology and to separate it altogether from catallactics, and still others could see in it only a materialistic theory of value and utility. The great problem with which economics has been incessantly occupied since its founding in the eighteenth century is the establishment of a relationship between human well-being and the valuing of the objects of economic action by economizing individuals. The older theory did not recognize that economic action in a social order based on private property is never an action of the whole of mankind, but always the action of individuals, and that it generally does not aim at the disposal of the entire supply of a good of a given type, but merely at the utilization of a definite part. Hence arose the problem of the paradox of value, which the earlier theory was helpless to resolve. Accordingly, in the treatment of the problem of value and price determination it was shunted onto a wrong track, became entangled more and more in a morass of untenable theorems, and finally failed completely.

The great service that modern economics performed consists in resolving the paradox of value. This was effected by the realization that economic action is always directed only toward the utilization of definite quantities of a good. "If I have to buy a horse," said Böhm-Bawerk,

it will not occur to me to form an opinion about how much a hundred horses, or how much all the horses in the world, would be worth to me, and then to adjust my bid accordingly; but I shall, of course, make a judgment of value about one horse. And in this way, by virtue of an inner compulsion, we always make exactly that value judgment which the concrete situation requires.[1]

Economic action is always in accord only with the importance that acting man attaches to the limited quantities among which he must directly choose. It does not refer to the importance that the total supply at his disposal has for him nor to the altogether impractical judgment of the social philosopher concerning the importance for humanity of the total supply that men can obtain. The recognition of this fact is the essence of the modern theory. It is independent of all psychological and ethical considerations. However, it was advanced at the same time as the law of the satiation of wants and of the decrease in the marginal utility of the unit in an increasing supply. All attention was turned toward this law, and it was mistakenly regarded as the chief and basic law of the new theory. Indeed, the latter was more often called the theory of diminishing marginal utility than the doctrine of the subjectivist school, which would have been more suitable and would have avoided misunderstandings.

2.

The fact that modern economics starts from acting man's subjective valuations and the action that is governed by these valuations, and not from any kind of objectively "correct" scale of values, is so familiar to everyone who is even slightly conversant with modern catallactics or who has thought only very little about the meaning of the terms "supply" and "demand" that it would be out of place to waste any more words on it. That it is frequently attacked by authors whose stand is opposed to that of subjective economics—for example, recently by Diehl [2]—is the result of such crass misunderstanding of the entire theory that it can be passed over without further discussion. Modern economics cannot be more clearly characterized than by the phrase "subjective use value." The explanation that the new theory gives of the phenomena of the market does not have as its basis any "scale of wants which is constructed on rational principles," [3] as Diehl maintains. The scale of wants or of values, of which the theory speaks, is not "constructed." We infer it from the action of the individual or even—whether or not this is permissible can remain undecided here—from his statements about how he would act under certain assumed conditions.

Diehl considers it obviously absurd to draw on "fanciful wishes, desires, etc." for an explanation and thinks that in that case value would be determined by "the subjective whims of each individual" and thereby "the theory of marginal utility would lose all meaning." [4] Here he has indeed been misled by the oft-lamented ambiguity of the term "value," whose meaning for catallactics must not be confused with the "absolute" values of ethics. For no one will want to doubt that market prices, the formation of which we have to explain, really are influenced by "fanciful wishes" and caprices in exactly the same way as by motives that appear rational in Diehl's eyes. Let Diehl try some time to explain, without referring to "fanciful wishes and desires," the formation of the prices of goods that fluctuate in response to changes in fashion! Catallactics has the task of explaining the formation of the exchange ratios of economic goods that are actually observed in the market, and not those which would come about if all men were to act in a way that some critic regards as rational.

All this is so clear, as has been said, that no one will doubt it. It cannot be the task of this essay to belabor the obvious by attempting to prove it in detail. On the contrary, what we intend is something altogether different. We have already pointed out that Menger and Böhm-Bawerk made statements in various passages of their writings that are utterly incompatible with the basic principles they advanced. It should not be forgotten that the two masters, like all pioneers and trail blazers, had first assimilated the old concepts and ideas that had come down from earlier days and only later substituted more satisfactory concepts and ideas for them. It is humanly excusable, even if it is not objectively justifiable, that occasionally they were not consistent in the elaboration of their great fundamental ideas and that in details they clung to assertions stemming from the conceptual structure of the old, objective theory of value. A critical consideration of this insufficiency of the work of the founders of the Austrian School is an absolute necessity, since they seem to present great difficulties to many readers who attempt to understand the theory. For this reason I wish to select a passage from the chief work of each.[5]

In the preface to the first edition of his *Principles of Economics,* Menger describes the "proper subject matter of our science," i.e., theoretical economics, as the investigation of the "conditions under which men display provisionary activity that aims at the satisfaction of their wants." He illustrates this in the following words:

Whether and under what conditions a thing is useful to me; whether and under what conditions it is a good; whether and under what conditions it is an economic good; whether and under what conditions it has value to me, and how great the measure of this value is to me; whether and under what conditions an economic exchange of goods between two parties can take place; and the margins within which prices can be formed in such an exchange; and so on.[6]

This, according to Menger, is the subject matter of economics. It should be noted how the subjectivity of the phenomena of value is repeatedly emphasized by means of the personal pronoun "me": "useful to me," "value to me," "measure of this value to me," etc.

Unfortunately, Menger did not adhere to this principle of subjectivity in his description of the qualities that make things goods in the economic sense. Although he cites Storch's beautiful definition (*l'arrêt que notre jugement porte sur l'utilité des choses . . . en fait des biens*), he declares that the presence of all four of the following prerequisites is necessary for a thing to become a good:

1. A human want.
2. Such properties of the thing as enable it to be placed in a causal relation with the satisfaction of this want.
3. Knowledge of this causal relation on the part of a human being.
4. The ability to direct the employment of the thing in such a way that it actually can be used for the satisfaction of this want.[7]

The fourth prerequisite does not concern us here. There is nothing to criticize in the first requirement. As far as it is understood in this connection, it corresponds completely to the fundamental idea of subjectivism, viz., that in the case of the individual he alone decides what is or is not a need. Of course, we can only conjecture that this was Menger's opinion when he wrote the first edition. It is to be noted that Menger cited Roscher's definition (everything that is acknowledged as useful for the satisfaction of a *real* human want) along with many definitions[8] of other predecessors, without going further into the matter.

However, in the posthumous second edition of his book, which appeared more than half a century later and which (apart from the section on money, published long before in the *Handwörterbuch der Staatswissenschaften*) can in no way be called an improvement over the epoch-making first edition, Menger distinguishes between real and imaginary wants. The latter are those which do not in fact originate from the nature of the person or from his position as a member of a social body, but are only the result of defective knowledge of the exigencies of his nature and of his position in human society.[9]

Menger adds the observation:

The practical economic life of men is determined not by their wants, but by their momentary opinions about the exigencies of the preservation of their lives and well-being; indeed, often by their lusts and instincts. Rational theory and practical economics will have to enter into the investigation of real wants, i.e., wants which correspond to the objective state of affairs.[10]

To refute this notorious slip it suffices to quote some of Menger's own words a few lines below those just cited. There we read:

The opinion that physical wants alone are the subject matter of our science is erroneous. The conception of it as merely a theory of the physical well-being of man is untenable. If we wished to limit ourselves exclusively to the consideration of the physical wants of men, we should be able, as we shall see, to explain the phenomena of human economic action only very imperfectly and in part not at all.[11]

Here Menger has said all that needs to be said on this subject. The case is exactly the same with regard to the distinction between real and imaginary wants as it is in regard to the distinction between physical and nonphysical wants.

It follows from the preceding quotations that the second and the third prerequisites for a thing to become a good would have to read: the *opinion* of the economizing individuals that the thing is capable of satisfying their wants. This makes it possible to speak of a category of "imaginary" goods. The case of imaginary goods, Menger maintains, is to be observed

where things which in no way can be placed in a causal relation with the satisfaction of human wants are nonetheless treated as goods. This happens when properties, and thus effects, are attributed to things to which in reality they do not belong or when human wants that in reality are not present are falsely presumed to exist.[12]

To realize how pointless this dichotomy between real and imaginary goods is, one need only consider the examples cited by Menger. Among others, he designates as imaginary goods utensils used in idolatry, most cosmetics, etc. Yet prices are demanded and offered for these things too, and we have to explain these prices.

The basis of subjective use value is described very differently, but completely in the spirit of the theories that Menger elaborated in the latter sections of his basic work, in the words of C. A. Verrijn Stuart: A man's valuation of goods is based on "his insight into their usefulness," in which sense anything can be conceived as useful "that is the goal of any human desire, whether justified or not. It is for this reason that such goods can satisfy a human want." [13]

3.

Böhm-Bawerk expresses the opinion that the treatment of the theory of price determination should be divided into two parts.

The first part has the task of formulating the law of the fundamental phenomenon in all its purity; that is, to deduce all propositions following from the law that lead to the phenomena of prices on the hypothesis that for all persons interested in exchange the only impelling motive is the desire to attain a direct gain in the transaction. To the second part falls the task of combining the law of the fundamental phenomenon with modifications that result from factual conditions and the emergence of other motives. This will be the place to . . . demonstrate the influence that such commonly felt and typical "motives" as habit, custom, fairness, humanity, generosity, comfort or convenience, pride, race and nationality, hatred, etc. have in the determination of prices.[14]

In order to arrive at a correct judgment of this argument, one must note the difference that exists between classical and modern economics in the starting points of their investigations. Classical economics starts from the action of the businessman in that it places exchange value, and not use value, at the center of its treatment of the problem of price determination. Since it could not succeed in resolving the paradox of value, it had to forgo tracing the phenomenon of price determination further back and disclosing what lies behind the conduct of the businessman and governs it in every instance, viz., the conduct of the marginal consumers. Only a theory of utility, i.e, of subjective use value, can explain the action of the consumers. If such a theory cannot be formulated, any attempt at an explanation must be renounced. One certainly was not justified in leveling against the classical theory the reproach that it starts from the assumption that all men are businessmen and act like members of a stock exchange. However, it is true that the classical doctrine was not capable of comprehending the most fundamental element of economics—consumption and the direct satisfaction of a want.

Because the classical economists were able to explain only the action of businessmen and were helpless in the face of everything that went beyond it, their thinking was oriented toward bookkeeping, the supreme expression of the rationality of the businessman (but not that of the consumer). Whatever cannot be entered into the businessman's accounts they were unable to accommodate in their theory. This explains several of their ideas—for example, their position in regard to personal services. The performance of a service which caused no increase in value that could be expressed in the ledger of the businessman had to appear to them as unproductive. Only thus can it be explained why they regarded the attainment of the greatest monetary profit possible as the goal of economic action. Because of the difficulties occasioned by the paradox of value, they were unable to find a bridge from the realization, which they owed to utilitarianism, that the goal of action is an increase of pleasure and a decrease of pain, to the theory of value and price. Therefore, they were unable to comprehend any change in well-being that cannot be valued in money in the account books of the businessman.

This fact necessarily led to a distinction between economic and noneconomic action. Whoever sees and grasps the opportunity to make the cheapest purchase (in money) has acted economically. But whoever has purchased at a higher price than he could have, either out of error, ignorance, incapacity, laziness, neglectfulness, or for political, nationalistic, or religious reasons, has acted non-economically. It is evident that this grading of action already contains an ethical coloration. A norm soon develops from the distinction between the two groups of motives: You should act economically. You should buy in the cheapest market and sell in the dearest market. In buying and selling you should know no other goal than the greatest monetary profit.

It has already been shown that the situation is altogether different for the subjective theory of value. There is little sense in distinguishing between economic and other motives in explaining the determination of prices if one starts with the action of the marginal consumer and not with that of the businessman.

This can be clearly illustrated by an example drawn from the conditions of a politically disputed territory, let us say Czechoslovakia. A German intends to join a chauvinistic, athletic-military organization and wants to acquire the necessary outfit and paraphernalia for it. If he could make this purchase more cheaply in a store run by a Czech, then we should have to say, if we make such a distinction among motives, that in buying at a slightly higher price in a store run by a German in order to give his business to a fellow national, he would be acting uneconomically. Yet it is clear that the whole purchase as such would have to be called uneconomic, since the procuring of the outfit itself is to serve a chauvinistic purpose just as much as helping a fellow national by not considering the possibility of making a cheaper purchase from a foreigner. But then many other expenditures would have to be called uneconomic, each according to the taste of whoever judges them: contributions for all kinds of cultural or political purposes, expenditures for churches, most educational expenses, etc. One can see how ridiculous such scholastic distinctions are. The maxims of the businessman cannot be applied to the action of the consumers, which, in the last analysis, governs all business.

On the other hand, it is possible for the subjective theory of value to comprehend from its standpoint also the action of the businessman (whether he is a manufacturer or only a merchant) precisely because it starts from the action of the consumers. Under the pressure of the market the businessman must always act in accordance with the wishes of the marginal consumers. For the same reason that he cannot, without suffering a loss, produce fabrics that do not suit the taste of the consumers, he cannot, without taking a loss, act on the basis of political considerations that are not acknowledged and accepted by his customers. Therefore, the businessman must purchase from the cheapest source, without any such considerations, if those whose patronage he seeks are not prepared, for political reasons, to compensate him for his increased expenses in paying higher prices to a fellow national. But if the consumers themselves—let us say in purchasing trade-marked articles—are prepared to compensate him, he will conduct his business affairs accordingly.

If we take the other examples cited by Böhm-Bawerk and go through the whole series, we shall find the same thing in each case. Custom requires that in the evening a man of "good" society appear in evening clothes. If somewhere the prejudices of the circle in which he lives demand that the suit not come from the shop of a radical tailor, where it can be bought more cheaply, but that it be procured from the more expensive shop of a tailor with conservative leanings, and if our man acts in accordance with these views, he follows no other motive in doing so than that of getting a suit in general. In both instances, in agreeing to purchase evening clothes in the first place, and in procuring them from the tailor with conservative leanings, he acts in accordance with the views of his circle, which he acknowledges as authoritative for himself.

What is that "direct gain in the exchange" which Böhm-Bawerk speaks of? When, for humanitarian reasons, I do not buy pencils in the stationery store, but make my purchase from a war-wounded peddler who asks a higher price, I aim at two goals at the same time: that of obtaining pencils and that of assisting an invalid. If I did not think this second purpose worthy of the expense involved, I should buy in the store. With the more expensive purchase I satisfy two wants: that for pencils and that of helping a war veteran. When, for reasons of "comfort and convenience," I pay more in a nearby store rather than buy more cheaply in one further away, I satisfy my desire for "comfort and convenience," in the same way as by buying an easy chair or by using a taxi or by hiring a maid to keep my room in order. It cannot be denied that in all these instances I make a "direct gain in the exchange" in the sense intended by Böhm-Bawerk. Why, then, should the case be any different when I buy in a nearby store?

Böhm-Bawerk's distinction can be understood only when it is recognized as a tenet taken over from the older, objective system of classical economics. It is not at all compatible with the system of subjective economics. But in saying this, we must emphasize that such a dichotomy had not the slightest influence on Böhm-Bawerk's theory of value and price determination and that the pages in which it is propounded could be removed from his book without changing anything significant in it. In the context of this work it represents nothing more than—as we believe we have shown—an unsuccessful defense against the objections that had been raised against the possibility of a theory of value and price determination.

Strigl expresses the matter more nearly in accordance with the subjective system than does Böhm-Bawerk. He points out that the scale of values "is fundamentally composed also of elements that popular usage treats as noneconomic in contrast to the economic principle." Therefore, the "maximum quantity of available goods cannot be opposed, as 'economic,' to the 'uneconomic' goals of action." [15]

For the comprehension of economic phenomena it is quite permissible to distinguish "purely economic" action from other action which, if one wishes, may be called "noneconomic," or "uneconomic" in popular usage, provided it is understood that "purely economic" action is necessarily susceptible of calculation in terms of money. Indeed, both for the scientific study of phenomena and for the practical conduct of men, there may even be good reason to make this distinction and perhaps to say that under given conditions it is not advisable, from the "purely economic" point of view, to manifest a certain conviction or that some course of action is "bad business," that is to say, it cannot involve a monetary gain, but only losses. If, nevertheless, one persists in acting in that way, he has done so not for the sake of monetary gain, but for reasons of honor or loyalty or for the sake of other ethical values. But for the theory of value and price determination, catallactics, and theoretical economics, this dichotomy has no significance. For it is a matter of complete indifference for the exchange ratios of the market, the explanation of which is the task of these disciplines, whether the demand for domestic products arises because they cost less money than foreign goods (of the same quality, of course) or because nationalist ideology makes the purchase of domestic products even at a higher price seem right; just as, from the point of view of economic theory, the situation remains the same whether the demand for weapons comes from honorable men who want to enforce the law or from criminals who are planning monstrous crimes.

4.

The much talked about *homo economicus* of the classical theory is the personification of the principles of the businessman. The businessman wants to conduct every business with the highest possible profit: he wants to buy as cheaply as possible and sell as dearly as possible. By means of diligence and attention to business he strives to eliminate all sources of error so that the results of his action are not prejudiced by ignorance, neglectfulness, mistakes, and the like.

Therefore, the *homo economicus* is not a fiction in Vaihinger's sense. Classical economics did not assert that the economizing individual, whether engaged in trade or as a consumer, acts as if the greatest monetary profit were the sole guiding principle of his conduct. The classical scheme is not at all applicable to consumption or the consumer. It could in no way comprehend the act of consumption or the consumer's expenditure of money. The principle of buying on the cheapest market comes into question here only in so far as the choice is between several possibilities, otherwise equal, of purchasing goods; but it cannot be understood, from this point of view, why someone buys the better suit even though the cheaper one has the same "objective" usefulness, or why more is generally spent than is necessary for the minimum —taken in the strictest sense of the term—necessary for bare physical subsistence. It did not escape even the classical economists that the economizing individual as a party engaged in trade does not always and cannot always remain true to the principles governing the businessman, that he is not omniscient, that he can err, and that, under certain conditions, he even prefers his comfort to a profit-making business.

On the contrary, it could be said that with the scheme of the *homo economicus* classical economics comprehended only one side of man—the economic, materialistic side. It observed him only as a man engaged in business, not as a consumer of economic goods. This would be a pertinent observation in so far as the classical theory is inapplicable to the conduct of the consumers. On the other hand, it is not a pertinent observation in so far as it is understood as meaning that, according to classical economic theory, a person engaged in business always acts in the manner described. What classical economics asserts is only that in general he tends to act in this way, but that he does not always conduct himself, with or without such an intention, in conformity with this principle.

Yet neither is the *homo economicus* an ideal type in Max Weber's sense. Classical economics did not want to exalt a certain human type—for example, the English businessman of the nineteenth century, or the businessman in general. As genuine praxeology—and economics is a branch of praxeology—it aspired to a universal, timeless understanding that would embrace all economic action. (That it could not succeed in this endeavor is another matter.) But this is something that can only be indicated here. To make it evident, it would have to be shown that an ideal type cannot be constructed on the basis of a formal, theoretical science like praxeology, but only on the basis of concrete historical data.[16] However, such a task goes beyond the scope of this discussion.

By means of its subjectivism the modern theory becomes objective science. It does not pass judgment on action, but takes it exactly as it is; and it explains market phenomena not on the basis of "right" action, but on the basis of given action. It does not seek to explain the exchange ratios that would exist on the supposition that men are governed exclusively by certain motives and that other motives, which do in fact govern them, have no effect. It wants to comprehend the formation of the exchange ratios that actually appear in the market.

The determination of the prices of what Menger calls "imaginary goods" follows the same laws as that of "real goods." Böhm-Bawerk's "other motives" cause no fundamental alteration in the market process; they change only the data.

It was necessary to expressly point out these mistakes of Menger and Böhm-Bawerk (which, as we have noted above, are also encountered in other authors) in order to avoid misinterpretations of the theory. But all the more emphatically must it be stated that neither Menger nor Böhm-Bawerk allowed themselves to be misled in any way in the development of their theory of price determination and imputation by consideration for the differences in the motives that lie behind the action of the parties on the market. The assertions that were designated as erroneous in the preceding remarks did not in the least detract from the great merit of their work: to explain the determination of prices in terms of the subjective theory of value.

NOTES

1. Cf. Böhm-Bawerk, "Grunzüge der Theorie des wirtschaftlichen Güterwerts," *Jahrb. f. Nationalökonomie und Statistik,* New Series, XIII, 16; also *Kapital und Kapitalzins* (3rd ed.; Innsbruck, 1909), Part II, p. 228.
2. Cf. Diehl, *Theoretische Nationalökonomie* (Jena, 1916), I, 287; (Jena, 1927), III, 82-87. Against this, cf. my essays in *Arch. für Geschichte des Sozialismus,* X, 93 ff.
3. *Loc. cit.,* Vol. III, p. 85.
4. *Ibid.*
5. With regard to the problem of the measurement of value and of total value, which will not be treated further here, I have attempted a critical examination of the works of a few of the older representatives of the modern theory of value in my book, *The Theory of Money and Credit* (Yale University Press), pp. 38-47.
6. Menger, *Grundsätze der Volkswirtschaftslehre* (Vienna, 1871), p. ix; (2nd ed.; Vienna, 1923), p. xxi.
7. Cf. Menger, *op. cit.* (1st ed.), p. 3.
8. *Ibid.,* p. 2.
9. *Ibid.,* 2nd ed., p. 4.

10. *Ibid.*, p. 4 *et seq.*
11. *Ibid.*, p. 5.
12. *Ibid.*, p. 4; 2nd ed., pp. 161 f.
13. C. A. Verrijn Stuart, *Die Grundlagen der Volkswirtschaft* (Jena, 1923), p. 94.
14. Cf. Böhm-Bawerk, *Kapital und Kapitalzins*, II, 354.
15. Strigl, *Die ökonomischen Kategorien und die Organisation der Wirtschaft* (Jena, 1923), p. 75 *et seq.* Cf. further *ibid.*, pp. 146 ff.
16. Cf. above pp. 75 ff.

6

The Psychological Basis
of the Opposition
to Economic Theory

Subjectivist economics would be guilty of an omission if it did not also concern itself with the objections that have been raised against it from political and factional standpoints.

There is, first of all, the assertion that the subjective theory of value is "the class ideology of the bourgeoisie." For Hilferding it is "bourgeois economics' final answer to socialism." [1] Bucharin stigmatizes it as "the ideology of the bourgeoisie, which even now no longer corresponds to the process of production." [2] One is free to think what one will about these two authors, but it is to be noted that they belong to the ruling groups of the two most populous states in Europe and are therefore very capable of influencing public opinion. The millions of people who come into contact with no other writings than those distributed by the Marxist propaganda machine learn nothing of modern economics beyond these and similar condemnations.

Then we must consider the views of those who believe it to be significant that subjectivist economics is deliberately not taught at the universities. Even Adolf Weber, who knew enough to criticize the prejudices of academic socialism, comes very close to resorting to this argument.[3] It is completely in accord with the etatist thinking prevalent everywhere today to consider a theory to be finally disposed of merely because the authorities who control appoint-

183

ments to academic positions want to know nothing of it, and to see the criterion of truth in the approval of a government office.

No one will argue that views so widespread can simply be passed over in silence.

1. THE PROBLEM

Every new theory encounters opposition and rejection at first. The adherents of the old, accepted doctrine object to the new theory, refuse it recognition, and declare it to be mistaken. Years, even decades, must pass before it succeeds in supplanting the old one. A new generation must grow up before its victory is decisive.

To understand this one must remember that most men are accessible to new ideas only in their youth. With the progress of age the ability to welcome them diminishes, and the knowledge acquired earlier turns into dogma. In addition to this inner resistance, there is also the opposition that develops out of regard for external considerations. A man's prestige suffers when he sees himself obliged to admit that for a long time he has supported a theory that is now recognized as mistaken. His vanity is affected when he must concede that others have found the better theory that he himself was unable to find.[4] And in the course of time the authority of the public institutions of compulsion and coercion, i.e., of state, church, and political parties, has somehow become very much involved with the old theory. These powers, by their very nature unfriendly to every change, now oppose the new theory precisely because it is new.

However, when we speak of the opposition that the subjective theory of value encounters, we have something different in mind from these obstacles, which every new idea must overcome. The phenomenon with which we are confronted in this case is not one that touches all branches of human thought and knowledge. The opposition here is not mere resistance to the new because it is new. It is of a kind to be found exclusively in the history of praxeological, and especially of economic, thought. It is a case of hostility to science as such—a hostility that the years have not only not dispelled or weakened, but, on the contrary, have strengthened.

What is at issue here is not alone the subjective theory of value, but catallactics in general. This can best be seen from the fact that today there is no longer a single theory of price determination that opposes that of subjectivism. Now and then a Marxist party official tries to defend the labor theory of value. For the rest, no one dares to expound a doctrine essentially different from the subjective theory. All discussions concerning the theory of price determination are based completely on the latter theory of value, even if many authors—like Liefmann and Cassel, for example— believe that what they are saying is very different. Today whoever rejects the subjective theory of value also rejects every economic theory and wants to admit nothing but empiricism and history into the scientific treatment of social problems.

It has already been shown in earlier sections of this book what logic and epistemology have to say about this position. In this section we shall deal with the psychological roots of the rejection of the subjective theory of value.

Therefore, we need not consider the hostility that the sciences of human action encounter from without. There is, to be sure, enough of such external opposition, but it is scarcely capable of arresting the progress of scientific thought. One must be very strongly prepossessed by an etatist bias to believe that the proscription of a doctrine by the coercive apparatus of the state and the refusal to place its supporters in positions in the church or in government service could ever do injury to its development and dissemination in the long run. Even burning heretics at the stake was unable to block the progress of modern science. It is a matter of indifference for the fate of the sciences of human action whether or not they are taught at the tax-supported universities of Europe or to American college students in the hours not occupied by sports and amusements. But it has been possible in most schools to dare to substitute for praxeology and economics subjects that intentionally avoid all reference to praxeological and economic thought only because internal opposition is present to justify this practice. Whoever wants to examine the external difficulties that beset our science must first of all concern himself with those which arise from within.

The results of praxeological and historical investigation encounter opposition from those who, in the conduct of their discussion, treat all logic and experience with contempt. This peculiar phenomenon cannot be explained merely by saying that whoever sacrifices his conviction in favor of views that are popular with the authorities is generally well rewarded. A scientific investigation may not descend to the low level at which blind partisan hatred has carried on the struggle against the science of economics. It may not simply turn against its opponents the epithets that Marx used when he described the "bourgeois, vulgar" economists as villainous literary hirelings. (In doing so, he liked to use the word "sycophant," which he apparently altogether misunderstood.) Nor may it adopt the bellicose tactics with which the German academic socialists seek to suppress all opponents.[5] Even if one were to consider oneself justified in denying the intellectual honesty of all those opposed to the subjective theory of price determination, there would still be the question why public opinion tolerates and accepts such spokesmen and does not follow the true prophets rather than the false.[6]

2. THE HYPOTHESIS OF MARXISM AND THE SOCIOLOGY
   OF KNOWLEDGE

Let us consider first the doctrine which teaches that thought is dependent upon the class of the thinker.

According to the Marxian view, in the period between the tribal society of the golden age of times immemorial and the transformation of capitalism into the communist paradise of the future, human society is organized into classes whose interests stand in irreconcilable opposition. The class situation—the social existence—of an individual determines his thought. Therefore, thinking produces theories that correspond to the class interests of the thinker. These theories form the "ideological superstructure" of class interests. They are apologies for the latter and serve to cover up their nakedness. Subjectively, the individual thinker may be honest. However, it is not possible for him to pass beyond the limitations imposed on his thinking by his class situation. He is able to reveal and unmask the ideologies of other classes, but he remains throughout his life biased in favor of the ideology that his own class interests dictate.

In the volumes that have been written in defense of this thesis the question is—characteristically—almost never raised whether there is any truth in the supposition that society is divided into classes whose interests stand in irreconcilable conflict.[7] For Marx the case was obvious. In Ricardo's system of catallactics he found, or at least believed that he had found, the doctrine of the organization of society into classes and of the conflict of classes. Today, Ricardo's theories of value, price determination, and distribution have long since been outmoded, and the subjective theory of distribution offers not the slightest basis of support for a doctrine of implacable class conflict. One can no longer cling to such a notion once one has grasped the significance of marginal productivity for income determination.

But since Marxism and the sociology of knowledge see in the subjective theory of value nothing more than a final ideological attempt to save capitalism, we wish to limit ourselves to an immanent critique of their theses. As Marx himself admits, the proletarian has not only class interests, but other interests that are opposed to them. The Communist Manifesto says: "The organization of the proletarians into a class and thereby into a political party is repeatedly frustrated by the competition among the workers themselves." [8] Therefore, it is not true that the proletarian has only class interests. He also has other interests that are in conflict with them. Which, then, should he follow? The Marxist will answer: "Of course, his class interests, for they stand above all others." But this is no longer by any means a matter "of course." As soon as one admits that action in conformity with other interests is also possible, the question is not one concerning what "is," but what "ought to be." Marxism does not say of the proletarians that they *cannot* follow interests other than those of their class. It says to the proletarians: You are a class and *should* follow your class interests; become a class by thinking and acting in conformity with your class interests. But then it is incumbent upon Marxism to prove that class interests ought to take precedence over other interests.

Even if we were to assume that society is divided into classes with conflicting interests and if we were to agree that everyone is morally obliged to follow his class interests and nothing but his class interests, the question would still remain: What best serves class interests? This is the point where "scientific" socialism and the "sociology of knowledge" show their mysticism. They assume without hesitation that whatever is demanded by one's class interests is always immediately evident and unequivocal.[9] The comrade who is of a different opinion can only be a traitor to his class.

What reply can Marxian socialism make to those who, precisely on behalf of the proletarians, demand private ownership of the means of production, and not their socialization? If they are proletarians, this demand alone is sufficient to brand them as traitors to their class, or, if they are not proletarians, as class enemies. Or if, finally, the Marxists do choose to engage in a discussion of the problems, they thereby abandon their doctrine; for how can one argue with traitors to one's class or with class enemies, whose moral inferiority or class situation makes it impossible for them to comprehend the ideology of the proletariat?

The historical function of the theory of classes can best be understood when it is compared to the theory of the nationalists. Nationalism and racism also declare that there are irreconcilable conflicts of interests—not between classes, of course, but between nations and races—and that one's thinking is determined by one's nationality or race. The nationalists form "Fatherland" and "National" parties, which boast that they and they alone pursue the goals that serve the welfare of the nation and the people. Whoever does not agree with them—whether or not he belongs to their nationality—is forever after regarded as an enemy or a traitor. The nationalist refuses to be convinced that the programs of other parties also seek to serve the interests of the nation and the people. He cannot believe that the man who wants to live in peace with neighboring countries or who advocates free trade rather than protective tariffs does not make these demands in the interests of

a foreign country, but likewise wishes to act, and thinks he is acting, in the interests of his own country. The nationalist believes so
adamantly in his own program that he simply cannot conceive
how any other could possibly be in the interests of his nation.
Whoever thinks differently can only be a traitor or a foreign
enemy.

Consequently, both doctrines—the Marxian sociology of knowledge as well as the political theory of nationalism and racism—
share the assumption that the interests of one's class, nation, or
race unequivocally demand a definite course of action and that
for the members of a class or nationality, or for the racially pure,
no doubt can arise about what this should be. An intellectual discussion of the pros and cons of different party programs seems
unthinkable to them. Class membership, nationality, or racial
endowment allow the thinker no choice: he must think in the
way his being demands. Of course, such theories are possible only
if one has drawn up beforehand a perfect program, which it is
forbidden even to doubt. Logically and temporally Marx's acceptance of socialism precedes the materialist conception of history, and the doctrine of militarism and protectionism logically
and temporally precedes the program of the nationalists.

Both theories also arose from the same political situation. No
logical or scientific arguments whatsoever could or can be brought
against the theories of liberalism, which were developed by the
philosophers, economists, and praxeologists of the eighteenth and
of the first half of the nineteenth centuries. Whoever wishes to combat these doctrines has no other means available than to dethrone
logic and science by attacking their claim to establish universally
valid propositions. To the "absolutism" of their explanations it is
countered that they produced only "bourgeois," "English," or
"Jewish" science; "proletarian," "German," or "Aryan" science
has arrived at different results. The fact that the Marxists, from
Marx and Dietzgen down to Mannheim, are eager to assign to
their own teachings a special position designed to raise them above
the rank of a mere class theory is inconsistent enough, but need
not be considered here. Instead of refuting theories, one unmasks
their authors and supporters.

What makes this procedure a matter of serious concern is that, if adhered to in practice, it renders impossible every discussion involving argument and counterargument. The battle of minds is replaced by the examination of opponents' social, national, or racial backgrounds. Because of the vagueness of the concepts of class, nation, and race, it is always possible to conclude such an examination by "unmasking" one's opponent. It has gone so far that one acknowledges as comrades, fellow countrymen, or racial brothers only those who share the ideas that are alone presumed adequate to such a status. (It is a sign of a special lack of consistency to appeal to the evidence of the existence of supporters for one's ideology who are outside the circle of members of one's own class, nation, or race, with such expressions as: "Even those not of our own class, nation, or race must share our view if they are enlightened and honest.") A rule for determining the doctrine that would be adequate to one's being is unfortunately not stated, nor, indeed, can it ever be stated. A decision by the majority of those belonging to the group is expressly rejected as a criterion.

The three axioms that these antiliberal doctrines all assume are:

1. Mankind is divided into groups whose interests are in irreconcilable conflict.

2. Group interests and the course of action that best serves them are immediately evident to every member of every group.

3. The criterion of the separation into groups is (a) membership in a class, (b) membership in a nationality, or (c) membership in a race.

The first and the second propositions are common to all these doctrines; they are distinguished by the particular meaning that they give to the third.

It is regrettable that each of these three propositions taken individually, or the conjunction of all three into one, is completely lacking in the self-evidence and logical necessity required of axioms. If, unfortunately, they are not capable of proof, one cannot simply say that they do not require proof. For in order to be proved, they would have to appear as the conclusion of an entire system of praxeology, which would first need to be drawn up. But how should this be possible when they logically and temporally precede every thought—at least every praxeological (the sociologists of knowledge would say "situationally-determined")— thought? If a man begins to take these axioms seriously in his thinking, he will fall into a skepticism far more radical than that of Pyrrho and Aenesidemus.

But these three axioms form only the presupposition of the theory; they are not yet the theory itself, and, as we shall see, their enumeration by no means exhausts all its axiomatic assumptions. According to the doctrine of the Marxian sociology of knowledge, to which we return and which is the only one we wish to consider in the rest of this discussion, a man's thought is dependent on his class membership to such an extent that all the theories which he may arrive at express, not universally valid truth, as their author imagines, but an ideology that serves his class interests. However, there can be no doubt that for members who want to further the interests of their own class as much as they can, the knowledge of reality, unclouded by any sort of ideological error, would be extremely useful. The better they know reality, the better will they know how to select the means for the promotion of their class interests. Of course, if knowledge of the truth were to lead to the conclusion that one's class interests should be sacrificed for other values, it could lessen the enthusiasm with which these alleged class interests are championed, and a false theory that avoided this disadvantage would be superior to the true one in tactical value. But once this possibility has been admitted, the basis of the whole doctrine has been given up.

Consequently, a class can be aided in its struggles by means of a false theory only in so far as it weakens the fighting power of opposing classes. "Bourgeois" economics, for example, helped the bourgeoisie in the struggle against the precapitalist powers, and then later in its opposition to the proletariat, in spreading among its opponents the conviction that the capitalist system must necessarily prevail. Thus we arrive at the fourth and last of the axiomatic presuppositions of Marxism: The help which a class gets from the fact that its members can think only in terms of apologetics (ideologies), and not in terms of correct theories, outweighs the consequent loss to it of whatever advantages a knowledge of reality unclouded by false ideas might have afforded it for practical action.

It must be made clear that the doctrine of the dependence of thought on the class of the thinker is based on all four of these axioms. This relation of dependence appears as an aid to the class in carrying on class warfare. That its thinking is not absolutely correct, but conditioned by its class origin, is to be attributed precisely to the fact that interest points the way for thought. Here we definitely do not in any way wish to challenge these four axioms, which are generally accepted without proof for the very reason that they cannot be proved. Our critique has to do only with answering the question whether a class theory can be used in unmasking modern economics as the class ideology of the bourgeoisie, and we must attempt to solve this problem immanently.

In spite of everything that has been said, one may still perhaps maintain the fourth of the axioms set forth above, according to which it is more advantageous for a class to cling to a doctrine that distorts reality than to comprehend the state of affairs correctly and to act accordingly. But at best this can hold true only for the time during which the other classes do not yet possess theories adequate to their own social existence. For later, the class that adjusts its action to the correct theory will doubtless be superior to the classes that take a false—albeit subjectively honest—theory as a basis for action; and the advantage that the class-conditioned theory formerly afforded, in that it weakened the opposition of enemy classes, would now no longer obtain, since the latter would have already emancipated their thinking from that of other classes.

Let us apply this to our problem. Marxists and sociologists of knowledge call modern subjectivist economics "bourgeois" science, a last hopeless endeavor to save capitalism. When this reproach was directed against classical economics and its immediate successors, there was a grain of truth in it. At that time, when there was not yet a proletarian economics, it might be thought that the bourgeoisie could, by means of its science, hinder the awakening of the proletariat to class consciousness.

But now "proletarian" science has entered the scene, and the proletariat has become class-conscious. It is now too late for the bourgeoisie to try anew to formulate an apologetic, to construct a new bourgeois science, to develop a new "ideology." All attempts to destroy the class consciousness of the proletarian, who can no longer think otherwise than in conformity with his class, can redound only to the detriment of those who would undertake them. Today the bourgeoisie could do nothing but harm to its own interests if it were to endeavor to concoct a new class ideology. The classes opposed to it could no longer be brought under the influence of such a doctrine. But because the action of the bourgeoisie would itself be determined by this false theory, the latter would necessarily endanger the outcome of the struggle against the proletariat. If it is class interest that determines thought, then today the bourgeoisie has need of a theory that expresses reality without contamination by false ideas.

Therefore, one could say to the Marxists and the sociologists of knowledge, if one wanted, in turn, to take one's stand on one's own viewpoint: Until the appearance of Karl Marx, the bourgeoisie fought with an "ideology," viz., the system of the classical and "vulgar" economists. But when, with the appearance of the first volume of *Capital* (1867), the proletariat was provided with a doctrine corresponding to its social existence, the bourgeoisie changed its tactics. An "ideology" could henceforth no longer be useful to it, since the proletariat, awakened to consciousness of its social existence as a class, could no longer be seduced and lulled to sleep by an ideology. Now the bourgeoisie needed a theory that, dispassionately viewing the true state of affairs and free from every ideological coloration, offered it the possibility of always availing itself of the most suitable means in the great decisive battle of the classes. Quickly the old economics was given up; and since 1870, first by Jevons, Menger, and Walras, and then by Böhm-Bawerk, Clark, and Pareto, the new, correct theory has been developed as now required by the changed class situation of the bourgeoisie. For it has become apparent that in this stage of its struggle against an already class-conscious proletariat the doctrine adequate to the existence of the bourgeoisie as a class, that is, best serving its class interests, is not an "ideology," but knowledge of the absolute truth.

Thus, with Marxism and the sociology of knowledge you can prove everything and nothing.

3. THE ROLE OF RESENTMENT

In his *De officiis* Cicero prescribed a code of social respectability and propriety that faithfully reflects the conceptions of gentility and merit that have prevailed in western civilization through the centuries. Cicero presented nothing new in this work, nor did he intend to. He availed himself of older, Greek standards. And the views that he expounded corresponded completely to those that had been generally accepted for centuries both in the Greek and Hellenistic world and in republican Rome. The Roman republic gave way to the empire; Rome's gods, to the Christian God. The Roman empire collapsed, and out of the storms created by the migration of entire populations a new Europe arose. Papacy and empire plunged from their heights, and other powers took their place. But the position of Cicero's standard of merit remained unshaken. Voltaire called the *De officiis* the most useful handbook of ethics,[10] and Frederick the Great considered it the best work in the field of moral philosophy that had ever been or ever would be written.[11]

Through all the changes in the prevailing system of social stratification, moral philosophers continued to hold fast to the fundamental idea of Cicero's doctrine that making money is degrading. It expressed the convictions of the great aristocratic landowners, princely courtiers, officers of the army, and government officials. It was also the view of the literati, whether they lived as paupers at the court of a great lord or were permitted to work in security as the beneficiaries of ecclesiastical prebends. The secularization of the universities and the transformation of the precarious posts of the court literati into publicly supported sinecures served only to aggravate the distrust that the intellectual who was paid a salary for his work as a teacher, scholar, or author felt toward the independent scholar, who had to support himself on the generally meager proceeds from his writings or by some other activity. Set apart by their position in the hierarchy of church, public office, and military service, they looked down with contempt upon the businessman, who serves Mammon. In this respect they took the view common to all who by virtue of an income derived from taxes are relieved of the necessity of earning a living on the market. This contempt turned to gnawing rancor when, with the spread of capitalism, entrepreneurs began to rise to great wealth and thus to high popular esteem. It would be a grievous error to assume that the hostility felt toward entrepreneurs and capitalists, toward wealth and quite especially toward newly acquired wealth, toward money-making and in particular toward business and speculation, which today dominates our entire public life, politics, and literature stems from the sentiments of the masses. It springs directly from the views held in the circles of the educated classes who were in public service and enjoyed a fixed salary and a politically recognized status. This resentment is, accordingly, all the stronger in a nation the more docilely it allows itself to be led by the authorities and their functionaries. It is stronger in Prussia and Austria than in England and France; it is less strong in the United States and weakest in the British dominions.

The very fact that many of these people in government service are related to businessmen by blood or marriage or are closely connected with them by school ties and social acquaintance exacerbates still further these sentiments of envy and rancor. The feeling that they are in many ways beneath the contemptible businessman brings about inferiority complexes that only intensify the resentment of those removed from the market. Standards of ethical merit are fashioned not by the active man of affairs, but by the writer who lives *procul negotiis*. A system of ethics whose authors are to be found in the circles of priests, bureaucrats, professors, and officers of the army expresses only disgust and contempt for entrepreneurs, capitalists, and speculators.

And now these educated classes, filled with envy and hatred, are presented with a theory that explains the phenomena of the market in a manner deliberately neutral with regard to all value judgments. Price rises, increases in the rate of interest, and wage reductions, which were formerly attributed to the greed and heartlessness of the rich, are now traced back by this theory to quite natural reactions of the market to changes in supply and demand. Moreover, it shows that the division of labor in the social order based on private property would be utterly impossible without these adjustments by the market. What was condemned as a moral injustice—indeed, as a punishable offense—is here looked upon as, so to speak, a natural occurrence. Capitalists, entrepreneurs, and speculators no longer appear as parasites and exploiters, but as members of the system of social organization whose function is absolutely indispensable. The application of pseudomoral standards to market phenomena loses every semblance of justification. The concepts of usury, profiteering, and exploitation are stripped of their ethical import and thus become absolutely meaningless. And, finally, the science of economics proves with cold, irrefutable logic that the ideals of those who condemn making a living on the market are quite vain, that the socialist organization of society is unrealizable, that the interventionist social order is nonsensical and contrary to the ends at which it aims, and that therefore the market economy is the only feasible system of social cooperation. It is not surprising that in the circles whose ethics culminate in the condemnation of all market activity these teachings encounter vehement opposition.

Economics refuted the belief that prosperity is to be expected from the abolition of private property and the market economy. It proved that the omnipotence of the authorities, from whom wonders had been hoped for, is a delusion and that the man who undertakes to organize social cooperation, the ζῷον πολιτιχόν, as well as the *homo faber*, who directs organic and inorganic nature in the process of production, cannot go beyond certain limits. This too had to appear to the servitors of the apparatus of violence, both those in the *imperium* and those in the *magisterium*, as a lowering of their personal prestige. They considered themselves as demigods who make history, or at least as the assistants of these demigods. Now they were to be nothing but the executors of an unalterable necessity. Just as the deterministic theories, entirely apart from the condemnation they received from the ecclesiastical authorities on dogmatic grounds, encountered the inner opposition of those who believed themselves to be possessed of free will, so these theories too met with resistance on the part of rulers and their retinue, who felt free in the exercise of their political power.

No one can escape the influence of a prevailing ideology. Even the entrepreneurs and capitalists have fallen under the sway of ethical ideas that condemn their activities. It is with a bad conscience that they try to ward off the economic demands derived from the ethical principles of the public functionary. The suspicion with which they regard all theories that view the phenomena of the market without ethical judgment is no less than that felt by all other groups. The sense of inferiority that arouses their conscience to the feeling that their acts are immoral is all too often more than compensated by exaggerated forms of antichrematistic ethics. The interest that millionaires and the sons and daughters of millionaires have taken in the formation and leadership of socialist workers' parties is an obvious case in point. But even outside of the socialist parties we encounter the same phenomenon. In the last analysis is it not the result of the efforts and activities of two entrepreneurs, Ernst Abbe and Walter Rathenau, that the intellectual leaders of the German people condemn the social order based on private ownership of the means of production?

4. FREEDOM AND NECESSITY

The ultimate statement that the theory of knowledge can make without leaving the solid ground of science and engaging in vague speculations on fruitless metaphysical concepts is: Changes in what is given, as far as our experience is concerned, take place in a way that allows us to perceive in the course of things the rule of universal laws that permit of no exception.

We are not capable of conceiving of a world in which things would not run their course "according to eternal, pitiless, grand laws." But this much is clear to us· In a world so constituted, human thought and "rational" human action would not be possible. And therefore in such a world there could be neither human beings nor logical thought.

Consequently, the conformity of the phenomena of the world to natural law must appear to us as the foundation of our human existence, as the ultimate basis of our being human. Thinking about it cannot fill us with fear, but, on the contrary, must comfort us and give us a feeling of security. We are able to act at all— that is to say, we have the power to order our conduct in such a way that the ends we desire can be attained—only because the phenomena of the world are governed not by arbitrariness, but by laws that we have the capacity to know something about. If it were otherwise, we should be completely at the mercy of forces that we should be unable to understand.

We can comprehend only the laws that are revealed in the changes in the given. The given itself always remains inexplicable to us. Our action must accept the given as it is. However, even knowledge of the laws of nature does not make action free. It is never able to attain more than definite, limited ends. It can never go beyond the insurmountable barriers set for it. And even within the sphere allowed to it, it must always reckon with the inroads of uncontrollable forces, with fate.

Here we encounter a peculiar psychological fact. We quarrel less with the unknown that comes upon us in the form of fate than with the result of the operation of the laws we have comprehended. For the unknown is also the unexpected. We cannot see its approach. We do not apprehend it until it has already taken place. Whatever follows from a known law we can foresee and expect. If it is inimical to our wishes, there is sheer torment in waiting for the approaching disaster that we cannot avoid. It becomes unbearable to think that the law is inexorable and makes no exceptions. We build our hopes on the miracle that this time, this one time, the law, contrary to all expectations, might not hold true. Faith in a miracle becomes our sole comfort. With it we resist the harshness of natural law and silence the voice of our reason. We expect a miracle to turn aside the foreseen course of events, which we find disagreeable.

It was thought that in the field of human conduct, and accordingly in that of society, men are free from the pitiless inexorability and rigor of law, which our thought and action had long since been compelled to recognize in "nature." Since the eighteenth century the science of praxeology, and especially its hitherto most highly developed branch, economics, has enabled "law" to be apprehended in this realm too. Before the dawn of the realization that the phenomena of nature conform to laws, men felt themselves to be dependent upon superhuman beings. At first these deities were thought to possess complete free will; that is, they were believed to be raised above all bounds in their acts of commission and omission. Later they were thought to be at least sovereigns who in individual cases are capable of decreeing exceptions to the otherwise universal law. Likewise in the domain of social relations, until that time men were aware of nothing but dependence on authorities and autocrats whose power over others seemed boundless. Everything and anything could be expected from these great and noble beings. In good as well as in evil they were bound by no earthly limitations. And one liked to hope that their consciences, mindful of retaliation in the life to come, would most often restrain them from misusing their power for evil purposes. This whole way of thinking was violently shaken in a twofold way by the individualist and nominalist social philosophy of the Enlightenment. The Enlightenment disclosed the ideological[12] basis of all social power. And it showed that every power is limited in its effect by the fact that all social phenomena conform to law.

The opposition to these teachings was even stronger than the resistance to the doctrine of the subjection of nature to law. Just as the masses want to know nothing of the inexorable rigor of the laws of nature and substitute for the God of the theists and the deists, who is subject to law, the free ruling divinity from whom mercy and miracles are to be eagerly expected, so they do not allow themselves to be deprived of faith in the boundless omnipotence of the social authorities. As even the philosopher catches himself hoping for a miracle when he is in distress, dissatisfaction with his social position leads him to long for a reform that, restrained by no barriers, could accomplish everything.

Nevertheless, knowledge about the inexorability of the laws of nature has so long since forced its way into the mind of the public—at least of the educated public—that people see in the theories of natural science a means by which they can attain ends that would otherwise remain unattainable. But, in addition, the educated classes are possessed by the idea that in the social domain anything can be accomplished if only one applies enough force and is sufficiently resolute. Consequently, they see in the teachings of the sciences of human action only the depressing message that much of what they desire cannot be attained. The natural sciences, it is said, show what could be done and how it could be done, whereas praxeology shows only what cannot be done and why it cannot be done. Engineering, which is based on the natural sciences, is everywhere highly praised. The economic and political teachings of liberalism are rejected, and catallactics, on which they are based, is branded the dismal science.

Scarcely anyone interests himself in social problems without being led to do so by the desire to see reforms enacted. In almost all cases, before anyone begins to study the science, he has already decided on definite reforms that he wants to put through. Only a few have the strength to accept the knowledge that these reforms are impracticable and to draw all the inferences from it. Most men endure the sacrifice of the intellect more easily than the sacrifice of their daydreams. They cannot bear that their utopias should run aground on the unalterable necessities of human existence. What they yearn for is another reality different from the one given in this world. They long for the "leap of humanity out of the realm of necessity and into the realm of freedom." [13] They wish to be free of a universe of whose order they do not approve.

CONCLUSION

The romantic revolt against logic and science does not limit itself to the sphere of social phenomena and the sciences of human action. It is a revolt against our entire culture and civilization. Both Spann and Sombart demand the renunciation of scientific knowledge and the return to the faith and the bucolic conditions of the Middle Ages, and all Germans who are not in the Marxist camp joyfully agree with them. The Marxists, however, are eager in this regard to transform their once sober "scientific" socialism into a romantic and sentimental socialism more pleasing to the masses.

Science is reproached for addressing only the intellect while leaving the heart empty and unsatisfied. It is hard and cold where warmth is required. It furnishes theories and techniques where consolation and understanding are sought. Yet it cannot be argued that the satisfaction of religious and metaphysical needs is the task of science. Science cannot go beyond its own sphere. It must limit itself to the development of our system of knowledge and with its help undertake the logical elaboration of experience. In this way it lays the foundations on which scientific technology —and all politics in so far as it is the technology of the domain of social phenomena comes under this head—constructs its system. In no way does science have to concern itself with faith and peace of soul. The attempts to establish metaphysics scientifically or to produce a kind of substitute for religion by means of "ethical" ceremonies copied from religious worship have nothing whatever to do with science. Science in no way deals with the transcendent, with what is inaccessible to thought and experience. It can express neither a favorable nor an unfavorable opinion about doctrines that concern only the sphere of the metaphysical.

A conflict between faith and knowledge develops only when religion and metaphysics pass beyond their proper domains and challenge science in its own realm. They do so partly out of the necessity of defending dogma that is not compatible with the state of scientific knowledge, but more often in order to attack the application of science to life if this does not conform to the conduct that they prescribe. It is not difficult to understand why, under such conditions, subjectivist economics is most vehemently attacked.

We should not deceive ourselves about the fact that today not only the masses, but also the educated public—those who are called intellectuals—are not to be found on the side of science in this controversy. For many this position may be a heartfelt necessity. However, a great many others justify their taking this point of view by arguing that it represents the "wave of the future," that one cannot cut oneself off from what the masses most passionately desire, that the intellect must humbly bow before instinct and the simplicity of religious emotion. Thus the intellectual voluntarily steps aside. Full of self-abnegation, he renounces his role as a leader and becomes one of the led. This reversal of roles on the part of those who regard themselves as the bearers of culture has been by far the most important historical occurrence of the last decades. It is with horror that we now witness the maturation of the fruits of the policy that results from this abdication of the intellect.

In all ages the pioneer in scientific thought has been a solitary thinker. But never has the position of the scientist been more solitary than in the field of modern economics. The fate of mankind—progress on the road that western civilization has taken for thousands of years, or a rapid plunge into a chaos from which there is no way out, from which no new life as we know it will ever develop—depends on whether this condition persists.

NOTES

1. Cf. Hilferding, "Böhm-Bawerk's Marx-Kritik," *Marx-Studien* (Vienna, 1904), I, 61.
2. Cf. Bucharin, *Die politische Ökonomie des Rentners* (Berlin, 1926), p. 27.
3. Adolf Weber, *Allgemeine Volkswirtschaftslehre* (Munich and Leipzig, 1928), p. 211. The passage referred to is no longer contained in the most recent (fourth) edition of this well-known textbook. That this refusal to admit economic theory into the universities has not led to satisfactory results in actual "practice" may be seen from the address of Dr. Bücher to the Frankfurt conference on the National Federation of German industry. Bücher objected that in the universities of Germany economists are being "falsely" educated because "German economics has lost feeling for the actual problems of the present day and in many ways has given up practical economic thought." It has "split itself into highly specialized branches concerned with detailed problems and has lost sight of the connections between them." (See the report in the "Frankfurter Zeitung," September 4, 1927.) This devastating judgment is all the more remarkable as Bücher is, as can be seen from the other statements in this speech, in economic and political matters thoroughly in accord with the opponents of laissez faire and the advocates of the

"completely organized economy" and consequently agrees with the interventionist-etatist school of German economists.

4. For a psychoanalytical examination of this stubborn resistance to the acceptance of new knowledge, cf. Jones, *On the Psychoanalysis of the Christian Religion* (Leipzig, 1928), p. 25.

5. Cf. the description of these methods by Pohle, *Die gegenwärtige Krisis in der deutschen Volkswirtschaftslehre* (2nd ed.; Leipzig, 1921), pp. 116 ff.

6. The opposition of which we speak is not confined to one country only; it is likewise to be found in the United States and England, though not perhaps as strong as in Germany and Italy.

7. This is true above all of those who, like the "sociologists of knowledge" and the school of Max Adler, want to consider Marxism "sociologically," that is to say, quite apart from all economics. For them, the irreconcilability of the conflict of class interests is a dogma the truth of which only the depraved can doubt.

8. *Das Kommunistische Manifest* (7th authorized German edition, Berlin, 1906), p. 30.

9. "The individual errs frequently in protecting his interests; a class never errs in the long run," says F. Oppenheimer, *System der Soziologie* (Jena, 1926), II, 559. This is metaphysics, not science.

10. Zielinski, *Cicero im Wandel der Jahrhunderts* (4th ed.; Leipzig, 1929), p. 246.

11. *Ibid.*, p. 248.

12. The expression "ideological" is used here not in the Marxist sense or in that in which it is understood by the sociologists of knowledge, but in its scientific meaning.

13. Engels, *Herrn Eugen Dührings Umwälzung der Wissenschaft* (7th ed.; Stuttgart, 1910), p. 306.

7

The Controversy Over
the Theory of Value[1]

We meet here to discuss a question of economic theory. But first of all we must be in agreement on two principles. Otherwise, every attempt at mutual understanding would be hopeless from the very outset.

Following in the footsteps of Kant, we must reject the common saying: "That may be true in theory, but not in practice." Though I do not think this point needs any further elaboration, I mention it nevertheless because at the last plenary meeting of our society the term "theorist" was used by one of the speakers with a trace of scorn, without immediately arousing disagreement.

For us to be able to have any discussion at all, it is far more important that we also acknowledge a principle that Kant, to be sure, did not explicitly state, but, like all his forerunners, implicitly assumed. We must take it for granted that the logical structure of human thought is immutable throughout the whole course of time and is the same for all races, nations, and classes. We know very well that the majority of the German people—and even most educated Germans—do not share this point of view. Indeed, I believe one might also say that most students of economics at the universities today hear lectures in which this idea is rejected. If we wish to study praxeology and economics, we cannot avoid dealing with doctrines which assert that temporal, racial, or "class" factors determine abstract thought. However, the discussion of such ideas can be meaningful only for those of us who assume that logic and thought are independent of time, race, nationality, and class. We who hold this view can attempt to carry

204

to their ultimate conclusions and examine the validity of the objections of those who say that thought is conditioned by the thinker's social existence. But those who maintain such doctrines may not, and indeed cannot, argue with us about our criticisms of them without at the same time giving up their own point of view.

This is no less true of epistemological discussions concerning the foundations of praxeological knowledge than it is of the discussion of the particular problems of our science. Yet we do want to deal with science, not with subjective value judgments; with questions of cognition, not of volition; with what is, not with what ought to be. If we wish to discuss the theory of value, we cannot do so in a manner that allows everyone to justify his position by appealing to considerations of nation, race, or class. And we certainly cannot tolerate reproaches that make reference to the class or racial determination of the opposing point of view, like the familiar characterization of Böhm-Bawerk's theory of interest as the theory of the Phaeacian city of Vienna, or of the subjective theory of value as the political economy of the *rentier*. Let the Marxist, if he can, "unmask" Böhm-Bawerk as the representative of "students snatching at amusement" and of "officers, resplendent, but always suffering from a lack of money." [2] But then let him tell his discovery to those whom he considers the comrades of his class, not to us, who in his eyes are only playboys. Phaeacians, and *rentiers*, or perhaps even worse.

A Marxist—and I understand by this term not only the members of a political party that swears by Marx, but all who appeal to Marx in their thinking concerning the sciences of human action—who condescends to discuss a scientific problem with people who are not comrades of his own class has given up the first and most important principle of his theory. If thought is conditioned by the thinker's social existence, how can he understand me and how can I understand him? If there is a "bourgeois" logic and a "proletarian" logic, how am I, the "bourgeois," to come to an understanding with him, the "proletarian"? Whoever takes the Marxist point of view seriously must advocate a complete division between "bourgeois" and "proletarian" science; and the same is also true, *mutatis mutandis,* of the view of those who regard thought as determined by the race or the nationality of the thinker. The Marxist cannot be satisfied with separating classes in athletic contests, with a "bourgeois" and a "proletarian" olympics. He must demand this separation above all in scientific discussion.

The fruitlessness of many of the debates that were conducted here in the Verein für Sozialpolitik as well as in the Gesellschaft für Soziologie are to be attributed more than anything else to the neglect of this principle. In my opinion, the position of dogmatic Marxism is wrong, but that of the Marxist who engages in discussions with representatives of what he calls "bourgeois science" is confused. The consistent Marxist does not seek to refute opponents whom he calls "bourgeois." He seeks to destroy them physically and morally.

The Marxist oversteps the bounds that he himself sets up by his avowal of Marxism if he wishes to take part in our discussion without first making sure that we are all comrades of his own class. The heart of Marxism is the doctrine that thought is determined by one's class. One cannot simply forget about this doctrine for the time being, to make use of it only occasionally when needed or to suit one's convenience. Without the materialist conception of history Marxist economics would be nothing but a garbled Ricardianism. Of course, no one will deny that we would have to come to grips with Ricardo's ideas if defenders of his labor theory of value were to appear here.

It is certainly not the purpose of a discussion such as ours to minimize or veil in any way the difference that exists between our points of view. At political rallies it may seem desirable to make the opposition between different schools of thought appear as slight as possible. The purpose of such tactics, to bring about a resolution for united action, can be achieved only when all are finally in agreement. Our purpose, however, is not action, but cognition. And cognition is furthered only by clarity and distinctness, never by compromises. We must endeavor to bring what divides us as sharply into relief as possible.

As soon as we do this we shall arrive at a very important

result. We shall discover that in the province we are dealing with here today there are and must be far fewer positions than there are labels and parties.

The task we have set for ourselves is the explanation of the phenomena of the market. We wish to investigate the laws that determine the formation of the exchange ratios of goods and services, i.e., of prices, wages, and interest rates. I know very well that even this has been challenged. The Historical School believes that there can be no universally valid economic laws and that it is therefore foolish to search for them. Prices, it is said, are determined not by "economic laws," but by the "conditions of social power."

It is clear that even this point of view must be analyzed if one wishes to pursue economics at all. And we are all acquainted with the immortal, masterful works of Menger, Böhm-Bawerk, and others in which such an analysis has been attempted. However, one cannot deal with all scientific problems at the same time. We took up this denial of the possibility of economic science at the conference at Würzburg. This question should not be considered here today if our discussion is not to wander off the topic we have agreed on.

This topic is the theory of the market. And the point at which we must begin is the question: Are we obliged to construct a special theory of value as the foundation of the theory of price determination?

In the theory of value we attempt to trace back the formation of prices to factors that are operative not only in a society acquainted with private property, and consequently with the market, but in every conceivable society, even in the self-sufficient economy in which there is no interpersonal exchange, such as the economy of the isolated household, on the one hand, and the economy of a socialist community, on the other. We shall not go into the question of whether these two types of economies —the isolated self-sufficient economy and the socialist collective economy—are merely imaginary constructions, or whether they are also historically realizable. Cassel has misunderstood the purport of this procedure in supposing that it is used with the intention of studying primitive society as the simplest case of economic action in order to be able to proceed from there—in Cassel's opinion, deceitfully—to the study of a money economy, which is regarded as more complicated.[3] By means of this imaginary construction we want to study not the simplest or the most primitive, but the most general case, and not so much in order to proceed to the historically later and more complicated, but to the more special cases. And we do not want to assume the existence and the use of money, as Cassel does. On the contrary, we want to comprehend and deduce the function of money from the more general case of an economy without money.

Catallactics has accomplished its task only when it has succeeded in this process of generalization, only when it has traced the formation of prices back to the point where acting man makes his choice and pronounces his decision: I prefer A to B.

However, economics also stops here. It does not go further back. It does not inquire into what lies behind the decisions of acting men, why they act precisely in the way they do and not otherwise. This self-limitation on the part of economics is not arbitrary. It finds its justification in the fact that the motives that actuate men are of no significance for the formation of prices. It is without importance whether the demand for weapons on the market comes from men who are on the side of law and order or from criminals and revolutionists. What is alone decisive is that a demand exists in a definite volume. Economics is distinguished from psychology by the fact that it considers action alone and that the psychic events that have led to an action are without importance for it.

It has been repeatedly pointed out that the term "value" is ambiguous. No one will choose to dispute this, and no one ever has disputed it. Every economist who wants to make use of this term has striven above all to eliminate the ambiguity of the word "value" by means of a strict definition designed to meet the requirements of scientific work. The assertion that modern economics has not undertaken to do this with all necessary rigor is to be emphatically denied. Cassel is quite wrong as far as scientific literature is concerned in maintaining that the notions of "use value" and "exchange value" sufficiently attest to the ambiguity of the concept of "value." [4] At least since the middle of the eighteenth century—and therefore as long as there has been any economics at all—economists have sharply distinguished between these two concepts. A difference of opinion concerning their significance for the explanation of the phenomena of the market has nothing to do with the alleged ambiguity of the idea of value. It is impermissible to declare that modern economics has not forged its concept of value with full clarity. One must ask Cassel, Gottl, and all the others to prove their charges by means of a thoroughgoing critique of the modern authors.

Unfortunately, the point must be made again and again that the greater part of the repeated criticism of the modern theory of value is based on gross misunderstanding or refers to difficulties that belong to an older stage in the development of the theory and that have long since been overcome. The science of the last forty years may not simply be ignored. Today one may no longer be satisfied with a cursory consideration of Menger and Böhm-Bawerk; one must also be familiar with Pareto and have read Čuhel and Strigl, not to mention the most recent works in this field. Cassel's criticism of a few peculiarities in Menger's and Böhm-Bawerk's presentation (which he made thirty-three years ago)[5] was justified in many respects, even if his positive arguments were completely erroneous. However, Cassel is wrong in thinking that his criticism refers not only to the form of presentation, but also to the substance of the theory. And it is unpardonable that even today he clings to his errors and ignores the scientific literature of the last generation as well. Everything that Cassel has to say about the problem of the measurement of value is untenable because it does not take into consideration the accomplishments of the last decades.

The most recent and most vehement criticism of the subjective theory of value comes from universalism. Spann maintains that the conduct of a household can change only "if production, payments, transportation, consumption, etc. have changed beforehand; in other words, only if the collective whole of the economy (taken in its strict sense) has first undergone a change." Therefore, no individual member can be conceived as an independent variable.[6] Daily experience contradicts this idea. When I change the habitual course of my conduct and begin to consume less meat, for example, and more vegetables, this must affect the market. The change originates in me and is not predicated on the supposition that consumption has previously changed. Indeed, the change in consumption consists precisely in the fact that I change my own consumption. That this is noticeable on the market only when not just one man changes his habits of consumption, but many, is a quantitative question that has nothing to do with the main problem. Equally irrelevant in this regard are general changes in consumption that have a common cause—e.g., a shift from the consumption of meat to the consumption of vegetables that may be caused by a change in the prevailing views concerning the physiology of nutrition. These changes concern motives, and we have already said why motives are of no concern to us.

What Spann expressly designates as the most important objections of universalism—the rejection of the assumption of the quantitative ascertainability of changes, the measurability of wants, and the quantification of value—can certainly not be cited as arguments against the subjective theory of value. For the starting point of the latter—which Spann, following the arguments of Čuhel and Pareto on this point, accepts when he speaks of the order of rank—is precisely the fact that values are not measured, but graded. No doubt there are unique and non-repeatable actions, but we may not so far disregard the facts that can be established in human experience as to assert that every action is unique and nonrepeatable and of a special character.[7] What we actually can observe is that certain actions are regarded as repeatable and replaceable. Spann thinks that he has proved his point when he states that an opera by Mozart is certainly more valuable—has a higher rank—than an opera by Flotow, but that one cannot say that it is ten and a half times more valuable. It is regrettable that such a gifted thinker should waste his ingenuity on theories that long before him had already been criticized and rejected by the founders of the subjective theory of value, and it is equally deplorable that thus far he has not seen fit to concern himself with the literature on that theory that has been published in the last forty years.

All the objections that Spann is able to advance against the subjective theory of value disintegrate when they are confronted with the simple fact that in life men again and again have to choose between various possibilities. The distinction in rank of which Spann speaks manifests itself precisely in the fact that a man prefers a concrete A to a concrete B, and nothing else. The market price comes into being as a result of such decisions on the part of men making exchanges on the market. If catallactics begins with the act of choice, it takes as its starting point a fact whose existence can be established in a manner that admits of no doubt —a fact that every human being knows and, because he himself acts, grasps in its essence. If catallactics were to begin, as Spann wants it to do, with totalities and imaginary constructions, its point of departure would be arbitrarily chosen. For totalities and imaginary constructions are not unequivocally precise, recognizable, and confirmable in such a way that agreement could be reached about their existence or nonexistence. Totalities and imaginary constructions are seen very differently by Spann from the way they are viewed by the Marxists, and Coudenhove-Kalergi certainly does not look upon them in the same light as Friedrich Naumann did.

Spann, to be sure, considers the concepts of the subjective theory of value to be arbitrarily chosen—for example, the concept of "quantity." Only in the figurative sense, he asserts, is there a "quantity." For "what unit should be taken? Should the unit be a sack of flour, a bale of cotton or a gram, one piece or a shock?" [8] We need not enter here into the epistemological question how the concept of "quantity" is to be formulated. For what is under discussion is not this, but the question what quantity the theory of the market has to start from. Unfortunately, Spann did not see that the subjective theory of value answers this question with the greatest precision. We always have to start from that quantity which is the object of the definite act of choice we have in view. I must let the matter rest here with this brief comment because I do not wish to repeat what I have said about total value in my theory of money.[9]

Where Spann is correct he follows the path pointed out by the subjective theory of value that he attacks. Where he opposes the subjective theory he becomes involved in metaphysical speculations that frequently hinder him even where he is right on his own account—as, for example, in rejecting the errors of those who want to make economics a mathematical science. However, we cannot deal with this point today. If our present discussion is fruitful and thus proves that the Verein für Sozialpolitik is an appropriate place to debate economic problems, then I think there is no other question that so urgently requires investigation as that of the mathematical method. But one cannot dispose of this subject in a cursory way. One must devote thorough preparation to its treatment and make sufficient time available for its discussion.[10]

Unfortunately, we shall never be able to reach an understanding with Spann because the goal of his work is different from ours. It is not his purpose to understand and explain things as they are. Instead, his object is to determine the correct, and, following from this, the *just* price.[11] He sees the failure of the old doctrines precisely in the fact that they do not aim at this goal and therefore cannot attain it. Our object is to comprehend things as they are, because we are well aware that this is the only task that science is capable of undertaking and the only matter about which agreement can be reached. Spann's object is to comprehend what ought to be. But if someone is of the opinion that something else ought to be, the adherent of universalism is helpless and can only repeat over and over again: I, however, consider my opinion right and wish to regard my solutions as just. All that universalism can say to its opponents is: You are simply inferior, and your inferiority makes it impossible for you to know what is true and what is just, as I, who am more meritorious, do. It is obvious that with such a deep-seated difference of viewpoint there can be no fruitful scientific discussion.

Whoever wishes to form some idea of the importance of the theory of marginal utility has only to look at any presentation of the theory of the market in one of the current textbooks on the subject and to try separating out all the ideas contained in it that we owe to the modern subjective theory of value. Let him pick up the leading books on business management—for example, the works of Schmalenbach—and he will understand the contribution that subjectivism has made to this subject. He will have to admit that today there is still only one economics. I should like to point out expressly that this is true also of the German-speaking countries.

For a very long time the solution of the fundamental problem of catallactics was prevented by the apparent antinomy of value. Not until this difficulty was overcome could one construct a comprehensive theory of value and price determination that, starting from the action of the individual, proceeds to the explanation of all the phenomena of the market. The history of modern economics begins with the resolution of the paradox of value by Menger, Jevons, and Walras. There is no period in the history of economics more important than the one in which these thinkers flourished. However, we recognize more clearly today than was yet possible a generation ago that the work of the classical economists was not useless and that the substance of what they accomplished could be incorporated into the modern system. In the theory of value, the opposition between subjectivism and objectivism, between utility theory and cost theory, has lost none of its distinctness. We see it merely in another light since we have understood the proper place of a modified concept of cost in the whole system of subjectivist economics.

In the classical doctrine, the theory of money occupies a separate position. Neither Ricardo nor his successors succeeded in giving an explanation of the phenomena of the market in which the same principles used to explain the exchange relationships in direct exchange could be used to explain money prices. If one starts from a cost theory like that of the classical economists and accepts the labor theory of value, one cannot, of course, master the problem of indirect exchange. In this way the theory of money and credit, and thus also of the trade cycle, came to assume a strikingly distinctive position in the whole system of classical economics. The triumph of the subjective theory of value deprived these theories of their separate position. It succeeded in developing the theory of indirect exchange in harmony with that of direct exchange without being compelled to accept the help of hypotheses that are not already contained in the fundamental concepts of its system. With the disappearance of the separate position of the theory of money and credit, the separate treatment of the theory of the trade cycle also disappeared. Here too we must again point out that the subjective theory of value has derived the greatest benefit from the intellectual heritage left by the classical economists. The modern theory of credit and the modern theory of the trade cycle can truly be designated as the successors to the currency theory, which, for its part, is in turn based on the ideas of Ricardo.

Within modern subjectivist economics it has become customary to distinguish several schools. We usually speak of the Austrian and the Anglo-American Schools and the School of Lausanne. Morgenstern's work,[12] which you have before you, has said almost all that is necessary about the fact that these three schools of thought differ only in their mode of expressing the same fundamental idea and that they are divided more by their terminology and by peculiarities of presentation than by the substance of their teachings.

The assertion is repeatedly made that there is not one economics, but many kinds. Sombart mentions three, and others profess to know still more. And many go so far as to say that there are as many kinds of economics as there are economists. This is just as incorrect as Sombart's declaration that economics does not know what its domain is in the *globus intellectualis*. On this point, however, there can be no argument: the problems of catallactics constitute the field of our science. We are faced with them and we have to solve them. Historicism, to be sure, disputes this, but only in principle. As soon as it begins to pursue the study of economic history, it defines its sphere. For out of the entire range of historical phenomena it takes upon itself the study of catallactic phenomena.

Today we have only one theory for the solution of the problems of catallactics, even if it makes use of several forms of expression and appears in different guises. It cannot be denied that there are also opponents of this theory who reject it or who maintain that they are able to teach something entirely different from it. The very fact that distinguished thinkers like Cassel, Otto Conrad, Diehl, Dietzel, Gottl, Liefmann, Oppenheimer, Spann, and Veblen believe that they must combat it makes our discussion necessary. Its purpose is the clarification of the points we do not agree on by means of their distinct and precise formulation. We shall not vote at the end of our discussion. We shall go our separate ways, unconverted even if perhaps not unadvised. If our conference today and the forthcoming publication of its proceedings help the younger economists in forming their opinions, it will have done the most that a conference of this kind can do.

The chairman of the subcommittee assigned to me the task of opening the discussion. I do not consider myself as one who has read a paper in a seminar. For this reason I shall not present a summary of the proceedings. To do so would be quite pointless at a conference like ours. I shall, however, reserve the privilege possessed by everyone present to engage in the open discussion, if circumstances permit. I know quite well that my opening remarks were not neutral and that the opponents of the subjective theory of value will regard them as partisan. But perhaps even they will agree with me when I say in conclusion: Is it not remarkable that this subjective theory of value, which in the German-speaking countries is condemned and decried as heresy, which was pronounced dead a thousand times, does not, for all that, cease to occupy the center of scientific debate? Is it not astonishing that the ideas of Menger and Jevons still arouse general interest, while all their contemporaries have long since been forgotten? Does anyone still dare today to mention in the same breath with Gossen, Menger, or Böhm-Bawerk the names of those contemporaries who during their lifetimes were much more famous? We feel it is a treatment thoroughly worthy of a great subject that today books still appear that are devoted to the struggle against the teachings of Menger and Böhm-Bawerk. For these theories, which have again and again been pronounced dead, still live. And the proof that they do is precisely the fact that they find opponents. Would we not consider it fighting windmills if someone were to choose to devote his efforts to refuting the long-dead theories of the contemporaries of these thinkers, who were much more renowned in their day? If it is true that the importance of an author consists in his effect on posterity, then the founders of the theory of marginal utility have attained far greater importance than any other economists of the postclassical period. Today, whoever attempts to deal with the problems of economics cannot avoid coming to grips with the much maligned subjective theory of value. In this sense it can be called the prevailing theory, in spite of the fact that anyone who acknowledges it in the German-speaking countries must be prepared to stand a great deal of hostility and even worse.

The most striking indication of the authority of a doctrine is the fact that it is the target of many attacks. The Marginal Utility School proves its sway over men's minds by freely inviting their criticism.

NOTES

1. Speech delivered in introduction to the discussion of the problem of the theory of value, September 30, 1932, at Dresden, before the panel on theory of the Verein für Sozialpolitik. (*Schriften des Vereins für Sozialpolitik*, Vol. CLXXXIII, Part II.)
2. Cf. Totomianz, *Geschichte der Nationalökonomie und des Sozialismus* (2nd ed.; Berlin, 1929), p. 132.
3. Cf. Cassel, *Grundgedanken der theoretischen Ökonomie* (Leipzig, 1926), p. 27.
4. Cf. Cassel, *ibid.*, p. 24.
5. Cf. Cassel, "Grundriss einer elementaren Preislehre," *Zeitschrift für die gesamte Staatswissenschaft* (1889).
6. Cf. Spann's contribution to Vol. CLXXXIII, Part I, p. 204, of the periodical of the Verein für Sozialpolitik. The contributions to this volume will hereafter be quoted as *Schriftenband*, with the page number.
7. Cf. Spann, *Schriftenband*, p. 217.
8. Spann, *Schriftenband*, p. 222.
9. Cf. my *Theory of Money and Credit*, pp. 45-47.
10. Concerning the mathematical method, cf. above pp. 116 ff.
11. Cf. Spann, *Schriftenband*, p. 250.
12. Cf. *Schriftenband*, pp. 3 ff.

8

Inconvertible Capital

1. THE INFLUENCE OF THE PAST ON PRODUCTION

Suppose that, making use of our entire store of technological skill and our present-day knowledge of geography, we were to undertake to resettle the earth's surface in such a way that we should afterwards be in a position to take maximum advantage of the natural distribution of raw materials. And suppose further that for this purpose the entire capital wealth of the present were at our disposal in a form that would allow us to invest it in whatever way was regarded as the most suitable for the end in view.

In such a case the world would certainly take on an appearance that would be very considerably different from the one it now presents. Many areas would be less densely populated; others, in turn, more densely populated, than they are today. Land that is now cultivated would be allowed to lie fallow, while other land that today lies fallow would be farmed. Many mineral deposits that are presently exploited would be left unused. Factories would exist in fewer number than they do today and often in different locations. The great trade routes would follow other courses. In the factories themselves only the most modern machinery would be employed. Economic and commercial geography would have to be completely rewritten, and many machines and types of equipment still used today would remain only in museums.

It has been a repeated subject of criticism that the present actual state of affairs does not correspond to this ideal picture that we construct with the help of our technological and geographical knowledge. The fact that production has not been "made completely rational" is regarded as a sign of backwardness and wastefulness inimical to the general welfare. The prevailing

217

Epistemological Problems of Economics

ideology, which makes capitalism responsible for all evils, sees in this situation a new argument in favor of interventionism and socialism. Everywhere commissions and councils are set up "for the efficient use of resources." An abundant literature occupies itself with questions of "the most efficient utilization of the factors of production," and "making the economy rational" has become one of the most popular clichés of the day. The treatment given this subject, however, scarcely touches upon the problems involved.

First of all, catallactics must take as the basis of its reasoning the proposition that only "true capital," in Clark's sense, has mobility, but that individual capital goods do not.[1] Capital goods as produced, material factors of production are intermediary steps on the way toward a definite goal—a consumer's good. If in the course of the period of production subsequent changes in the entrepreneur's goals are caused by a change in the data of the market, the intermediary products already available cannot always be used for the attainment of the new goals. This holds true both of goods of fixed and goods of circulating capital, although in greater measure of the former. Capital has mobility in so far as it is technologically possible to transfer individual capital goods from one branch of production to another or to transport them from one location to another. Where this is not possible, "true capital" can be shifted from branch to branch or from place to place only by not being replaced as it is used up and by the production of other capital goods elsewhere in its stead.

In accordance with the purpose of our investigation, we do not wish to take up the question of the mobility of goods of circulating capital any further. And for the time being, in considering the mobility of fixed capital, we shall disregard the case of a decrease in demand for the final product. The two questions that concern us are: What consequences are brought about by limitations in the convertibility of fixed capital in the event of a change in the conditions determining the location of industries or in the case of technological progress?

First, let us consider the second, simpler case. A new machine, more efficient than those used previously, comes on the market.

Whether or not the plants equipped with the old, less efficient machines will discard them in spite of the fact that they are still utilizable and replace them by the new model depends on the degree of the new machine's superiority. Only if this superiority is great enough to compensate for the additional expenditure required is the scrapping of the old equipment economically sound. Let p be the price of the new machine, q the price that can be realized by selling the old machine as scrap iron, a the cost of producing one unit of product by the old machine, and b the cost of producing one unit of product by the new machine without taking into account the costs required for its purchase. Let us further assume that the advantage of the new machine consists merely in a better utilization of circulating capital—for example, by saving labor—and not in manufacturing a greater quantity of products, and that thus the annual output z remains unchanged. Then the replacement of the old machine by the new one is advantageous if the yield $z(a - b)$ is large enough to compensate for the expenditure of $p - q$. We may disregard the writing off of depreciation in assuming that the annual quotas are not greater for the new machine than for the old one. Consequently, the case can very well occur that plants equipped with the older model are able to compete with those equipped with the better, more recent model. Every businessman will confirm this.

The situation is exactly the same in the first case. When more propitious natural conditions of production are made accessible, plants change their location only if the difference in net proceeds exceeds the costs of moving. What makes this a special case is the fact that obstacles standing in the way of the mobility of labor are also involved. If the workers do not also migrate and if there are no workers available in the regions favored by nature, then neither can production migrate. However, we need not go into this further, since we are interested here only in the question of the mobility of capital. We need merely establish the fact that production would change its location, even if labor were perfectly mobile, only if the conditions described above were met. This too is confirmed again and again by experience.

With regard to choice of location and technological performance, new plants appear most efficient in the light of the existing situation. But in both cases that have been discussed, consideration for capital goods produced in the past under certain circumstances makes the technologically best method of production appear uneconomical. History and the past have their say. An economic calculation that did not take them into account would be deficient. We are not only of today; we are heirs of the past as well. Our capital wealth is handed down from the past, and this fact has its consequences. What is involved here is not the play of irrational factors in the rationality of economic activity, as we might perhaps be inclined to say were we to follow a fashion in science that is hardly to be recommended. Nor are we confronted here with an instance of alleged "noneconomic" motives. On the contrary, it is precisely strict rationality that induces the entrepreneur to continue production in a disadvantageous location or with obsolete equipment. Therefore it would also be a mistake to speak in this connection of "symptoms of friction." This phenomenon can be most appropriately described as the effect of the influence of the past upon production.[2]

If technologically obsolete machines are retained, or if production is continued at an unfavorable location, it may still be profitable to invest new capital in these plants in order to increase their efficiency as much as the situation permits. Then a production aggregate that, from the purely technological point of view, appears outclassed can continue to compete profitably for a long time to come.

The merely technological view, which neglects the consideration of the influence of the past, finds it inexplicable, from the rational standpoint, how backward production methods can continue to exist alongside the more advanced. It resorted to all kinds of inadequate attempts at an explanation. One would think that the procedure of drawing upon the factors of the past to explain present conditions would have appeared especially obvious to the Historical School. Yet here too it failed completely. It could see in this problem nothing but ammunition for its attack upon capitalism.

This came very opportunely for the socialists of all varieties. On the one hand, the knowledge was growing that socialism could keep its promise of improving the lot of everybody only if it were a more productive system than capitalism. On the other hand, it was becoming increasingly evident that a sharp decline in productivity would very definitely have to be expected in the socialist planned economy. To the extent that people were becoming aware of these facts it became important for the socialists to collect seeming arguments with which one could justify the prophecy of abundance in the socialist community of the future. It seemed useful for this purpose to point repeatedly to the fact that under capitalism there is still technological backwardness everywhere. That the equipment of some enterprises does not conform to the ideal picture presented by the most advanced establishments was attributed, not to the influence of the past upon production or to the scarcity of available capital, but to the inherent shortcomings of capitalism. To it one contrasted the utopian vision of a socialist planned economy. It was assumed unhesitatingly and as a matter of course that under socialism all plants will be equipped with the most modern machinery and will be situated in the most favorable locations. We are not told, of course, where the resources for their construction and equipment are to come from.

Very characteristic of this method of providing a deceptive proof of the higher productivity of socialism is the book of Atlanticus-Ballod.[3] This work attained great renown in the recent past precisely because it harmoniously combines the bureaucratic socialism of the public functionary and Marxism. Here the attempt is made simply "to point out in an approximate way what could be accomplished with present-day science and technology under the natural conditions given today in a socialist-operated community."[4] To appreciate his method of treating the subject that he embarks on with this declaration, it is enough to mention his statement that in German agriculture there will be "nothing left" for the socialist state to do "but to rebuild completely almost all farms." In place of the existing farms 36,000 new ones are to be set up, each with approximately 400 hectares of arable land.[5] Similar measures are to be taken in industry. How simply the question of obtaining capital is answered by Ballod is shown by his observation: "It is therefore quite out of the question for the individualist state to pay for the electrification of the railways. The socialist state can do so without great difficulties." [6] The entire book demonstrates no appreciation whatsoever of the fact that investment of capital is possible only within given limits and that in view of the scarcity of capital it would be the greatest waste to abandon still utilizable plants that have come down from the past solely because they would have been equipped differently if they were to be designed for the first time today.

Even a socialist community could not proceed differently from the capitalists of the economic order based on private property. The manager of a socialist economy would also have to take account of the fact that the means of production available are limited. He too would have to consider carefully, before abandoning a still utilizable plant to erect a more modern one in its place, whether there is not a more urgent need for the resources that the new plant must require. That a socialist community could by no means make this comparison of input and output, of costs and proceeds, because economic calculation is not possible under socialism, does not further come into question here. The impossibility of economic calculation makes a socialist economy based on the division of labor altogether unfeasible. A completely socialist economy can exist only in thought, not in reality. However, if one seeks, in spite of this, to describe the communist paradise in an imaginary construction, one must, in order not to become involved in self-contradictory nonsense, assign to the scarcity of capital the same role it plays in the economic life of capitalism.

In business practice the problem before us usually appears as the opposition between the viewpoint of the businessman, who coolly and calculatingly examines the profitability of investments, and that of the visionary engineer, who declares himself for the "technologically most perfect plant," even if it is unprofitable under the given circumstances. Wherever the pure technologist has his way, capital is malinvested, i.e., squandered.

2. TRADE POLICY AND THE INFLUENCE OF THE PAST

The infant industries argument advanced in favor of protective tariffs represents a hopeless attempt to justify such measures on a purely economic basis, without regard to political considerations. It is a grievous error to fail to recognize the political motivation behind the demand for tariffs on behalf of infant industries. The same arguments as are advanced in favor of protecting a domestic product against foreign competition could also be adduced in favor of protecting one part of a general customs area against the competition of other parts. The fact that, nevertheless, protection is asked only against foreign, but not also against domestic, competition clearly points to the real nature of the motives behind the demand.

Of course, it may happen in some cases that the industry already in existence is not operating in the most favorable of the locations that are presently accessible. However, the question is whether moving to the more favorable location offers advantages great enough to compensate for the cost of abandoning the already existing plants. If the advantages are great enough, then moving is profitable and is carried out without the intervention of a tariff policy. If it is not profitable in itself and becomes so only by virtue of the tariff, then the latter has led to the expenditure of capital goods for the construction of plants that would otherwise not have been constructed. These capital goods are now no longer available where they would have been had the state not intervened.

Every tariff under whose protection new plants come into existence that otherwise would not have been built so long as the older plants established elsewhere were still utilizable leads to the squandering of capital. Of course, the fanatics on both sides of the ocean who want to "make the economy rational" do not care to see this.

Under the protection of tariffs—and other interventionist measures that bring about the same result—industries come into existence in places where they would not have been established in a world of free trade. If all tariff walls were now to fall at one blow, these plants would prove to be malinvestments. It would then become evident that it would have been more practical to have erected them in more favorable places. Nevertheless, they are there now, and the question whether they should be abandoned in order to set up new ones in more advantageous places is again to be decided by examining whether or not this would be the most profitable application for the employment of capital available for new investments. Consequently, the transfer of production from the places to which it has been brought by the interference of the tariff policy to the locations it would have chosen in a free economy, and which are now still regarded as the most favored by nature, will take place only gradually. The effects of the protectionist policy still continue even after its abandonment and disappear only in the course of time.

If one country alone removes its tariffs while all other countries continue to adhere to protectionism and retain their immigration barriers, its economy would have to adjust itself by concentrating on those branches of production for which conditions in that country are relatively most advantageous. Such an adjustment requires the investment of capital, and the profitability of this capital is again dependent on whether the difference in the costs of production between the enterprises to be abandoned and the ones to be newly established is great enough to justify the necessary expenditure of capital at that time. In this case too the effects of the protectionist policy continue for a certain period after its abandonment.

Everything that has been said concerning protection in foreign trade is, of course, equally true of the protection of one group of domestic enterprises against another. If, for example, tax rates favor savings banks over commercial banks, consumer cooperatives over businessmen, agricultural producers of alcohol over industrial producers, small business over big business, all those consequences appear that are brought about by the protection of the less efficient domestic industry against its more efficient foreign competitor.

3. THE MALINVESTMENT OF CAPITAL

The malinvestment of capital goods can have come about in several ways.

1. The construction of the plant was economically justified at the time it was established. It is not so any longer because since then new methods of production have become known or because today other locations are more favorable.

2. Though originally a sound investment, the plant has become uneconomic because of changes that have occurred in the data of the market, such as, for example, a decrease in demand.

3. The plant was uneconomic from the very first. It was able to be constructed only by virtue of interventionist measures that have now been abandoned.

4. The plant was uneconomic from the very first. Its construction was an incorrect speculation.

5. The incorrect speculation (case 4) that led to the malinvestment has been brought about by the falsification of monetary calculation consequent upon changes in the value of money. The conditions of this case are described by the monetary theory of the trade cycle (the circulation-credit theory of cyclical fluctuations).

If the malinvestment is recognized and it nevertheless proves profitable to continue in business because the gross revenue exceeds the current costs of operation, the book value of the plant is generally lowered to the point where it corresponds to the now realizable return. If the necessary writing off is considerable in relation to the total capital invested, it will not take place in the case of a corporation without a reduction in the original capital. When this happens the loss of capital occasioned by the malinvestment becomes visible and can be reported by statistics. Its detection is still easier if the firm collapses completely. The statistics of failures, bankruptcies, and balance sheets can also provide much information on this point. However, a not inconsiderable number of investments that have failed elude statistical treatment. Corporations that have sufficient hidden reserves available can sometimes leave even the stockholders, who are, after all, the most interested parties, completely in the dark about the fact that an investment has failed. Governments and local administrative bodies decide to inform the public of their mistakes only when losses have become disproportionately great. Enterprises that are not under the necessity of giving a public accounting of their activities seek to conceal losses for the sake of their credit. This may explain why there is a tendency to underestimate the extent of losses that have been brought about by the malinvestment of fixed capital.

One must call special attention to this fact in view of the prevailing disposition to overrate the importance of "forced saving" in the formation of capital. It has led many to see in inflation in general, and in particular in credit expansion brought about by the policy of the banks of granting loans below the rate that would otherwise have been established on the market, the power responsible for the increasing capital accumulation that is the cause of economic progress. In this connection we may disregard the fact that inflation, though it can, of course, induce "forced saving," need not necessarily do so, since it depends on the particular data of the individual case whether dislocations of wealth and income that lead to increased savings and capital accumulation really do occur.[7] In any case, however, credit expansion must initiate the process that passes through the upswing and the boom and finally ends in the crisis and the depression. The essence of this process consists in rendering the appraisement of capital misleading. Therefore, even if more capital is accumulated to begin with than would have been the case in the absence of the banks' policy of credit expansion, capital is lost on the other hand by incorrect appraisement, which leads it to be used in the wrong place and in the wrong way.

Whether or not the increase in capital is equalled or even exceeded by these losses is a *quaestio facti*. The advocates of credit expansion declare that there is always an increase in capital in such cases, but this certainly cannot be so unhesitatingly asserted. It may be true that many of these plants were erected only prematurely and are not by nature malinvestments, and that if there had been no trade cycle they would certainly have been constructed later, but not otherwise. It may even be true that in the last sixty to eighty years, especially during the upswing of the trade cycle, plants were built that surely would have been constructed later—railroads and power plants in particular—and that therefore the errors that had been committed were made good by the passage of time. However, owing to the rapid progress of technology in the capitalist system, we cannot reject the supposition that the later construction of a plant would have influenced its technical character, since the technological innovations that appeared in the meanwhile would have had to be taken into account. The loss that results from the premature construction of a plant is then certainly greater than the above optimistic opinion assumes. Very many of the plants whose establishment was due to the falsification of the bases of economic calculation, which constitutes the essence of the boom artificially inaugurated by the banks' policy of credit expansion, would never have been built at all.

The sum total of available capital consists of three parts: circulating capital, newly formed capital, and that part of fixed capital which is set aside for reinvestment. A shift in the ratio of circulating capital to fixed capital would, if not warranted by market conditions, itself represent a misdirection of capital. Consequently, the circulating capital in general must not only be maintained, but also increased by the allocation of a part of the newly formed capital. Thus only an amount that is quite modest in comparison with total capital is left over for new fixed investment. One must take this into consideration if one wishes to estimate the quantitative importance of the malinvestment of capital. It is not to be measured by comparison with the total amount of capital, but by comparison with the amount of capital available for new fixed investments.

Without doubt, in the years that have elapsed since the outbreak of the World War, very considerable amounts of fixed capital have been malinvested. The stoppage of international trade during the war and the high-tariff policy that has since prevailed have promoted the construction of factories in places that certainly do not offer the most favorable conditions for production. Inflation has operated to produce the same result. Now these new factories are in competition with those constructed earlier and mostly in more favorable locations—a competition that they can sustain only under the protection of tariffs and other interventionist measures. These extensive malinvestments took place precisely in a period in which war, revolution, inflation, and various interferences of the political authorities in economic life were consuming capital in very great volume.

One may not neglect all these factors if one wishes to investigate the causes of the disturbances in the economic life of the present day.

The fact that capital has been malinvested is visibly evident in the great number of factories that either have been shut down completely or operate at less than their total capacity.

4. THE ADAPTABILITY OF WORKERS

Economic progress in the narrower sense is the work of the savers, who accumulate capital, and of the entrepreneurs, who turn capital to new uses. The other members of society, of course, enjoy the advantages of progress, but they not only do not contribute anything to it; they even place obstacles in its way. As consumers they meet every innovation with distrust, so that new products at first are unable to command the price that they could reach if the buyers were less conservative in their tastes. This is the reason for the not inconsiderable costs of introducing new articles. As workers, the masses fight against every change in the accustomed methods of production, even though this opposition only seldom leads today to open sabotage, to say nothing of the destruction of the new machines.

Every industrial innovation must take into account the fact that it will encounter opposition from those who cannot easily accustom themselves to it. The worker lacks precisely the nimbleness of mind that the entrepreneur must have if he is not to succumb to his competitors. The worker is unable and often is even unwilling to adapt himself to the new and to meet the demands that it makes upon him. Precisely because he does not possess this ability he is an employee and not an entrepreneur. This slowness on the part of the masses works as an obstacle to every economic improvement. It too represents the effect of the influence of the past upon labor as a factor of production, and as such it must be taken into account in every calculation of new undertakings. If it is not taken into consideration, then there is just as much malinvestment in this case as in all other cases in which an enterprise proves to be unprofitable. Every enterprise has to adapt itself to the given situation, and not reckon on the situation it would like to be given.

This applies in particular to enterprises established in regions in which suitably qualified workers are not to be found. However, it is no less valid for those that have been established with the purpose of utilizing workers of inferior ability, as soon as this inferiority disappears—that is to say, from the moment in which "cheap labor" is no longer available. A great part of European agriculture was able to withstand competition from farmers working on better land abroad only so long as culturally backward masses could be employed as workers. As industry was able to attract these workers and the "flight from the land" began, the wages of agricultural laborers had to be increased in order to make remaining on the farms more attractive. Consequently, the profitability of running these farms dwindled, and the great amounts of capital that were invested in them in the course of time now proved to be malinvested.

5. THE ENTREPRENEUR'S VIEW OF MALINVESTMENT

The foregoing discussion makes quite clear the conduct of the individual entrepreneur and of the individual capitalist in the face of losses that come about through the commitment of inconvertible capital in enterprises in which a person having complete knowledge of all the relevant circumstances would no longer invest it today. Nevertheless, the way in which businessmen and the press generally discuss these matters differs markedly in many respects from our description. Yet it is only the businessman's view of the situation that is different; his conduct, however, is in complete conformity with our description of it.

Let us suppose that it becomes obvious that the earning capacity

230 Epistemological Problems of Economics

of an enterprise will be permanently diminished in the future or that a diminution of revenue that had hitherto been regarded as temporary proves to be lasting. This fact is appraised in different ways—particularly in the case of corporations and other similar associations for raising capital—according to whether it is necessary to make clear in the books the loss of fixed capital that has taken place, or whether this can be avoided because the fixed investments do not at present appear in the books with higher appraisements than correspond to their now diminished values. It is hardly necessary to point out that this has nothing to do with the question whether the enterprise should be abandoned altogether in view of the new state of affairs. It is obvious that what gives this secondary decision such great importance is merely consideration for what the stockholders may think of the achievements of the responsible management, for the credit of the firm, and for the price of its stock.

One often hears the view expressed that when a concern writes off a great part of its investment this very fact offers it the possibility of entering into competition with other firms that operate under more favorable conditions. Here too the situation is no different from the case just mentioned. The book value of a concern's fixed investment has no bearing whatever on the question of its ability to withstand competition. What is alone decisive is whether, after covering all current operating costs and after paying interest on the circulating capital, there is still so much left over from the gross revenue that something more can be reaped than an adequate return on the value which, after discontinuation of the enterprise, the fixed capital would have in view of the possibility of using it for other production (occasionally this will be only the scrap value of the machines and bricks). In that case the continuation of the enterprise is more profitable than its discontinuation. If the fixed capital has a higher book value than corresponds to its present and probable future earning capacity, then the book value must be lowered to that extent.

What the businessman wants to say in using his mode of expression is nothing else than that an enterprise whose investment has already been written off either wholly or to a great extent out of previous earnings appears, when considered in regard to the entire duration of its life, as still profitable even in the later periods of its existence if only it is still able to pay interest on the circulating capital.

The case is similar where, as is generally said, competition with enterprises operating for the rest under more favorable conditions is possible because a source of special advantage not within their reach is available—like the value of a popular brand name. If the remaining conditions of production were perfectly equal, then this advantage would constitute the source of a differential rent. As the situation stands, the resources needed to make up an existing disadvantage are obtained from it.

NOTES

1. Cf. Clark, *The Distribution of Wealth* (New York, 1908), p. 118.
2. The influence of the past is also operative in the two cases that we have not considered: obstruction of the mobility of circulating capital and a decrease in demand for the final product. But this need not be gone into any further because the relationship is obvious from what has been said. Equally simple is the application to "durable goods" in Böhm-Bawerk's sense.
3. Cf. Atlanticus-Ballod, *Der Zukunftsstaat, Produktion und Konsum im Sozialstaat* (2nd ed.; Stuttgart, 1919).
4. *Ibid.,* p. 1.
5. *Ibid.,* p. 69.
6. *Ibid.,* p. 213.
7. Cf. my *Geldwertstabilisierung und Konjuncturpolitik,* p. 45 *et seq.*

Index

(Prepared by Vernelia A. Crawford)